OPERATION SEA LION

Peter Fleming was born in London in 1907, the son of an MP. He was educated at Eton, where he was Captain of the Oppidans, and at Oxford, where he got a first-class degree in English. He then took up journalism and wrote at first under the name "Moth". Subsequently he travelled in Mexico, Brazil, China, Japan and other countries, often as special correspondent for *The Times*. During World War II he served in the Grenadier Guards and was mentioned in dispatches. He is famous chiefly for his travel books which include *Brazilian Adventure*, *News from Tartary*, *A Forgotten Journey* and *Bayonets to Lhasa*. The brother of Ian Fleming, he used to describe himself as "a kind of uncle of James Bond's". He died in 1971.

Operation Sea Lion

An account of the German preparations
and the British counter-measures

originally published as *Invasion 1940*

Peter Fleming

PAN BOOKS

First published 1957 as *Invasion* 1940 by Rupert Hart-Davis

First published by Pan Books 1975

This edition published 2003 by Pan Books
an imprint of Pan Macmillan Ltd
Pan Macmillan, 20 New Wharf Road, London N 1 9RR
Basingstoke and Oxford
Associated companies throughout the world
www.panmacmillan.com

ISBN 0 330 42057 7

3 5 7 9 8 6 4 2

A CIP catalogue record for this book is available from
the British Library.

Printed and bound in Great Britian by
Mackays of Chatham plc, Chatham, Kent

Contents

List of Illustrations

List of Illustrations in the Text

Foreword

IN the summer of 1940 the Germans prepared to launch, and the British to repel, an invasion of England. In this book these preparations are described and placed in relation to each other. An attempt is made to show how the strong, elaborate German expedition would have fared if its orders had not been countermanded at a late hour; and the reasons for the abandonment of a project, whose success would have altered the course of history, are analysed in some detail.

The period (roughly from May to September 1940) is veiled already in a not unbecoming mist of legend. In the German camp the mounting of the invasion, though it went forward feverishly, occupied only twelve weeks of a war which raged for five and a half years; it involved but a part of the armed forces, and of these only the airmen saw action; it did not affect the civilian population at all. Knowledge of the plans was confined to a very small circle, and the abortive episode made little impression on the minds of the German nation. By them it is for the most part remembered as a mild aberration of Hitler's strategy, a cross between a daydream and a hoax, a jousting match staged in lists which proved unsuitable for the purpose. It was in fact something quite different.

On the British the threat of invasion had a more vivid, direct and comprehensive impact, for the danger, and the precautions taken to avert it, affected the whole population. Yet legend plays a large part in their memories of that tense and strangely exhilarating summer, and their experiences, like those of early childhood, are sharply rather than accurately etched upon their minds. The stories they tell of the period have become better, but not more veracious, with the passage of time. Rumours are remembered as facts, and—particularly since anti-invasion precautions continued in force for several years after the Germans had renounced their project—the sequence of events is blurred.

All this is natural. In 1940 most people in the United Kingdom lived, like small children, in a small world. Petrol-rationing restricted travel. The use of the telephone was discouraged. The newspapers, drastically reduced in size, worked under a censorship. Large-scale evacuations had disrupted many normal patterns of social inter-course. Men of the fighting services, as they were shifted unpre-dictably about the country, preserved in the interests of security a taciturn demeanour. In Parliament the gravest issues were debated in secret session.

As a result the average citizen knew less than usual about what was happening, and why it happened. Like a child who is excluded from the confidence of the grown-ups, he accepted the existence of a sphere of knowledge into which he could not expect to be admitted, even though within it his own destinies were being decided; and like a child he tended afterwards to remember events without a full understanding of their significance (which, it may be added, often eluded the grown-ups).

The main purpose of this book is to set down what actually did happen, in both the German and the British camps, while Hitler after swiftly overrunning Europe prepared the annihilation of his only remaining enemy. One day the definitive history of this curious interlude will be written; and when it is I hope that my narrative will prove of value to the writer. The short period is not well documented, for both belligerents were hastily improvising measures to deal with a situation which neither had foreseen (the mustering of the German barge-fleet, for instance, left records almost as frag-mentary as did the raising of the Home Guard); and I have had access to sources—the memories of British and German participants in the affair—which will not be available to the historian of the future.

In this field I have not confined my researches to the recollections of important persons but have, especially among the Germans, also questioned those who in 1940 held junior ranks or posts; for from them it was often possible to gain some impression of how Hitler's strategical directives, which have long been familiar to students of the period, were translated into action by the men who were to carry them out. It is inevitable that both British and German reminiscences should include a high proportion of striking or amusing anecdotes; austerely, but I hope wisely, I have made sparing use of these, on the grounds that after sixteen years they are likely to be nearer to legend than to truth.

A private individual has no right of access to British official archives, which in this case include a quantity of captured German documents; and even permission to see an advance copy of *The Defence of the United Kingdom*, one of the volumes of the Official History of the Second World War, was granted only on conditions which I felt unable to accept. But I have been fortunate in obtaining, from German and American sources, the German documentary material which I needed; and on the British side I seem, in one way or another, to have come by a good deal of enlightenment without incurring the obligation to submit my manuscript to anybody for approval.

Part of Chapter 9 has, however, undergone scrutiny. I must express my respectful gratitude both to Her Majesty the Queen for granting me permission to include in it certain material dealing with the Royal Family, and to Her Majesty Queen Elizabeth the Queen Mother for allowing me to consult her own memories of the period.

History cannot be adequately written sixteen years after the event. Except for Hitler, I have not attempted to assess the parts played by the leading personages in either camp, for to do so without knowledge of their motives would have been impertinent and foolish. I have however assembled all the available evidence about what each side intended, hoped and did; I have placed upon it my own interpretations; and I have here and there filled out the picture with details which may help the reader to reconstruct the manner of life in the British Isles during one of the oddest and most critical episodes in their history.

My book can hardly claim a higher status than that of an interim report; but perhaps some of those who live in that interim, which covers the gap in time between the event and the final verdict on it, will find in these pages the image, not wilfully distorted, of a strange reality.

PETER FLEMING

Nettlebed, Oxfordshire. 1957

Acknowledgements

Published sources are acknowledged in footnotes to the text. A bibliography will be found at p. 311.

Privately communicated testimony from British and German sources is not acknowledged, except in three places (pp. 117, 120 and 261) where particular informants have thrown light on events not referred to in the documents of the period or in the literature based on them. This should not be taken to imply that my debt to such sources is a small one. It is very large, and I must here express my gratitude to the many individuals who have allowed me to ransack their memories during the past two and a half years. I know that some would prefer not to be named; and I hope that the others will recognise the impossibility of identifying all the eggs in an omelette, and will accept my thanks for contributing to such flavour as it has.

I owe several debts which must be more plainly acknowledged. Captain Stephen Roskill, DSC, RN, the Royal Navy's official historian, has given me generous help and guidance. So has Mr Denis Richards, MA, Principal of Morley College and co-author with the late Hilary St George Saunders of *The Royal Air Force, 1939-45* (London, 1949). On the researches conducted by Mr Charles Graves while the wartime Home Guard was still in being, and embodied in *The Home Guard of Britain* (London, 1943), I have relied extensively in Chapter 13.

For his friendly advice I would like to thank Captain Karl Klee, whose *Das Unternehmen Seelöwe: Die geplante deutsche Landung in England. Ein Beitrag zum Verhältnis zwischen Politik und Kriegführung in Deutschland im Sommer and Herbst des Jahres 1940* (Göttingen) was unfortunately completed too late for me to be able to consult his able study of the German records; and among the countless people who have helped me in various ways I must mention Mr Brian Melland, of the Historical Section of the Cabinet Office: Mr J. C. Nerney, head of the Air Historical Branch of the Air Ministry: Mr J. S. Maywood, head of *The Times* Intelligence Department: and the staffs of the Imperial War Museum and the Henley-on-Thames Public Library.

For their zeal and resource in many unlikely quests I am grateful to Mrs Joan St George Saunders and Mrs Joan Bright Astley, of "Writer's and Speaker's Research"; and I am indebted to Mr Anthony G. Powell for his services as a translator.

I must also thank Miss Kathleen M. Laidler for making available the originals of the three drawings by her late brother, "Pont" (Graham Laidler), which appear among the illustrations; I owe gratitude on similar grounds to my friend Mr Osbert Lancaster. Admiral K. J. von Puttkamer, who was Hitler's naval adjutant in 1940, has obligingly allowed me to use—facing p. 32—a photograph from his private collection. The captured German maps, from which the frontispiece has been reconstructed with (if I may say so) great skill and fidelity by Mr K. C. Jordan, were lent to me by the Historical Section of the Cabinet Office.

This list could, and should, be considerably prolonged; but I must end it somewhere, and I will do so with a tribute to Sir Norman Brook, GCB, until recently Secretary to the Cabinet. He dealt with all my requests for access to the archives of the last war, over which, for fortuitous reasons, the Cabinet Office has control. Protocol demanded that almost all these requests should be refused; but Sir Norman refused them with such courtesy that, instead of appearing an obstructive ogre, he seemed to be—like myself—the victim of a system which must appear to the private historian unreasonable and at times absurd. I thank him for his considerate attitude.   P. F.

NOTE: As these pages go to press, I learn that after ruminating upon the matter for three years the authorities have decided to permit the publication of a monograph on the German invasion plans by Mr R. R. A. Wheatley, of the Historical Section of the Cabinet Office. During the period of my researches Mr Wheatley's work was a restricted document, but I was, by a bureaucratic oversight, given access to it for a few hours. It is a scholarly and exhaustive study of the original documents, and in acknowledging my debt to Mr Wheatley I cannot help expressing a wistful envy of his readers, who will not need to digest the rich fruits of his research in a single afternoon with the shadow of the Official Secrets Act hanging over them.

JOYOUS GARD.
"Surrender, or die".
Punch, 24 July 1940

CHAPTER ONE

Seconds Out of the Ring

Down, down, down. Would the fall *never* come to an end!

Lewis Carroll: *Alice in Wonderland*

ON 16 July 1940 Adolf Hitler, in his capacity as Chancellor of the German Reich and Supreme Commander of its Armed Forces, issued his Directive No. 16. It began:

As England, in spite of the hopelessness of her military position, has so far shown herself unwilling to come to any compromise, I have decided to begin to prepare for, and if necessary to carry out, an invasion of England.

This operation is dictated by the necessity of eliminating Great Britain as a base from which the war against Germany can be fought, and if necessary the island will be occupied.

I therefore issue the following orders . . .

These orders will be examined in detail at a later stage. For the present it is enough to note that they required preparations for the invasion (most of which had been put in hand a fortnight earlier) to be completed by the middle of August, and that the code-name *Sea Lion* was allotted to the operation.[1] A brief account must now be given of the principal events from which Hitler's decision stemmed; their cumulative effect had placed his only remaining adversary in a position which it was not unreasonable to describe as hopeless.

The Second World War, the shadow of whose imminence had darkened life in Europe for the best part of two years, began at first light on 1 September 1939 when, without warning or provocation,

[1] In the draft of Directive No. 16 the code-name appears as *Lion*. It is reasonable to suppose that Hitler made the change himself. See p. 48.

the German armed forces launched a furious attack upon Poland. Orders for this operation to be mounted had been issued five months earlier, and of the two main political dangers attending the adventure one had, with equal adroitness and effrontery, been eliminated by the conclusion on 23 August 1939 of the Nazi-Soviet Pact.

The other danger Hitler, who in this matter had been ill-served by his advisers and his intuition, was not successful in avoiding. France and Great Britain honoured their pledges to their Polish ally, and both countries declared war on Germany on 3 September. To say that they were powerless to intervene at this stage is not quite true; but neither nation was prepared to risk the consequences of initiating air warfare against objectives in Germany, and the commitment of their puny bomber forces against targets hundreds of miles from the battlefield would not in fact have made the smallest difference to the outcome of the campaign, or even to its duration.

This was brutally short. A new word, *Blitzkrieg*, took its place in the vocabularies of Europe. The Poles fought with desperate gallantry; but the Germans were superior in numbers, in training and in equipment, and the Luftwaffe swiftly established and ruthlessly exploited complete supremacy in the air. To crown all, Stalin, setting an example which Mussolini was timidly to emulate in France, stabbed in the back a nation already mortally stricken. The Red Army began on 17 September to occupy Eastern Poland; Russia's action was sanctioned by secret protocols annexed to the Nazi-Soviet Pact. On 27 September Warsaw surrendered, and Hitler's first campaign was over less than four weeks after it had begun. The butchery of their ally, and their own impotence to avert it, did nothing to increase either the prestige or the self-confidence, which were not at that time substantial, of France and Great Britain.

Hitler now made certain ineffective attempts to wind up a war in which—save at sea, and by his executioners in Poland—no shots were being fired. These tentatives failing, he prepared for the summary destruction of the Allied armies in France. On 9 October Directive No. 6 set in motion urgent preparations for *Operation Yellow, "an offensive action on the northern flank of the Western Front crossing the area of Luxemburg, Belgium and Holland"*. Hitler's definition of his strategic purpose at this stage has some relevance to the theme of this book. It reads:

> *The object of this attack is to defeat as strong sections of the French Army as possible, and her ally and partner in the fighting [i.e. Great Britain], and at the same time to acquire as great an area of Holland, Belgium and Northern France as possible, to use as a base offering good prospects for waging aerial and sea warfare against England and to provide ample coverage for the vital district of the Ruhr.*

In any military order, at whatever level it is given, nothing exceeds—indeed nothing equals—in importance a precise definition of the object which the commander giving the orders intends to achieve. Hitler's practice in this respect was always sound, and Directive No. 6 provided his three commanders-in-chief with a clear, though general, statement of his aims in undertaking *Operation Yellow*. From this it is evident that in October 1939 he did not regard the blow which he was about to deliver as one which would knock France out altogether; *Operation Yellow* was intended to win the first round only, not the whole bout.

Taken by itself, the fact that Directive No. 6 contains no reference to the possibility of invading England has small significance; for if Hitler's western offensive had been launched (as he meant it to be when he wrote the orders issued on 9 October) within a very few weeks, the winter would have ruled out any question of following it up with cross-Channel operations. There is however much evidence from other sources that the impression produced by Directive No. 6 is correct, and that the idea of an invasion of England as a possible sequel to *Operation Yellow* had not crossed Hitler's mind. It was fortunate for Western civilisation that this was so.

Hitler's orders for *Operation Yellow* had recognised the possibility that bad weather might retard its launching. D-Day, originally fixed for 12 November, was postponed five days earlier because of adverse weather reports. Thereafter it was postponed about a dozen times in all. Not only was the winter an exceptionally hard one, but the German General Staff, several of whose leading members were actively if ineffectually plotting to remove their Fuehrer from power and stop the war before it was too late, had a vested interest in putting off *Operation Yellow* for as long as possible; and even commanders who were not disaffected tended to view the campaign, on purely professional grounds, with apprehensions which the event proved groundless.

The last postponement took place in January, shortly after a German aircraft carrying a complete set of orders for *Operation Yellow* had landed inadvertently in Belgian territory; this made available to the Allied High Command an accurate preview of Hitler's intentions, a forewarning which for various reasons failed to produce its proverbial effect. After this *Operation Yellow* was put off until the spring, and Europe, in the grip of frost, of fear and of an eerie sense of anticlimax, settled down to endure what America had taught it to call the Phoney War, the *drôle de guerre*. Along the Maginot Line patrol activity only sporadically disturbed the almost neighbourly relations which had grown up between the occupants of the French casemates and the German bunkers. The RAF dropped leaflets on Berlin and other German cities. In England, where the black-out was causing casualties but no bombs had yet fallen, people grew easily querulous; the well-meant activities of the Ministry of Information were a favourite target for indignation. As the long, ominous, aggravating lull persisted, the embattled democracies began to feel as if—like the wedding-guests in the nonsense-story—the gunpowder was running out of the heels of their boots. Only the Royal Navy, stretched to the uttermost to meet commitments of sovereign importance, felt no frustration.

Hitler, though temporarily baulked in the west by forces beyond his control, still held the initiative; no gunpowder was running out of *his* boots. In December Russia had attacked Finland. The leading formations of the Red Army were outfought by the Finns, and in the respite thus gained Allied plans for using the despatch of military aid to Finland as a pretext for the (it was hoped) peaceful occupation of certain Norwegian ports began to mature. One of these ports was Narvik, in the far north; Narvik was the bottleneck through which German industry received the bulk of its indispensable supplies of iron ore from the Swedish mines at Gallivare.

The Germans were not directly aware of these plans; but it required little imagination to see that they might be made, and less to see that they must at all costs be frustrated. Grand-Admiral Raeder, the Commander-in-Chief of the German Navy and probably the soundest strategist, though by no means the strongest personality, among Hitler's military advisers at this period, had in October sought, but failed, to interest the Fuehrer in the seizure of Norwegian bases. He now reverted to the project. His new proposals had behind them the compulsion, not of strategic desirability, but of strategic necessity; and the action they recommended was garnished with a sub-plot well calculated to appeal to Hitler's devious mind.

Rosenberg, a leading Nazi ideologist who specialised in quack racial theories, had made contact with a Norwegian politician whose name was shortly to enlarge the scope of European invective. The traitor Quisling, who had three interviews with Hitler in mid-December, canvassed a *coup d'état* in Oslo, backed if necessary by limited German support; when he and his associates were in power, the Germans could have all the bases and facilities they wanted. The backstairs approach appealed to Hitler, who relished all forms of trickery, deceit and subversion; neither the risks involved in nor the resources required for the enterprise were large. Quisling was encouraged to go ahead; but an alternative plan, envisaging the occupation of Norway by force, was prepared in case of necessity.

By the end of January the second plan had taken precedence over the first. Quisling's arrangements for a *pronunciamiento*, furthered—not always very helpfully—by what Rosenberg called "seasoned National Socialists who are experienced in such matters", had made disappointing progress. More important, Hitler was no longer immediately preoccupied with *Operation Yellow*, whose postponement until the spring had released (in particular) powerful air forces for employment elsewhere. On 3 March 1940 Hitler signed a directive which sealed the fate of both Norway and Denmark; the invasion of both countries began (and that of Denmark ended) on 9 April.

Though their basic purpose was defensive, or at any rate preventive, the conception of the Norwegian operations was extremely bold. It was however stealth and dissimulation, as much as audacity, which enabled the Germans to achieve surprise, and without surprise they must have failed.

Various *ruses de guerre* helped to get ships past the coastal batteries before the gun-crews realised that something was amiss, and at Narvik the invaders took advantage of parleys under the white flag to massacre the crews, totalling some 300 officers and men, of two coastal-defence vessels. Quisling's few but active adherents did not, as was generally supposed at the time, play any part in facilitating the invasion of their country, for the Germans told them nothing about their plans, and Quisling narrowly escaped being arrested by the German divisional commander in Oslo[1]; but here and there traitors proved serviceable in minor ways after the troops had come ashore. Favoured by luck and by several follies committed by the British, the Germans were able to seize all their main objectives; the first phase of the operation, though the German Navy suffered crippling losses, was a complete success.

So was the second. An Allied but preponderantly British force had been on the point of sailing to do, by more overt and humane methods, very much what the Germans did on 9 April. After a brief interlude of confusion and cross-purposes, this force was despatched to extrude the Germans from Narvik and from Trondheim and to strengthen the gallant but ill-found resistance which the Norwegians, under their King, were putting up in the south. It seemed that the Phoney War had ended. Later a phrase used, four days before the Germans invaded Norway, by the British Prime Minister came to be misremembered as an unforgivably foolish comment on the launching of the feeble Allied counter-stroke. "After seven months of war", Chamberlain told an influential Conservative gathering on 5 April, "I feel ten times as confident of victory as I did at the beginning. Hitler", he added with homely hubris, "has missed the bus."

It was an inapt diagnosis of the situation. The British forces were ill-equipped and for the most part ill-trained. The Allied campaign was directed, from London, with a blithe disregard for the realities of the situation, of which the most unpleasant, and the most decisive, was the Luftwaffe's almost unchallenged supremacy in the air. Less

[1] Louis de Jong: *The German Fifth Column in the Second World War*. London, 1955.

than three weeks after its leading elements had landed, the expedition to Central Norway, resourcefully extricated by the Royal Navy, was sailing for home, where its dazed survivors were hailed by the Press, with unconscious sarcasm, as "Norway veterans".

It is true that at Narvik, where the Luftwaffe's supremacy was less complete, British, French, Polish and Norwegian contingents remained behind to exert a slow and in the end unbearable pressure on the German garrison; the place was captured at the end of May. But by then *Operation Yellow* was in full swing, and under its manifold stresses the Allies had to renounce the fruits of the only victory they won on land during the first fifteen months of the war. The decision to evacuate Narvik was taken before it fell.

It is difficult, even in the light of after-knowledge, to cast an accurate balance-sheet of Hitler's gains and losses in Norway; it is at least arguable that the losses (and in particular the casualties suffered by the German Navy) offset, or perhaps more than offset, the gains.[1] But in April 1940 not even the staunchest casuist in the Allied camp could place upon the swift and total German victory an interpretation remotely favourable to the losers. At last, after the immolation of Austria, Czechoslovakia and Poland, the democracies had intervened to rescue a neutral state from aggression; the contemptuous ease with which they had been sent packing was a source of deep and bitter humiliation. One of Britain's sea-flanks had been turned; her Navy had formed, for the first time, a just and most disturbing appreciation of its limitations in the face of air-power; and soldiers who had taken part in the fiasco found in this Crimean curtain-raiser few reasons to look forward with confidence to the great drama which all vaguely knew was impending.

[1] "A fleet had been sacrificed to gain a base, but the base had little value without the fleet." (Dr Stefan T. Possony, *United States Naval Institute Proceedings*, July 1946.) This is a succinct statement of a view not likely to commend itself unreservedly to historians of the Allied convoys to North Russia. German naval losses off Norway were:

> one 8-inch cruiser
> two light cruisers
> ten destroyers
> eight submarines

These were all sunk. Many other vessels were damaged.

It began, as usual without an overture, almost before the quarter-masters had relieved late arrivals from Central Norway of the un-suitable Arctic equipment with which they had been cumbered. At dawn on 10 May 1940 the German juggernaut rolled forward, without the shadow of a pretext, across the Dutch and Belgian frontiers. What followed reduced the Norwegian disaster to the dimensions of a minor contretemps.

Hitler deployed eighty-nine divisions in *Operation Yellow*, with a further forty-seven in reserve. Armoured and motorised formations, boldly and ably handled, formed the spearhead of an advance for which, as in Poland and Norway, the Luftwaffe did much to pave the way. Airborne troops seized and neutralised key-points in the elaborate system of fortifications behind which the Low Countries had hoped, against all probability, somehow to preserve their neutrality.

The Dutch gave up after five days' fighting, the Belgians after seventeen. A powerful, unforeseen thrust through the Ardennes pierced the French front, reached the coast west of Abbeville and cut off the British Expeditionary Force and the French troops who were fighting alongside it. The attempts of the Allied High Command (at the apex of which Weygand had now succeeded Gamelin) to restore order out of something approaching chaos were altogether ineffectual. The encircled forces, British and French, began to fall back towards the coast.

What happened at Dunkirk scarcely needs to be recapitulated. By what seemed at the time a miracle but can in retrospect be more plausibly attributed to a failure in generalship on the Germans' part, 338,226 Allied troops, mostly British, were evacuated to England, some in small craft but the bulk of them in destroyers and transports. This operation, which was carried out under continuous air-attack and artillery fire in heavily mined waters, ended on 4 June.

The German error lay in halting, on 24 May, the advance of powerful armoured forces on Dunkirk from the south, when they were only a few miles from the as yet unorganised defensive perimeter of the Allied bridgehead. The order (for whose issue there were sound administrative reasons, since the tanks were in sore need of maintenance and their crews of rest) was given by von

Rundstedt, commanding Army Group A, and was approved by Hitler on the 24th; but it was not, as many German authorities have asserted, initiated by Hitler, although he did support von Rundstedt when, on the 25th, the latter resisted attempts by the Army High Command to have the advance resumed forthwith. It was not in fact resumed until 27 May, by which time improvised defences, held with a desperate tenacity, protected the embarkation area. This delay cost the Germans dear.

When men escape from mortal danger the mere act of survival has a curiously moving and even exhilarating effect upon them. The whole of Britain shared vicariously in these primitive emotions, and, for a few days at any rate, a wave of gratitude and relief served to blur the harsh outlines of the country's predicament.

But only for a few days. The Germans, swiftly reorganising their tired but triumphant forces, lost no time in striking south against the French, who had now, on land, only token support from the British. Their front on the Somme crumbled. When the Germans entered Paris (which had been declared an open city) on 14 June, their leading armoured units were already far south of the capital, driving almost unopposed into the bowels of France. Five weeks' campaigning had sufficed to give Hitler's directive for *Operation Yellow* the status of a collector's piece.

On 11 June Mussolini brought Italy into the war. His decision to do so had long been expected, and its timing earned him contempt in both camps. His forces, committed to gingerly operations against the French positions in the Alps, soon found themselves in difficulties; and for a time the Italian High Command toyed with the idea of flying troops into German-held airfields in the south of France, so that they could chalk up a victory of sorts against the broken French armies before an armistice was signed.

France was down and out. On 16 June Pétain replaced Reynaud and on 21 June, in the forest of Compiègne, an armistice was signed. Hitler caused the old restaurant-car which had witnessed a similar ceremony at the same spot on 11 November 1918 to be brought out from its museum for the occasion. The armistice came into force on 25 June.[1]

Hitler, striding past the news-reel cameras with the jaunty assurance which was his nearest approach to *panache*, left the formalities in the old restaurant-car at an early stage and led his retinue of notables and myrmidons down an avenue of tall trees towards waiting cars. There were, for once, few doubts about what he would do next.[2]

There had been none in Britain since Dunkirk. It was as obvious to her citizens as to her leaders that she was due for the *coup de grâce*. There was, to the best of their knowledge, only one way in which this could be delivered; and ever since Dunkirk—for more than six weeks, in other words, before Hitler issued his orders for *Operation Sea Lion* on 16 July—the British had been feverishly, but with a curious cheerfulness, improvising defences against invasion by a military machine which in three brisk imperious campaigns had shown itself to be irresistible, and indeed scarcely worth resisting.

[1] In the early hours of that day—the incident is recorded only for its symbolic value—a small, amateurish party of British Commandos, transported across the Channel in motor-boats manned by civilians, landed on the French coast. They killed two German soldiers (whose personal documents it did not occur to them to sequester) and returned to England. They suffered no casualties, but one of the boats was for some hours denied admittance to Folkestone harbour because none of her complement could establish his identity. (Christopher Buckley: *Norway: The Commandos: Dieppe*. London, 1951.)

[2] The German radio concluded its account of the proceedings at Compiègne by broadcasting *Wir fahren gegen Engelland*, a ditty to which in those days the Germans were often obliged to listen. It yielded pride of place a few weeks later to *Bomben auf Engelland*, an orgiastic melody which the Luftwaffe disliked.

CHAPTER TWO

A Bugbear in Eclipse

Many able writers have forcibly depicted the frightful sufferings which would follow the presence of hostile soldiery among us.

E. S. Creasy: *The Invasions and Projected Invasions of England, from the Saxon Times: with Remarks on the Present Emergencies.* 1852

THE behaviour of the British, once they realised that they were threatened with invasion, can fairly be called characteristic. What was however strangely out of character, and indeed scarcely capable of a rational explanation, was their complete failure to take the possibility of invasion into account at any time before the middle of May 1940. It is as though a kind of black-out had expunged from their minds, and even from their instincts, the lessons of history and the inherited promptings of tradition and experience. This odd phenomenon merits examination.

English history begins, for all save its more serious students, in 1066. Every Englishman knows that the successful Norman expedition to his shores was followed, more than 500 years later, by the stirring, but from the aggressor's point of view disastrous, episode of the Spanish Armada; and he knows too that Napoleon made certain preparations—which he suspects, wrongly, to have been of a ridiculous nature—for the invasion of the British Isles. On the basis of one successful invasion and a couple of major false alarms in nearly 900 years, the average Englishman had, as Hitler's war loomed up and at last broke over him, some excuse for not worrying unduly about the violability of his sea-girt frontiers.

Yet this was what his ancestors had always worried about when war broke out on the Continent. Since the end of the sixteenth century comparatively few generations had lived out their time immune from the threat—real or fancied—of invasion. Considering with what morbid ingenuity the best brains in England had mulled over, through the late Thirties, the dread consequences of the impending conflict: considering how hard the leaders of her armed services had striven to make the most appropriate types of brick with the little straw allowed them: considering the plain implications of Total War (a phrase then newly fashionable), it seems odd that no atavistic impulse in the islanders should have been stirred, that no school of thought should have advocated precautions against the traditional danger, that no one should have murmured: "Supposing he tries to invade us?" No one, so far as can be ascertained, did.

Tradition, precedent, experience—the British, facing an uncertain future, do not normally relinquish their hold on the three intertwined threads which have guided them through the labyrinth of the past. In 1798, several years before a French invasion became an imminent threat, the keeper of the State Paper Office was ordered to

discover what arrangements were made, for the internal defence of these Kingdoms, when Spain, by its Armada, projected the invasion and conquest of England; and how far the wise proceedings of our ancestors may be applicable to the present crisis of public safety.[1]

Why was something which seemed automatically worth doing in 1798 not pondered, not even mentioned, in roughly similar circumstances less than a century and a half later?

A comparison with the First World War can hardly be called instructive; it is, rather, baffling. Throughout that war, and despite the continuous and often desperate need to reinforce the Western Front, the British General Staff allocated to the defence of the east coast, first (for a few weeks in 1914) one of the six divisions of the Regular Army, and later forces of the Territorial Army which were never allowed to fall below four divisions of infantry and one of cavalry. During 1915 official estimates of the forces which the Germans might be able to land without being intercepted at sea rose from 70,000 to 160,000.[2] Though the threat of invasion—which was then envisaged rather as a large-scale raid than as an all-out attempt

[1] *Report on the Spanish Armada.* State Paper Office, 1798.
[2] In May 1915 a reporter on the staff of *The Times* wrote in his diary: "Early in the war the danger of invasion was seriously borne in mind. I have been kept on duty in the office all night in readiness to be sent to the East Coast if necessary, to describe a landing of the Germans. This precaution was taken on the advice of our Military Correspondent." (Michael MacDonagh: *In London during the Great War.* London, 1935.)

to conquer the country—receded as the war went on, it was never officially discounted by the British[1]; while by the Germans it was never officially entertained.

It is curious that what was almost a reflex action in 1914 should have been nowhere reflected in the thoughts, let alone the deeds, of Britain's military leaders when they went to war against the same adversary twenty-five years later; the verdict of an official historian of the Second World War that the danger of invasion was "so remote in experience as to be hard to conceive"[2] does not square with the facts. Still more curious is the contrast to be noted if we turn from the realm of strategical doctrine at the outbreak of both wars to that of popular literature and public opinion in the years which led up to each.

At the turn of the century the Boer War had shown Britain's military arrangements to be inadequate, obsolete and bad. More than a decade of peace followed, but throughout it, as Germany's shadow across their path lengthened and broadened, Englishmen, both in politics and outside it, strove to rouse the country to a realisation of the perils implicit in her weakness. Among those who did so, three novelists and one amateur playwright, using the medium of popular entertainment for purposes—avowed by all save one of them—of propaganda, made a German invasion of England the theme of works, each of which had in its own way a considerable impact upon the minds of their fellow-countrymen. If in those Edwardian days you wanted to sound the tocsin, it was invasion that, as the saying is, rang the bell; yet when war did come, invasion was never more than a bogey. In the anxious Thirties, though here and there a writer sought to depict the nation writhing in the grip of a totalitarian régime, none took a military assault upon the islands as the raw material for a novel or a play, or even

[1] As late as 25 October 1917 *The Times* reported an announcement by the Board of Trade in which the issue of petrol licences was made conditional on the licensee placing himself, his driver and his car or cars "at the disposal of the military authorities for use in the event of a national emergency". The emergency here contemplated, *The Times* explained, was "that which would be caused by the invasion . . . of our shores by an enemy force". The situation on the Western Front was critical at the time.

[2] T. H. O'Brien: *Civil Defence*. London, 1955.

for a pamphlet. "Unimaginable horrors" is a phrase which recurs in contemporary references by orators and leader-writers to the gradually impending Second World War. The old, fell, decisive contingency, which was imminently to threaten Britain within ten months of its outbreak, received no attention at all. It was a horror which no previous generation had found unimaginable.

The first and easily the best of the four pre-1914 works dealing with invasion did not, it is true, postulate a German landing, but only preparations for a landing which might not be undertaken for another decade. In *The Riddle of the Sands* (published in 1903) Erskine Childers described an amateur reconnaissance by two English yachtsmen of the north Frisian coast, in whose remoter interstices they found a flat-bottomed invasion-fleet under construction. The author, whose manner suggests an agreeable blend of Anthony Hope and John Buchan, backs up his exciting story with much local and technical knowledge which give it a compelling plausibility; and, quite apart from its enduring appeal to yachtsmen, the book can still be read with pleasure to-day. Despite the racy, unpretentious style in which it was written, it was a *roman a thèse*; and if the *roman* achieved a wider popularity than the *thèse*, the latter did not by any means go unheeded. The book was remembered long after the stir created by its appearance had died down, and it created, if anything, an even greater stir when it was reissued in a fresh edition in August 1914.

The next successful book dealing with the threat to Britain's territorial integrity was by William le Queux, a prolific writer of sensational fiction. *The Great Invasion of 1910, with a Full Account of the Siege of London*, appeared in 1906. "The object of this book", wrote its author, "is to illustrate our utter unpreparedness for war, to show how, under certain conditions which may easily occur, England can be successfully invaded by Germany, and to present a picture of the ruin which must inevitably fall upon us on the evening of that not far-distant day." An introductory letter in Field Marshal Lord Roberts's own hand (reproduced in facsimile) recommended the work "to the perusal of everyone who has the welfare of the British Empire at heart". The book gives a full-blooded account of a successful German invasion following a surprise landing in East Anglia. Le Queux's approach is documentary. He had—"by means of a motor-car"—carried out a careful survey of all his imaginary battlefields, and he had also studied German occupation methods during the Franco-Prussian war. The result belongs fundamentally to journalism rather than to literature; but, though the history of a campaign is perhaps easier to write before, rather than after, it has taken place, this one contains no inherent improbabilities and much verisimilitude. It seems fair to infer that Lord Roberts, the idol of the country and its leading soldier-statesman, would hardly have sponsored a book whose theme was regarded as fantastic or even unduly alarmist.

In the spring of 1909 a melodrama called *An Englishman's Home* was produced at Wyndham's Theatre and was received with enthusiasm. It depicted the impact on a comfortable but spineless lower-middle-class family in Essex of a foreign invasion. The invaders were called "Nearlanders" and said to be in the service of "Her Imperial Majesty the Empress of the North", a euphemism by which nobody in the audience allowed himself to be misled. "By a Patriot" was all it said about the playwright on the first-night programmes, but he was soon identified as Major Guy du Maurier, a regular officer in the Royal Fusiliers, a son of the artist George du Maurier and a brother of the actor Gerald. *An Englishman's Home*, rigged out with a happy ending in which, to the skirl of bagpipes, blue jackets drove the Nearlanders from the stricken suburban scene, had a long and successful run.[1] "A remarkable little play", *The Times* called it; and the *National Review*, after reporting that recruiting for the newly formed Territorial Army had risen sharply after the play's appearance, congratulated the author on "accomplishing what others have vainly tried to do by more humdrum methods". Du Maurier was killed on active service in Flanders in March 1915; his play is possibly less well remembered than the irreverent echo it

[1] A Berlin production of the play in the same year did not survive—did not, indeed, complete—its first performance; but this seems to have been due rather to bad acting than to any offence which its theme may have given to the Nearlanders. A scene from the original London production is reproduced opposite p. 65.

evoked in *Ruthless Rhymes for Heartless Homes*, by Harry Graham, where the following lines appeared under the title "The Englishman's Home":

> I was playing golf the day
> That the Germans landed;
> All our troops had run away,
> All our ships were stranded;
> And the thought of England's shame
> Very nearly spoilt my game.

The last of the four works was *When William Came*, published in 1913.[1] In this "Saki" (H. H. Munro) drew, for the benefit of a more sophisticated public than the others could be sure of reaching, a picture of fashionable society in a German-occupied London. It is an acute, satirical study of what came, much later, to be called collaboration. The writer's touch is light, but there is no mistaking his implicit purpose, or the contempt and hatred he felt (and wanted others to share) for the people in high places who refused to recognise Britain's need to be strong in an hour of danger. Like du Maurier, Munro was killed in action in Flanders.

From 1933, the year in which the German people voted the Nazi Party into power, until the outbreak of war in 1939, the British became increasingly aware of the peril in which they stood. Although at first the true prophets, few in number, were scouted as alarmists, the nation as a whole slowly awoke—the process being deprecated rather than encouraged by its leaders—to the realisation that it was threatened, that it was weak, that the worst was almost bound to happen. The urgency of the situation and the need to rearm were widely, ably and imaginatively canvassed; yet it occurred to no one, as it had to Le Queux, du Maurier and the others, that invasion was a drum worth beating in this cause.

It was, oddly enough, left to a German writer to raise the subject, and he did so in such a way as to stir up the maximum of con-

---

[1] In the same year *Chums* concluded, after six months, the run of a serial called *The Swoop of the Eagle: A Story of the German Invasion*. Each instalment was prefaced by an editorial note: "This story is not intended to stir up race hatred, but is written as a true picture of what would happen if a great Continental nation attacked our country."

troversy and discussion. In February 1934 a book called *Germany, Prepare for War!* by Dr Ewald Banse was published in London. Strenuous efforts had been made by the German authorities to prevent its appearance in an English translation, for its publication in Germany—under the title of *Raum und Volk im Weltkriege*—in the previous November had already caused a scandal; and the German Embassy in London made haste to issue a statement branding Banse as an "irresponsible theoretician" whose absurd ideas were not taken seriously in Germany. "The German Government", said the statement, "will have nothing to do with his nonsensical views, and are determined not to allow their policy of peace to be frustrated by the propagandist exploitation of private views."

Banse, though depicted in some quarters as the *éminence grise* of German military doctrine, was in fact an obscure professor at Brunswick Technical College. The lubberly arrogance of his book, with its plea for the breeding by eugenics of a race of military *Herrenvolk* and its advocacy of bacteriological warfare and other extreme measures as a means of crushing Germany's foes, seems to-day a fairly typical product of the higher National Socialist thinking; but in February 1934 the true nature of this demented philosophy was scarcely apprehended in Germany, let alone outside it, and there was some excuse for dismissing Banse as a crank.

An embittered crank; for of Britain he had written (and it was this sentence which ensured a hearing for his views among the British): "We confess that it gives us pleasure to meditate on the destruction that must sooner or later overtake a proud and seemingly invincible nation, and to think that this country, which was last conquered in 1066, will once more obey a foreign master." [1]

In 1934 Germany was not a first-class military power, or anything like one; and it was natural that Banse's strategy, outlined in pathological language, should then have been ignored as the ravings

[1] Thirty years earlier the same sentiment, rather more urbanely expressed, had won a minor *succès de scandale* in London for another German author, August Niemann. *The Coming Invasion of England* (a title freely translated from *Der Weltkrieg: Deutsche Träume*) was a work of fiction falling—in technique—midway between Childers and le Queux. In this agreeably preposterous novel the Germans, assisted by the Russians and the French, subdue Britain without much difficulty after an unopposed landing in the Firth of Forth.

of a splenetic visionary. Yet it does seem odd that his open advocacy of invasion found nowhere lodgement in a pigeon-hole of the national consciousness, should never have been remembered and re-examined in the deepening twilight of the years that followed, until at last, on 4 June 1940 (the day on which evacuation from Dunkirk ended), a letter to *The Times* (beginning "Never has Great Britain had an enemy who has told her so plainly and in so much detail as Herr Hitler what he intends to do") recalled with the help of one of his own maps the Professor's recipe for a British defeat.

Banse's lust to invade England was not, as will appear, reflected in German strategy until the summer of 1940; but the British, who could not know this, had no good reason for ignoring his spirited attempt to raise a subject on which they had always held strong and almost instinctive views. The very speed with which Banse was officially disowned might have seemed in retrospect suspicious. But no; he was forgotten. Five years before the First World War a crude melodrama by an amateur playwright had awakened thousands of Englishmen to the need to defend their shores against the Germans; five years before the Second World War a considered, hate-charged, widely publicised book by a serious German writer prophesying the invasion of England wholly failed to remind its inhabitants that invasion might one day again be a military possibility.

Yet although Banse was a prophet without honour, one at least of his prophecies was not far off the mark. A descent upon the east coast formed the main basis of his plan for the conquest of England, but he examined also the prospects for a cross-Channel operation. "To get an army across the Channel to the Kent coast [he wrote] should prove a relatively simple business, particularly if the attacker is in possession of the French Channel ports of Dunkirk, Calais and Boulogne, from which he can clear the Channel of English ships with artillery."

In 1940 not only did the Germans settle for an attack across the Channel, but a misplaced faith in the value of coastal artillery as an antidote to the Royal Navy was almost an obsession with Hitler and the German General Staff through all the stages of planning for *Sea Lion*.

Just as *The Riddle of the Sands* had seemed worth republishing in

August 1914, so in May 1939 the tense atmosphere was thought propitious to a revival in London of *An Englishman's Home*, refurbished and brought up to date. The melodrama is of primitive craftsmanship, and it is not surprising that the venture should have failed. What is surprising is that the play's theme should have struck the critics as devoid of topicality. "To-day", wrote *The Times*, "the picture of invasion had lost its power to startle." The *News Chronicle* deduced "from the presence in the theatre last night of a guard of honour from the RAF" that the play was "seeking to revive its old appeal". This time its message not only failed to sound the tocsin; it did not even ring a bell.

Dramatic critics can perhaps be forgiven if their grasp of strategic possibilities is infirm. A less ample margin of error is allowable to the leading military writer of the day, who had served from 1937 to 1938 as personal adviser to the Secretary of State for War. Yet in *The Defence of Britain*, published in July 1939, these were the conclusions reached by Captain Liddell Hart: "England . . . is . . . more secure than ever before against invasion. . . . There is sound cause for discounting the danger of invasion." The dramatic critic of *The Times* had spoken something less than the truth. The picture of invasion not merely no longer startled; it was no longer descried.

Was there a reason, or an excuse, for the blindness which seems to have afflicted the British at this period, obliterating so many of the lessons of experience and causing them, as they peered anxiously into the future, to leave altogether out of account the contingency to which those lessons pointed? Why did nobody entertain the possibility, so soon to become a near-certainty, that the islands would be invaded?

The aberration seems inexplicable, but certain things which probably contributed to it may be noted as a pendant to this digression. In the First World War, though precautions were taken against an invasion, the Germans neither carried out nor contemplated one; this must have had some subconscious influence on men's minds. The relative weakness of the German Navy lessened the risks of seaborne assault (though it can hardly be said to have precluded discussion of those risks). Finally, as war approached, people at all levels became increasingly obsessed with the part which air power, and bombers in particular, would play in it; had it been advanced, the idea that the coasts might need defending would have seemed obsolete and irrelevant while shelters were being hastily excavated in Hyde Park. Total war—unimaginable horrors—grass growing in the streets of London: the cant phrases passed from mouth to mouth, and counsel was darkened by a general fear of unknown, untried ordeals. Few, in their hearts, ruled out the possibility of Britain's defeat; it occurred to none that their new enemy might at some stage have an opportunity of encompassing it by the methods to which almost all their old enemies had attempted to seek recourse in the end.

CHAPTER THREE

The Background to the German Plan

We may therefore be sure that there is a plan—perhaps built up over years—for destroying Great Britain, which after all has the honour to be his main and foremost enemy.

Winston Churchill, on 14 July 1940

Hitler could no longer defer consideration of how the war against England was to be continued once the Channel coast was reached. It was a thought he had hitherto avoided.

General Franz Halder

We might, had the plans been ready, have crossed to England with strong forces after the Dunkirk operation.

General Guenther Blumentritt

ALTHOUGH Hitler's directive for *Operation Sea Lion* was not issued until 16 July, the idea of an invasion first received his attention nearly two months earlier, on 21 May; this was the day on which German spearheads reached the French coast. Raeder, the Commander-in-Chief of the German Navy, was responsible for bringing it forward. It was coolly received.

Raeder had an interview with Hitler on 21 May. It was Hitler's unpractical custom to rely upon the *tête-à-tête* rather than the inter-service conference when dealing with his commanders-in-chief, and there was only one occasion in the summer of 1940—on 14 September—when he saw all three of them together.[1] He trusted nobody. Things had not yet reached the stage when every visitor to his headquarters, no matter how distinguished, was searched for arms by SS guards before being admitted to his presence; but one puppet is always easier to manipulate than three, and doubtless—remote though the contingency was at this stage—Hitler thought it possible that his military triumvirs, if dealt with as a triumvirate, might one day sink their differences and combine to oppose his designs. He intensely disliked being disagreed with.

[1] Goering was represented by his chief of staff, Jeschonnek, at this conference.

The need for inter-service planning when a combined operation is being mounted is to-day axiomatic; it requires an effort of the imagination to remember that in 1940 this was a novel conception, untried and scarcely recognised on either side of the Channel or the Atlantic. It would be unfair to criticise the staffs of the three German armed services for failing to integrate themselves more effectively than they did; but it must be pointed out that their Supreme Commander set them a bad example. Inter-service rivalries and misunderstandings were a factor, though only a contributory one, in Hitler's failure to implement his plans for invading England; if he himself did not actively help to promote them, he did a great deal less than a Supreme Commander should to reduce the handicap which they imposed on his forces.

Raeder's motives for raising the question of invasion on 21 May (and again, with more effect, a month later) are not known. To say that he never viewed the operation with enthusiasm is to give a very mild idea of the assiduity with which, as will appear, he drew attention to its hazards and difficulties at every stage of the planning; and on the documentary evidence alone there is an obvious contradiction between the Grand-Admiral's status as the "onlie begetter" of *Sea Lion* in May and June and his less than lukewarm attitude to the project throughout the following three months. Why did Raeder blow hot (when there was no need for him to blow at all) and thereafter consistently blow cold?

The navy had been out of the running, and the limelight, in *Operation Yellow*; but to attribute, as one authority tentatively does,[1] Raeder's misplaced zeal to "self-importance and professional jealousy" is to underrate the man and to over-simplify the situation. It is well to remember that on 21 May 1940 the idea of an invasion of England, although as far as we know entirely novel to Hitler, was by no means so to Raeder. What had happened was this.

On 15 November 1939 Raeder gave an order for "the possibility of invading England to be examined". In his testimony at Nuremberg (where he was sentenced to imprisonment for life)[2] Raeder said, in effect, that he did this as a precautionary measure, fearing

[1] F. H. Hinsley: *Hitler's Strategy*. Cambridge, 1951.
[2] He was released in 1955.

that some quirk of Hitler's intuition might suddenly confront him with a demand for an invasion-plan. This is a plausible explanation of Raeder's action.

A fortnight later the naval planners had reached the conclusion that a sea-borne assault "on a grand scale" across the North Sea "appears to be a possible expedient for forcing the enemy to sue for peace". The ball was passed in November to the Army, whose comments and suggestions included some which were unacceptable to the Navy; and in the following month the Luftwaffe made known their views, which were uncompromisingly sceptical. All variants of this early plan envisaged landings on the east coast. At no stage was it referred to OKW,[1] and there is no reason to suppose that Hitler knew that any preliminary planning for invasion had been done until Raeder told him about it on 21 May.[2]

Why did Raeder tell him about it? The preliminary planning had revealed, in addition to the inherent and formidable difficulties of the undertaking, a wide measure of disagreement between the three services. Events, furthermore, had overtaken the plan, many of whose basic assumptions had been rendered obsolete by the welcome but unforeseen scope of *Operation Yellow's* success. Raeder was not in the happy and meritorious position of a bridge-player who lays down a dummy hand with several aces in it; he was revealing, rather, the weakness of cards which he had no wish to play.

Raeder was shrewd, tidy-minded, provident and conscientious. He had responsibilities both to Hitler, as his senior adviser on naval affairs, and to the German Navy, as its Commander-in-Chief. It was his duty in his first capacity to call his Fuehrer's attention to a strategy which, if successful, would end the war; it was his duty in his second capacity to ensure as far as possible that the German Navy

---

[1] OKW stood for *Oberkommando der Wehrmacht* (Armed Forces Supreme Command). This abbreviation has been used throughout, for convenience and to avoid confusion with its three subordinate *Oberkommandos*. A diagram showing the organisation of the German High Command will be found in the Appendix on p. 310.

[2] A comprehensive list of "the general tasks of the German Navy" in the forthcoming war had appeared in May 1939 in a secret directive headed *Battle Instructions for the Navy*. It included no reference to landing operations.

was not hazarded either in a last-minute gamble or in a combined operation over whose mounting and execution it had less than its fair share of control. On both these counts Raeder seems to have done the right thing by raising the question of invasion at the earliest moment after the enterprise began to transfer itself from the realm of long-range planning to that of operational expediency; and it may well have been lucky for Great Britain that his distrust of Hitler's military genius deterred him from mentioning the project while it was still only a long-range plan.

On 21 May Hitler's reactions to the idea were negative. Raeder's record of what transpired reads: "The Fuehrer and the Commander-in-Chief, Navy, discuss in private[1] details concerning the invasion of England, on which the Naval Staff has been working since November." Just before broaching the subject, Raeder, ostensibly or perhaps genuinely (and certainly not for the first time) seeking guidance as to the right policy to follow in regard to U-boat construction and training, had asked a leading question: was the war going to be decided quickly, or was it wiser to assume that it would "last some time"? Hitler favoured the second assumption. His forces were, after all, engaged in heavy fighting against the Allied armies; the fog of war still hung over a confused and far-flung battle-front. (Halder, the Chief of Staff at OKH, wrote in his diary that evening: "The overall picture of the day shows that the big battle is in full swing.") Through this fog the glint of golden, unsuspected opportunities, which might have been discerned by a Great Captain, failed to catch Hitler's eye.[2] It is possible, too, that the "details concerning the invasion of England" which Raeder brought for the first time to his attention were not of an alluring

[1] Generals Keitel and Jodl, of OKW, as well as Hitler's naval adjutant, Commander von Puttkamer, had as usual been present throughout the rest of the interview, at which this was the last item discussed.

[2] On 6 June Halder was complaining: "The Fuehrer . . . wants to play absolutely safe. . . . On top, there just isn't a spark of the spirit that would dare to put high stakes on a single throw. Instead, everything is done in cheap, piecemeal fashion." Admittedly the occasion for this criticism was the rejection of certain proposals made by the critic for a change in the plan of campaign in France; but Halder was a loyal and self-effacing staff-officer, whose objectivity was not easily impaired by pique.

kind. At any rate he showed no interest, and at Raeder's next
interview—on 4 June—the matter was not mentioned at all. The
fact that it had been discussed on 21 May was never disclosed to the
Army High Command nor, as far as is known, to anyone outside
Raeder's own headquarters.

Raeder did however bring it forward again on 20 June. The
French had asked for an armistice two days earlier, Italy was safely
in the war, and Europe lay at Hitler's feet. This, surely, was the
moment for him to press on with plans which—unless the British
lost their nerve and gave in—represented his best chance of bringing
the war to a speedy and triumphant end. But once more, when
Raeder reported on "the preparations for an invasion of England
... the locality chosen for landing ... mines ... shipping ... special
craft ... air supremacy", Hitler made no comment which Raeder
found worthy of recording. He spoke, instead, of a project for
settling Jews on Madagascar, and listened while Raeder, after
complaining about a "rude telegram" which Goering had sent him,
went on to explain the impracticability of a plan which Hitler had
ordered to be made for invading Iceland. For this operation, to
which the unhopeful code-name *Icarus* had been allotted, "the entire
Navy", said its Commander-in-Chief, "will have to be used".
Hitler does not, on 20 June 1940, seem to have been at the height
of his powers as a strategist.

Nevertheless, things began to move after this. On 17 June
Warlimont, the deputy Chief (under Jodl) of the Operations Staff
at OKW, had noted that "with regard to a landing in Britain, the
Fuehrer ... has not up to now expressed such an intention, as he
fully appreciates the unusual difficulties of such an operation. Therefore, even at this time, no preparatory work has been carried out at
OKW." Only the Navy had begun—by, for instance, provisionally
earmarking shipping and collating a mass of topographical intelligence about the English coast from the Isle of Wight to the Wash—
to do certain things which would have to be done, and done in a
hurry, if an invasion was to be launched that year.

At this stage—late June—the Army were still completely in the
dark. On 15 June OKH had been ordered to reduce the Army's

strength to 120 divisions; this meant demobilising roughly a fifth
of the men under arms and returning them to industry and
agriculture, where they were badly needed. Halder deduced that
this order was "based on the assumption that with the now imminent
final collapse of the enemy [i.e. France] the Army will have
fulfilled its mission" and that "the Air Force and the Navy will be
carrying on the war against Britain alone".

On 22 June, however, his diary mentions "preparations against
England" in connection with an OKH regrouping programme; and
it would be natural to assume—since Keitel and Jodl had been
present when on the previous day Raeder had given Hitler an
account of the Navy's arrangements for invasion, and since OKW's
main *raison d'être* was to co-ordinate the activities of the three
services—that the Army had been given by the Supreme Command
at least an inkling of what might be in the wind.

If they had, it must have been an imprecise inkling. On
26 June the commander of Army Group A (von Rundstedt) sent
an emissary to Halder to criticise the dispositions allotted to him
under the regrouping programme. This officer got no satisfaction,
and when he had gone Halder recorded his view that von Rundstedt
"from sheer ego wants a strip of the Channel coast. The contention
that the new dispositions, as ordered, would not form a sufficient
threat against England is childish. The threat to England is in the
number of divisions drawn up opposite her coast, and not in the
boundary line between Army Groups." Halder was too good a
soldier, and too intelligent a man, to have written those words if
he knew that the Army was going to be ordered to cross the Channel.
He would never have attributed to "sheer ego", or dismissed as
"childish", a soldierly anxiety not to be left out of a difficult and
decisive operation; and it is clear that at this stage he regarded the
"threat to England" as being limited to a demonstration in force,
a sort of minatory window-dressing, similar to, but solider than,
the bluff against the Austrian frontier which had produced such
satisfactory results in February 1938.

Colour is lent to this interpretation by the fact that, when planning
for *Operation Sea Lion* did start, Army Group A, so far from being
denied whatever of prestige or amenity went with the occupation

of a strip of the Channel coast, was made responsible for the main assault on England.

A week later the whole machine was put into gear and set in motion by an OKW order dated 2 July 1940, headed *The War Against England*, and signed by Keitel. It began:

> *The Fuehrer and Supreme Commander has decided . . . that a landing in England is possible, provided that air superiority can be attained and certain other necessary conditions fulfilled.*

No date had been fixed, but all preparations were to begin at once; they were, however, to "be undertaken on the basis that the invasion is still only a plan, and has not yet been decided upon". One point about this plan must be noted now, for it will gain in significance as the story unfolds. The plan called for the landing in England of 25–40 divisions; "the invading forces", Keitel insisted, "must be highly mechanised and numerically superior to the opposing armies".

A fortnight later the OKW order was ratified and expanded by Hitler's Directive No. 16.

CHAPTER FOUR

Directive No. 16

Lear. I will do such things—
What they are yet I know not; but they shall be
The terror of the earth.

Shakespeare

"How can I get in?" asked Alice again, in a louder tone.
"Are you to get in at all?" said the Footman. "That's the first question, you know." It was, no doubt! only Alice did not like to be told so.

Lewis Carroll: *Alice in Wonderland*

IN the preamble to this document[1] it is possible to detect petulance and irresolution. The words in which Hitler defined his intentions ("*I have decided to begin to prepare for, and if necessary to carry out, an invasion of England*") lack the crisp, compulsive, off-with-his-head ring which was a normal feature of his style in these contexts.[2] It would however be wrong to suppose that Hitler's mealy-mouthed statement of his operational aims was due *mainly* to his misgivings about the feasibility of the operation. He was still not only hoping for, but actively working to bring about, that compromise which the beaten British had—"*so far*", as the Directive noted—shown themselves unwilling to accept. His strategy at this stage was schizophrenic. Dr Jekyll, wistfully titivating his olive-branch, ought not to have prevented Mr Hyde from sharpening his sword; but this is what did happen, and the duality of Hitler's purpose, reflecting the strange mixture of esteem and spite which underlay his attitude to England, will merit closer appraisal at a later stage.

[1] See p. 15.
[2] The first paragraph of Hitler's directive for the attack on Poland ends "*I have decided on a solution by force*". The corresponding words in the directive for Yugoslavia are "*Yugoslavia . . . must be crushed as speedily as possible*". The warning order for *Barbarossa* begins: "*The German Armed Forces must be ready to crush Soviet Russia in a rapid campaign.*"

From a practical point of view, easily the most important thing about Directive No. 16 is its date. Eight weeks had elapsed since Raeder had first discussed the invasion of England with Hitler; six weeks since the BEF had been driven into the sea, four weeks since the fall of France, two weeks since Hitler had ordered preparations to begin "*on the basis that the invasion is still only a plan, and has not yet been decided upon*". For the attack on Czechoslovakia (which in the end did not need to be delivered) Hitler had issued his orders four months in advance: for Poland five months in advance : for France and the Low Countries five weeks before the planned D-Day and seven months before the actual operation. Even for the impromptu aggression against Norway his commanders had been given five weeks' warning. Now he was allowing them (on paper) four weeks, and in practice—since the season imposed a limit on postponements—a maximum of nine or ten, in which to carry out an operation, more hazardous and unfamiliar than any that had gone before it, for which they were neither equipped nor trained. And it must be remembered that now his land and air forces were not poised and fresh, but were sorting themselves out after an arduous campaign which had carried them far from their supply bases in Germany.

There can be little doubt that Hitler would have improved *Operation Sea Lion*'s prospects of success if he had given the necessary orders earlier than he did. Had he, for instance, ordered planning to start, and certain administrative measures to be put in hand, at the end of May, his commanders would have come to grips with their problems at a much earlier stage of the proceedings. A plan less disfigured by controversy and compromise could have been evolved, the assault formations would have benefited from two or three weeks' extra training, and less empirical answers could have been found to such important technical questions as that (for instance) of artillery support for the first wave during the critical phase of disembarkation on the beaches. Given the fact that Hitler did not in 1939 foresee the possibility of invasion in 1940, the Germans were bound to be dangerously short of time; but they need not have been as short as they were if Hitler had welcomed the possibility when it was first put before him.

In fairness to Hitler, however, it is necessary to remind the reader that in 1940 combined or amphibious operations were not recognised, as they soon came to be, as a well-established branch of the art of war. During the First World War the only combined operation carried out by the German Army had been a landing, in approximately divisional strength, on the island of Oesel in the Baltic, a sea in which tides do not seriously complicate the problems of the assault. The date chosen coincided, whether by accident or design, with the anniversary celebrations of the day on which the islanders had been granted permission to malt barley for brewing purposes, and opposition by the Russian garrison was easily overcome. But this small side-show was carried out by the same unstudied, *ad hoc* methods as the British had used on a larger scale at Gallipoli two years earlier.

Between the wars, though river-crossing exercises were regularly included in the training programmes of most European armies and important harbours were still defended by coastal artillery, the problems of landing a large force on a hostile coast in the face of opposition received scant attention. When in 1938 Japanese forces directed on Hankow carried out landings in the middle reaches of the Yangtse, using ships and landing-craft specially designed for the purpose, a wave of interest swept through the small world of peacetime military intelligence; the curiosity aroused was a measure of the neglect in which the study of amphibious operations, and the design of equipment for them, had languished since Napoleon's *Grande Armée* struck its tents at Boulogne and turned its back on its familiar training-grounds on the Channel coast.[1] It would be wrong to blame Hitler too severely for his brash approach to the problem of putting a large expedition across a narrow but intransigent sea.

[1] In 1899, when Anglo-French relations were strained by the Fashoda Incident, a French writer advocated the building of a large number of armoured landing craft of about 80 tons displacement. They were to draw less than three feet and to be equipped with landing-ramps. He pointed out that 1,500 of these vessels would cost less than five battleships, which would soon be obsolete anyhow: that—unlike battleships—they could be used in peacetime for coastal and riverine trade: and that they would make the successful invasion of England not only possible but certain. Nobody took any notice of his sensible ideas. (Admiral Sir Herbert W. Richmond: *The Invasion of Britain*. London, 1941.)

On July 13 von Brauchitsch and Halder—who found his Fuehrer still "greatly puzzled by Britain's persisting unwillingness to make peace"—had conferred with Hitler at the Berghof, his mountain retreat near Salzburg, and the operation orders contained in Directive No. 16 were based largely on their recommendations. (At this stage of the war OKW's function was to approve rather than to initiate plans.) The Army, after a fortnight's study of the problem, had taken over the running from the Navy, and as a result the Directive made a number of assumptions and demands which were to prove, in the light of inter-service scrutiny, unrealistic.

Paragraph 1 postulated "a surprise crossing on a broad front extending approximately from Ramsgate to a point west of the Isle of Wight." Long before the *Sea Lion* plans reached their final version all hopes of surprise (save in the pettiest sense of the word) had been abandoned, and a narrow front had perforce been substituted for a broad one.

This paragraph also required each of the fighting services to "consider the advantages . . . of preliminary operations such as the occupation of the Isle of Wight or the Duchy of Cornwall before the full-scale invasion". No more was heard of this project which, if adopted, would hardly have improved the prospects for a "surprise crossing".

Paragraph 2 demanded the elimination of effective opposition by the RAF: the sweeping of mines from the sea-routes: the laying of impassable minefields on "both flanks of the Straits of Dover and the western approaches to the Channel, approximately on a line from Alderney to Portland": the domination and protection of "the entire coastal front area" by heavy coastal guns: and the "pinning down" of the Royal Navy in the North Sea and (by the Italians) in the Mediterranean.

A streak of Maginot-mindedness, as well as the ignorance of landsmen, is here apparent in the German plans for a sea-crossing; it was to remain a feature of all later variants. Their faith in what Churchill called "balustrades" of mines to protect their sea-flanks was misplaced and callow. It was not for a night or two, but for weeks on end, that their flanks would need protection; it is inconceivable that their minefields (of which the more westerly was to be some sixty miles long) would not have been breached by sweeping or if necessary by more drastic methods.[1]

Equally unsound was the reliance on heavy guns, firing both from the French coast and, later, from the German bridgeheads in southern England, to keep the Royal Navy at a respectful distance. Artillery was not in those days equipped with radar, and could therefore only engage a target which it could see; this meant that at night or in bad visibility (when the air force was equally impotent) the guns were useless against ships at sea. Moreover, the bigger a gun the slower its rate of fire, the shorter the life of its barrel, and the less, after every round, the accuracy of its performance.

Minefields were better than nothing; coastal artillery could have appropriately formed an embellishment to the main plan. Neither expedient deserved, or was capable of supporting, the leading role which Hitler (like the "irresponsible theoretician", Banse) allotted to it.

But the key to the misapprehensions which throughout vitiated the German plans, even when they became better laid, is contained in the second sentence of paragraph 1. The first sentence called for a "surprise crossing on a broad front"; the second sentence explained that "elements of the Air Force will do the work of the artillery, and elements of the Navy the work of the engineers".

This homely over-simplification, though apt enough for use by an instructor addressing a cadre of young officers or senior NCOs, is not the language of high strategy in which a Supreme Commander

[1] The Germans had already exploited the element of surprise which the British, by neglect, had allowed the magnetic mine to retain. The British had used an unsatisfactory version of this weapon at the end of the First World War. Before the Second World War broke out they had a standard magnetic mine ready for production, and an Admiralty Committee was actively studying the protection of ships against this form of attack. Nevertheless, German magnetic mines sank a quarter of a million tons of shipping in three months during the winter of 1939-40 before their secrets were mastered. In April and May 1940 British magnetic mines, making a tardy début, sank just over a tenth of this tonnage. (Captain S. W. Roskill, DSC, RN: *The War at Sea*, Vol. I. London, 1954.)

Acoustic mines were brought into service by the Germans during August 1940. These had, initially, the same power to disconcert and to delay which is inherent in the cunning use of all such weapons; but the supply of them was not enough to stiffen or even to diversify importantly the long, wide balustrades with which the Germans hoped to protect their sea-lanes.

issues directives to his commanders-in-chief. Behind it lay the fallacy—in which there was perhaps as much of wishful thinking as of true delusion—that *Sea Lion* was only a glorified river-crossing. The analogy recurs throughout the soldiers' first reactions to the project. A river-crossing was something they understood, had practised, could look up in their manuals. There was comfort, both for the generals and for the former infantry corporal who now commanded them, in the thesis that there was not much difference between a narrow sea and a wide river: that instead of firing shells across the latter you achieved the same result by carrying bombs across the former: and that the Navy's task was merely to provide the facilities which the drill-book required of the sappers, with their rafts and pontoons. If you looked at the operation in that way, you felt that you knew where you were.

Between the making of a military plan and its execution, it is normal for some counsels of perfection to be abandoned, some assumptions to be found erroneous and some requirements impossible to meet. There is however a limit to the extent to which the *essentials* of a plan can be sacrificed on the altar of necessity. The element of surprise, which Directive No. 16 rather piously invoked, was a counsel of perfection and as such expendable. The substitution of a narrow front for a broad front might have impaired, but did not obliterate, the prospects for successful landings. And there was clearly some scope for reduction in the size of the forces to be put ashore.

But not unlimited scope. The OKW "warning order" of 2 July had prescribed 25-40 divisions, and on 21 July—five days after he had issued Directive No. 16—Hitler reaffirmed to Raeder (who had submitted a memorandum on *Sea Lion* which was so gloomy as to be almost a *non possumus*) that "40 divisions will be required".

In the event, as we shall see, this figure was reduced to 13. Obligatory though it was, this huge reduction lends an air of whimsy to the whole project; you cannot decide on the size of an army by the empirical methods with which you guess the weight of a cheese at a fair. During August and September the Germans over-estimated the strength of British forces in the United Kingdom by roughly 8 divisions,[1] and they realised that their equipment and training were improving every day. It is impossible to see realism, logic or even common sense in the two incompatible theses that (a) 40 divisions were needed to conquer the island in mid-August and (b) 13 would suffice to do the trick a month later. This is strategy only in the sense that Procrustes was a surgeon.

Before we leave Directive No. 16, the arrangements under which command was to be exercised during *Sea Lion* require to be examined. Hitler decreed that:

The Commanders-in-Chief of the respective branches of the Armed Forces will lead their forces, under my orders. The Army, Navy and Air Force General Staffs should be within an area of no more than 50 km from my Headquarters (Ziegenberg) by 1 August. I suggest that the Army and Naval General Staffs establish their Headquarters at Giessen.

This order has certain claims upon our interest. The first is that it was almost certainly (more certainly even than the promotion of the code-name *Lion* to *Sea Lion*) the product of Hitler's own brain and will and owed nothing to the promptings of his advisers. The operational content of Directive No. 16 followed closely the recommendations of the OKH planning staff, put forward by von Brauchitsch and Halder in their interview with Hitler on 13 July. The orders for the move of the headquarters of the three commanders-in-chief to the Giessen area took even OKW by surprise. "*Is this right about Giessen?*" Keitel wrote in the margin of the draft Directive. (He meant: Is Giessen within 50 km of Ziegenberg? Schloss Ziegenberg, though it had been earmarked and equipped for occupation as a headquarters, had not yet been used as one by OKW or anyone else; there was no particular reason for Keitel to know exactly where it was.) Jodl set his superior's small mind at rest.

"*Yes,*" he wrote, lower down in the margin, "*it is 30 km away.*" Giessen, then, was Hitler's own idea. Was it a good one?

Both in theory and in practice, the closer the contact between a

---

[1] The actual strength of Home Forces and the garrison of Northern Ireland in these months was 29 divisions and 8 independent brigades. All were below their establishment in men and equipment. See page 179.

commander and his immediate subordinates, the better. But to move any headquarters creates difficulties and delays, not merely for the small number of officers and men directly involved, but for the units or formations under their control. However smoothly the move is carried out (and the Germans excelled at this sort of thing) a staff is a sensitive machine which in the process of being transplanted suffers a temporary loss of efficiency; and this is particularly true when the staffs concerned are not those of field formations, who are inured to a nomadic existence, but belong to exalted, static, bureaucratic organisations, accustomed only to the comfortable ruts of routine.

No doubt everyone would have settled in quite quickly at Giessen, where extensive but not altogether satisfactory accommodation for a headquarters had been built by the Germans before the war. No doubt all three commanders-in-chief would have brought with them—Raeder from Berlin, von Brauchitsch from Fontainebleau and Goering from Potsdam—only the minimum number of staff officers, clerks, draughtsmen, cipher personnel, cooks, batmen, drivers and so on. But no one who has had experience of such matters will find it easy to believe that to uproot and transplant the four [1] most important military headquarters in Germany could have been done without *some* prejudice to the preparations which they had been ordered to complete—and to complete within thirty days. All three services were working against time. The Army had scarcely begun amphibious training, the Luftwaffe was regrouping and reorganising, and the Navy knew already that it had no hope of getting the invasion-fleet assembled, adapted and manned by the required date in mid-August. To impose upon his commanders-in-chief (without consulting them) the distractions and delays inseparable from a move of their operational headquarters was a minor act of folly on Hitler's part [2]; and in fact the moves never took place, being postponed by an OKW order of 1 August until "immediately before the beginning of the operation" and thereafter

[1] Including OKW.

[2] Halder's diary shows that on 20, 21, 22 and 26 July (a period of intense activity at OKH) he spent part of each day discussing matters relating to the move to Giessen, receiving—among other things—unfavourable reports on the internal telephone system and the lay-out of the offices. A Chief of Staff may feel himself obliged to devote some time to inessentials; he should never be compelled to do so.

fading, with the rest of *Operation Sea Lion*, into the limbo of the unfulfilled.[1]

If the orders for Giessen appear unsound within the context of Directive No. 16, a study of Hitler's own movements during the two preceding months heightens the impression of eccentricity.

In Poland his field headquarters had been in, or based on, a special train called "Atlas", and he continued to use this convenient mobile command-post during the campaign in the west.[2] On 10 May he opened his headquarters at Rodert, a hamlet perched inaccessibly on a steep hill above the old walled city of Muenstereifel; this place is not far south of Cologne, and opposite the junction of the Dutch and Belgian frontiers. It was a sensible, logical place to go to, close behind, and roughly in the centre of, the front of the land forces under his command.

From Muenstereifel (*Felsennest*[3]) the Fuehrer's headquarters moved on 6 June to Bruly de Pêche, an obscure village on the Franco-Belgian frontier north of Rocroi. This, again, was a location whose choice chimed with the natural desire of a Supreme Commander to be easily accessible to those who most needed his guidance or his inspiration.

On 25 June, however (the day on which the armistice with France came into force), Hitler withdrew the *Fuehrerhauptquartier* the best part of 200 miles in a south-westerly direction: to Kniebis (*Tannenberg*) near Freudenstadt in the Black Forest. Here a command-post had been prepared for use by OKW if, in the course of *Operation Yellow*, it had been found necessary to shift the main emphasis from

---

[1] Ziegenberg was occupied by the *Fuehrerhauptquartier* in the winter of 1944. From it Hitler, by then a physical and nervous wreck, launched the Ardennes offensive which was to have restored the situation on Germany's crumbling front along the Rhine.

[2] According to Heinrich Hoffmann, who was Hitler's crony as well as his official photographer, Hitler never allowed his engine-drivers to exceed a speed of 35 m.p.h. This followed an accident in 1936, when a special train in which the Fuehrer was being conveyed at 80 m.p.h. collided at a level crossing with a coach carrying a theatrical touring company and killed all the occupants. (H. Hoffmann: *Hitler Was My Friend*. London, 1955.)

[3] *Felsennest* means "eyrie". Throughout the war the code names of the *Fuehrerhauptquartier* retained Wagnerian overtones (*Tannenberg*, *Wolfsschanze*) which became, as doom and a creeping dementia settled in, progressively less apposite.

the right wing of the German armies to the left wing, further south; but the Supreme Commander was now considerably further away than he had been since the western offensive began, both from the front-line troops and the field headquarters (at Fontainebleau) of the Army and from the commanders-in-chief and staffs of his naval and air forces, who were firmly based on the Berlin area.

It is true that fighting had stopped when Hitler withdrew to the recesses of the Black Forest, and that therefore—theoretically—it did not greatly matter where he was in relation to the headquarters of his three commanders-in-chief. But if at this juncture there was any point in remaining "in the field" at all, why shift to a remote and not readily accessible part of it, where his staff had to lodge in an inn on a wooded plateau 2,700 feet above sea-level? If it was privacy and seclusion that he needed, he could have gone to the Berghof (where he did in fact spend much of July and August, the OKW staff train being berthed in Salzburg station). In those victorious days at the end of June there were doubtless strong arguments against returning to Berlin, against staying where he was (in Belgium), against establishing himself in Paris or its environs. It is extraordinarily difficult to reconstruct a single argument in favour of flitting off at a tangent into the Black Forest.

It is held in some German quarters that Hitler went to Kniebis in order to study the layout of the Maginot Line and the effect of German attacks on it; and on 30 June the German wireless reported that he had inspected the damage done to the forts in one sector. But eleven days seems a disproportionate time to devote to a post-mortem on technical problems which no longer had immediate relevance to the conduct of the war, and although Hitler did not reach *Tannenberg* in person until the 29th his headquarters were established there from 25 June to 5 July. The period produced no major military or political decisions. Save for his excursion to meet Mussolini at the Brenner, the rest of the summer was spent between the Berghof and Berlin, where on 24 October incendiary bombs dropped by the RAF fell on the OKW staff-train in the Grunewald Station. The resulting fires were extinguished without difficulty.

The projected concentration of headquarters in the Giessen area was less eccentric than the snipe-like vagaries of the Supreme

Command; yet it too has a strong flavour of the arbitrary. Can it have been that Hitler, conning through the undynamic draft of Directive No. 16, felt that it would be improved by an unexpected, autocratic crack of the whip? This is a possible explanation for a measure which offered few practical advantages.

"*The Commanders-in-Chief . . . will lead their forces, under my orders.*" Was it going to make it easier for von Brauchitsch to "lead" the Army by trebling the distance which separated his head-quarters from the Channel coast and installing them in premises where, as his Chief of Staff noted, "facilities for directing a major operation are not nearly as good as those in our former GHQ"? What were Goering and Raeder going to gain by being displaced from the well-equipped buildings whence they had directed, with complete success, the risky, remote operations against Norway? Seen in terms of Hitler's need to assert himself, the orders for the move to Giessen make a certain amount of sense; as a measure designed to facilitate the conquest of England, they make none.

On the other side of the Channel Hitler's adversary was given, before the summer ended, weighty reasons for moving his head-quarters. But Churchill, the War Cabinet, the Chiefs of Staff and the central bureaucracy of which they were the apex, remained in Whitehall. Here, since after 7 September an average of 200 German bombers attacked London every night for 57 nights, the no longer unimaginable horrors of aerial bombardment made life always diffi-cult, often dangerous, and on paper quite insupportable. A "citadel" bearing the un-Wagnerian code-name *Paddock* had been constructed near Hampstead, and into its austere catacombs the War Cabinet were ordered, on 29 September, for "a dress rehearsal, so that everybody should know what to do if it got too hot".[1] After par-taking of "a vivacious luncheon" they returned to Whitehall, where they somewhat unimaginatively remained until victory was won five years later.

[1] Churchill: *Their Finest Hour*. London, 1949.

CHAPTER FIVE

The Threat from Above and the Threat from Within

There is Nothing makes a Man Suspect much, more than to Know little.
Bacon

IF Hitler was slow to grasp the possibilities of invasion, the British began by misconceiving their nature.

The intervention of German airborne forces at various widely separated places in the Low Countries during the early hours of 10 May produced upon them an almost hypnotic effect. The un-reasoning conviction that a horde (or more probably a number of small, desperate parties) of highly trained parachute troops, many of them wearing disguises of one kind or another, might be de-posited by an air-fleet of limitless dimensions at any moment on any corner of the kingdom took firm root in the official and the public mind. Even when, three weeks later, the magnitude of the continental disaster had become apparent and every Channel port north of the Somme was in the enemy's hands, the airborne bogey continued to hold sway, and only very slowly yielded up part of its grip on men's imaginations to the ancient danger of invasion by sea.

"We expect to be attacked here ourselves, both from the air [i.e. by bombing] and by parachute and airborne troops, in the near future, and are getting ready for them", Churchill was writing to Roosevelt on 15 May. On the previous day *The Times* had published a selection from "a large number" of letters to the Editor urging the nation-wide enrolment and arming of volunteers to deal with airborne incursions; and that evening (14 May) the mustering of the Local Defence Volunteers was announced in a War Office statement and a broadcast by Anthony Eden. On 16 May a general warning against parachutists was included in the BBC's news bulletins, and on the following day guards were posted outside Broadcasting House and most of the Ministries in Whitehall.

The Home Guard (as the LDV were renamed in July) must be dealt with more amply later. Here we need only pause to note, as typical of the misapprehensions prevailing at the time, that the first step towards their embodiment was taken as a result of information, in itself of extremely doubtful value, which reached London *before* it was known that the Germans were employing airborne troops in *Operation Yellow*.

At noon on 10 May the following urgent message went out from the Air Ministry to the Admiralty, War Office and Ministry of Home Security:

Information from Norway shows that German parachute troops, when descending, hold their arms above their heads as if surrendering. The parachutist, however, holds a grenade in each hand. These are thrown at anyone attempting to obstruct the landing. To counter this strategem, parachutists, if they exceed six in number, are to be treated as hostile and if possible shot in the air. The largest crew carried in any British bomber is six persons.[1]

That this message was, not to put too fine a point upon it, nonsense would have been instantly apparent to anybody with a rudimentary knowledge of airborne operations. While in the air parachutists always "hold their hands above their heads as if surrendering", since they have to cling to the cords of their parachute in order to preserve equilibrium and a measure of control. When they land, they hit the ground with considerable violence and normally roll over several times before coming to rest. Even the most fanatical *Fallschirmjäger* would hardly carry in one, let alone in both of his hands a live grenade on the chance that he might find somebody waiting to "obstruct" his landing; if he did there would be no point in obstructing it.

These simple truths were not however apparent to the British at the time, and the message resulted in a meeting being arranged for the following day, 11 May, between representatives of the War

[1] Quoted by Charles Graves in *The Home Guard of Britain*, London, 1944.

Office and the Ministry of Home Security to consider measures for dealing with parachute troops. By the time the meeting assembled, reports—confused, exaggerated but incontestably alarming—of the successes of the German airborne operations in the Low Countries were flooding into London; the Home Office had already issued a warning to the public that the arrival of parachutists should be reported to the nearest police station; and if there had ever been any doubts about the need for some measure roughly corresponding to the anti-Napoleonic *levée en masse* of 1803, they were now peremptorily banished. Immediately after Eden's broadcast on 14 May the police stations were besieged by ardent citizens; the only qualifications for joining the Home Guard were that volunteers must be male, British, aged between seventeen and sixty-five, and (in an agreeably unbureaucratic definition) "capable of free movement".

The fact that the Press dubbed these embattled burghers "Parashots" is only one of many reminders that at this early stage the threat to British soil was thought of exclusively as coming from the skies above it. This delusion, though it led to some diversion of effort, was salutary; for, since there was no telling where the attacks might fall, it had the effect of putting the whole country in the front line, of giving everybody a more or less equal sense of urgency and purpose.

This undoubtedly helped to strengthen the very marked sense of national unity which sustained the British through a critical summer. No previous threat of invasion had seemed to impinge directly on every parish in the islands. In the 1914–18 war, though precautions had been taken in the coastal areas supposedly menaced, the population as a whole was unaffected by them. A shrewd and well-informed observer,[1] week-ending in Surrey in May 1915, recorded thus his dismay at seeing

a poster . . . giving directions as to what was to be done by the inhabitants of the district should the Germans come. What a catastrophe is here boded forth! . . . Here are the arrangements for the evacuation of the district when the order is given by the Military Authorities. Local gentry and clergy are to be in charge and the people are strictly enjoined

[1] MacDonagh.

"AM I AN ISLAND?"
Punch, 22 May 1940

to do as they are told. Cattle and livestock are to be driven to places of security and concealment, known only to the leaders. In their flight the people are to keep as far as possible to the highest ways, leaving the main roads free for the movement of the military.

That a man closer than most to the centre of affairs should have been taken aback by this poster shows how restricted was the scope of the instructions printed on it; twenty-five years later precautions against invasion made an impact on the lives of every household in the country.

Linked to, and destined to prove as groundless as, the fear of airborne attack was the fear of treachery. On 22 May a measure known as the Treachery Bill was rushed through Parliament. It superseded the Treason Acts, which since the fourteenth century had been found adequate to deal with this danger to the community. Besides blocking a legal loophole affecting non-resident aliens, the new Act curtailed and simplified the elaborate and ceremonious procedure prescribed for the trial of a suspected traitor. Under the new law anyone committing acts "designed or likely to give assistance to the naval, military, or air operations of the enemy, to impede such operations of His Majesty's forces, or to endanger life" was liable to the death penalty. Capital punishment was then, as it is to-day, an issue which touched the conscience of the House of Commons nearly; yet more than one lifelong abolitionist supported, or at least refrained from opposing, the measure. Among those who sacrificed their conscience to their country's need was the Labour leader J. R. Clynes; in the course of a moving speech he crystallised the nation's misgivings in these words: "There are [to-day] tendencies, conspiracies and movements totally unknown in the case of previous encounters between countries." He was speaking of the Fifth Column.

The expression dates from the Spanish Civil War. In the first week of October 1936 General Franco's forces, known to themselves as Nationalists and to their enemies as Insurgents, were closing in on Madrid from four directions. In a broadcast on 4 October General Mola, one of Franco's principal lieutenants, proclaimed that, in addition to their four columns in the field, the Nationalists had a fifth in Madrid.

The revelation was of questionable value to the Nationalist cause and had tragic consequences for its real or supposed adherents in Madrid, large numbers of whom were rounded up and executed. But the expression caught the imagination of the world and, torn from its forgotten context, survived to trouble men's minds in an age of violence and double-dealing.

The Fifth Column created in effect a new conception of treachery. Coined for purposes of psychological warfare, the phrase had a certain cogency, a technical bravura; it was intended to promote uneasiness and mutual distrust in a situation of danger, and it went on promoting them. Treachery and espionage had hitherto been regarded as the province of specialists; they represented a risk inherent in war, and the fact that this risk existed had always been liable to give rise (as, for instance, in England during the First World War) to exaggerated spy-scares with their attendant injustices, bad blood and diversion of effort.

But the phrase "the Fifth Column" sanctioned a new and more pervasive concept of the dangers to be feared from the traitor or the secret agent. It directed vigilance not to suspicious characters, but to those not outwardly suspicious. The bearded *Espion*, who in the game of "L'Attaque" lurks conspicuously behind a shrub waiting for his chance to eliminate the opposing Commander-in-Chief, had already been outmoded. Now people switched their suspicions from the strangers or half-strangers on the fringe of their community to those hitherto esteemed its backbone. In Britain the churchwarden or the local philanthropist attracted that searching scrutiny which in the First World War had been reserved for the bearded vagrant or the nocturnal collector of moths.[1]

Dictatorship, propaganda and subversion were not new things in the experience of mankind; but by 1940 the techniques involved in all three forms of human endeavour had, by comparison with

[1] "My experience is that the gentlemen who are the best behaved and the most sleek are those who are doing the mischief. We cannot be too sure of anybody." The Commander-in-Chief, Home Forces (Ironside), addressing LDV commanders on 5 June 1940.

those employed a quarter of a century earlier, improved out of recognition. The confused loyalties of the preceding decade made it easy for the British to postulate the existence in their ranks of an unobstrusive clique devoted to an alien dogma. In Norway, and in their technically bloodless conquests before the war, the Germans were believed to have relied to an important extent on prearranged treachery, or anyhow on preconditioned traitors; and reports—easy to believe and impossible to disprove—of the role played by Fifth Columnists, particularly as the accomplices of airborne troops, in the early stages of *Operation Yellow* wildly exaggerated both the incidence and the scope of traitorous activities on the Continent.

It would have been rash to assume that, in their designs on Britain, the Nazis would forgo the use of this valuable ancillary to aggression. Their motive for having a Fifth Column in the British Isles was clearly established. The Fifth Column was a weapon of war, and the Germans had all the best weapons. In the view both of the man in the street and of the authorities in Great Britain, there had, more or less, got to be a Fifth Column; in the uneasy climate of those times traitors had come to be regarded as not less indispensable to aggression than chorus girls are to a musical comedy.

It is true that the wireless transmitter, the aeroplane and the trained parachutist had greatly reinforced a traitor's potential ability to harm his own country and to succour her enemies. It is true that in a modern industrial community there are innumerable opportunities for sabotage (a form of activity whose practical difficulties are however underestimated by the layman). It is true that at the outbreak of the war there was known to be a small number of Britons who actively sympathised with Fascism, and that in view of Russia's alliance with Germany even less trust than usual could be placed in members of the Communist Party. It is true that in the years immediately before the war many thousands of refugees from Nazi oppression had been given asylum in England, and that this influx might, in part, have been used by the Germans as a sort of Trojan horse. And it is true that throughout the latter part of May still more refugees—from Holland, Belgium and France—were landing at British ports in circumstances which made it virtually impossible to check their *bona fides*.

These were all facts with inescapable implications. But they gave grounds rather for doubt whether all was sound within the State than for the conviction that something must be rotten; and it was this conviction, firmly held rather than clearly formulated, which gripped the British now. To find themselves in so grave a predicament without a Fifth Column was, they obscurely felt, a kind of solecism. Their perceptions were moreover heightened by acute anxiety and by a sense of public duty. Many a humble Dr Watson was promoted, by the access of self-importance which comes to patriots in an hour of crisis, to the status of a Sherlock Holmes. Police stations and military headquarters were inundated with reports of suspicious activities. The Government was not immune from the nation's bout of spy-fever; its policy for the internment of aliens had, as we shall see later, some of its roots in this unbecoming malady. The demand, universal at the time of Dunkirk, for more vigorous and better co-ordinated counter-espionage precautions was not ignored by the nation's leaders.

These precautions marched with, but normally a pace or two behind, precautions against the less clandestine operations upon which the enemy's airborne forces were expected to be launched. On 31 May orders were given for all signposts throughout the kingdom to be taken down, all milestones uprooted and all names of streets, railway stations and villages obliterated.[1] *The Times*'s comment on the removal of signposts reflected the general tendency of the Press at that time to discern, wherever possible, a silver lining in the darkest cloud; it began "Citizens venturing 'off the beaten track' will be able to experience the exhilarating feeling of being explorers." German broadcasts, not less characteristically, detected in this measure a callous attempt by the British Government to enforce their "Stay Put" policy by making it difficult for the populace to remove themselves to a place of safety when the invaders came.

The British are a people with a very high regard for privacy;

[1] Authority for signposts to be re-erected in urban areas was given in October 1942 and in rural areas in May 1943. All emergency restrictions on the exhibition of place-names were not cancelled until October 1944.

"I'll tell nobody where anywhere is."
Punch, 24 July 1940

"Mind your own business" has with them almost the force of an Eleventh Commandment. As a consequence, when they start looking at their neighbours with curious or suspicious eyes they are apt to find much that is unaccountable in their habits and behaviour. A chance remark, an unexplained absence, a visitor arriving after dark, an unusual hobby, the wearing of dark glasses or a beard—for a brief period clues such as these led many well-intentioned folk down many blind alleys.

For a time people were jumpy, and had some excuse for being so. On 31 May an offshoot of the Joint Intelligence Committee, known (at that stage) as the "Invasion Warning Sub-Committee",[1] held its first meeting. After noting, among other things, evidence that "extensive German plans for a descent on Eire have been in preparation for a considerable time", the Sub-Committee recorded in its minutes the

[1] See also pp. 171–174.

following summary of a report telephoned to the Admiralty by the Vice-Admiral in command at Dover[1]:

Indications of numerous acts of sabotage and 5th Column activity [are evident] in Dover, e.g. communications leakages, fixed defences sabotage, second-hand cars purchased at fantastic prices and left at various parking places.

This was all so much moonshine; but throughout the land equally disturbing reports, based on equally nebulous evidence, were being passed from mouth to mouth and from Ministry to Ministry, from the police to the military and from the military to the police.[2] Opinions differed widely as to the numbers, effectiveness and probable tactics of the Fifth Column; the one theory which nobody was prepared to entertain was that the Fifth Column did not exist.

All this was in part a legacy of the military disasters on the Continent. Treachery did in fact play a small but serviceable part in the opening phases of *Operation Yellow*, but its contribution to German victory was nowhere so decisive as the vanquished were only too ready to assert. In France and the Low Countries the Fifth Column had established itself, and was to remain throughout the war, a partial excuse for defeat.

Flashing lights,[3] poisoned sweets, bridges blown too soon or not

---

[1] It must in fairness be recorded that this officer (Admiral Ramsay) was then preoccupied with a critical phase of the Dunkirk evacuation, to the success of which he made an outstanding contribution.

[2] On 5 June the Commander-in-Chief, Home Forces, told an important meeting of LDV commanders: "We have got examples of where there have been people quite definitely preparing aerodromes in this country. . . . We want to know from you what is going on. Is there anything peculiar happening? Are there any peculiar people?" General Ironside's statement about "people preparing aerodromes" failed to survive scrutiny of the information on which it was presumably based.

[3] It is impossible to compute how many times the police, the Civil Defence organisations, the fighting services, and the Home Guard, to say nothing of patriotic individuals acting on their own initiative, took some form of action in the United Kingdom on the basis of reports that lights had been seen flashing during air-raids. It is probably true that the flashing of lights as navigational aids might have proved of some assistance to Julius Caesar, to William the Conqueror, and to Philip II of Spain; but to believe that an agent or a disaffected person could,

at all, punctured tyres, cut telephone-lines, misdirected convoys—in whatever went amiss the hand of the Fifth Column was detected, never the normal workings of muddle or mischance, confusion or plain cowardice. In Greece in 1941, in Hong Kong, Malaya and Burma in the succeeding year, it won (but hardly earned) its place in intelligence summaries and situation reports and, later, its shrine in regimental histories. Only in the Western Desert, where the armies fought in lists where, since there were no men, there could be no traitors, was the Fifth Column never reckoned a factor in the fluctuating campaigns.

The twin fears of airborne attack and of treachery were essentially complementary to each other; the heading on a column of letters in *The Times* of 18 May—"Parachutes and Traitors: More Suggestions"—reflects the way people's minds were working. Without the traitor to succour him, guide him to his objective and further his purpose by cutting telephone-wires, spreading rumours and initiating bogus telephone messages, the parachutist was not in the general opinion likely to achieve a great deal; and without the parachutist the traitor's usefulness to his country's enemies was similarly limited. At one point both fears overlapped.

This was in the matter of disguise, an expedient to which (it was firmly believed) both the enemy's main forces and their agents and collaborators were likely to resort. A completely baseless legend that in Holland German parachute troops had descended from the skies tricked out as nuns had caught the world's fancy and in Britain was proving a godsend to humorists and comedians; it was supplemented by stories of Germans dressed as French staff officers

by flashing a torch in his back garden, have rendered any service to the Luftwaffe is to overstrain credulity. Such a supposition involves the unthinking acceptance of, among other far-fetched assumptions, the following:

(*a*) that the Fifth Columnist knows which unit or formation of the hostile air force he is signalling to, what target they wish to attack that night, and from which direction they will be coming;

(*b*) that he therefore has two-way communication with the enemy by wireless;

(*c*) that the hostile air force both needs, and is able to identify, the speck of light which he offers as guidance.

Perhaps the fact of the matter is that men's fear of traitors, like their fear of snakes, is seldom based on a realistic estimate of either's power to inflict harm.

"Of course at the moment it's just a suspicion." *Daily Express*, 31 March 1941

misdirecting movements of British troops.[1] These fairy-tales strengthened a belief—which was after all both prudent and natural—that disguise was a contingency which ought not to be left out of account; and as early as 14 May the BBC, broadcasting in German to Germany, warned listeners in that country that parachutists descending in Britain in attire "other than recognised German uniform" would be shot out of hand.

To put a nation on its guard against masqueraders is one of those undertakings which is easily begun but not easily stopped. The possibility, once adumbrated, that the citizens and their defenders might be duped by impostors in not readily penetrable disguise led to the adoption of more precautions than the danger seems, even at the time, to have warranted. "Most of you", an official pamphlet told the populace in mid-June, "know your policemen and your ARP wardens by sight. If you keep your heads you can also tell whether a military officer is really British or is only pretending to be so."[2] Wisely, though perhaps not deliberately, the pamphlet ignored the presence in the United Kingdom of considerable numbers of Polish, French, Norwegian, Dutch, Belgian, Danish and Czechoslovakian officers, all by this time wearing British

[1] No less a person than the Dutch Foreign Minister told a Press Conference in London on 21 May that the Germans had descended attired as nuns, Red Cross nurses, monks and tramcar conductors. (*The Times*, 22 May 1940.) Nobody questioned the utility of these disguises to troops engaged in an overt military operation.

[2] On 28 May, as a result of a question in the House of Commons, the Government had undertaken to prohibit the sale to unauthorised persons of officers' uniforms. The questioner pointed out that, whereas the issue of battledress to private soldiers was strictly controlled by the authorities, anybody could go out and dress himself up as an officer for a few pounds.

uniforms; there were enough of these, as someone mildly pointed out in a letter to *The Times*, "to confuse people considerably".[1]

The removal of signposts and milestones raised a kindred problem which was also inconclusively thrashed out in the columns of *The Times* and elsewhere. What should a citizen do if a motorist asked him the way? The short answer was that the motorist should be requested to produce his identity card.[2] But since everyone had been warned never, in any circumstances, to show his identity card to persons not authorised to see it, this solution got neither the benighted traveller nor the would-be Good Samaritan out of their dilemma.

Though they could not have known it at the time, the use of disguise by their enemy was not a danger which the British need have taken seriously. (They were, however, right to assume that the Germans had no scruples about using disguise. One of their less perfunctory attempts to justify their aggression against Poland was a faked attack on the German radio station at Gleiwitz, near the Polish frontier. For this a dozen prisoners from a concentration camp were dressed in Polish uniforms, given lethal injections and, after being riddled with bullets, left lying about for the benefit of journalists and other observers who were conducted to the spot.[3]) But the few secret agents introduced into the islands during 1940 were, as we shall see later, imperfectly if at all skilled in the arts of masquerade.

It is true that the massive armies of invasion included two sub-units, controlled by the *Abwehr*,[4] some of whose personnel might

[1] The approximate strengths of Allied contingents serving with Home Forces in October 1940 were: Polish, 18,000; French, 850; Norwegian, 15,000; Dutch, 1,500; Belgian, 800; Czechoslovakian, 3,000. These figures, quoted in an authoritative lecture to the Staff College at the time, do not include Allied sailors and airmen; and they overlook a handful of Danes, to one of whom the Victoria Cross was later awarded.

[2] As a means of readily identifying the bearer these cards were all but valueless, since no photograph was affixed to them. They were however a convenience to bureaucrats; and their use continued, under protest, to be compulsory until seven years after the war had ended.

[3] Alan Bullock: *Hitler: A Study of Tyranny*. London, 1952. Walter Schellenberg: *Memoirs*. London, 1956.

[4] The German Intelligence Service, at that time directed by Admiral Canaris.

have been ordered to carry out impostures after the establishment of a bridgehead on British soil. These sub-units were detached from Special Unit 800, whose three battalions (the first of which was raised at Brandenburg) were eventually expanded into the Branden-burg Division; it was this equivocal formation which, in the winter of 1944, intervened abortively against the 1st United States Army in the Ardennes wearing American uniforms.

No evidence survives to show what role would have been allotted to these Protean soldiers in *Operation Sea Lion*.[1] One of them, captured much later in the war, recalled that they were moved up to the coast in August 1940, after undergoing training in "sabotage and English etiquette". Instruction in the latter subject included the information that the British—a "phlegmatic, conservative and some-what juvenile" race—had a snobbish attitude towards foreigners. He had been warned to agree with statements made by the working classes, but to lose no opportunity of contradicting the upper classes, since they respected argument; and he was to dress "very soberly but fashionably". Table manners were much the same as in Germany; but at table (he was encouragingly told) "it is not necessary to exercise so much restraint".

In fact the nearest the Germans got to making operational use of disguise in their tentatives against the United Kingdom was to play upon the anxieties and uncertainties which—as they could readily deduce from a study of the British Press—were being auto-matically created by the possibility that it would be employed. In a typical transmission on 9 August 1940 the "New British Broadcasting Station"[2] announced that German parachutists would descend either wearing some of the 100,000 (*sic*) British uniforms captured in France or else dressed as miners.

The British never really brought their fears of airborne attack into focus. Estimates of its potential strength varied, and were bound to vary, widely. On 4 June the Prime Minister referred in

[1] In *Operation Yellow*, wearing Dutch uniform and aided by traitors, Special Unit 800 had done useful work. Its failures included an attempt to capture the bridge near Arnhem, which was carried out by twenty-five men whose makeshift disguises were crowned by cardboard helmets. (De Jong.)

[2] See Chapter 8.

the House of Commons to the possibility of parachutists "taking Liverpool or Ireland", but a more usual conception seems to have been that of comparatively small bodies of men dropped, or landed by means of gliders or troop-carrying aircraft, to destroy or capture some specific objective. It was not thought necessary to relate these bold operations to the enemy's main strategy. The ubiquity of the threat sanctioned even the most far-fetched theories about the objectives it was supposed to threaten. When on 28 May the Secretary of State for War (Sir Edward Grigg) told the House of Commons that "imminent peril may descend on us from the skies at any moment", he came as near as anyone could to putting the danger into perspective. All that people knew, or thought they knew, was the direction from which the attack would come; its scale, its purpose, its timing, the localities in which it would be delivered remained matters of the purest conjecture.

"Waiter, just go and ask those fellows if they're members." *Daily Express*, 10 August 1940

In this disconcerting situation there was only one thing to do, and the British did it as best they could. All over the country fields, downland, golf-courses and other open spaces began to bristle with baulks of timber, and the contractors responsible for their erection waxed rich. Road-blocks—at first improvised from farm-carts but later made of stout concrete obstacles—barred the approaches to towns and villages not only on the coast but far inland; these were soon found to impose so much delay on military and industrial traffic that their design had to be drastically modified. It became a punishable offence to leave a car unattended without immobilising it by removing the rotor-arm. The road-blocks were manned by Local Defence Volunteers, eager for the fray and empowered to examine the identity cards of all travellers[1]; and several instances occurred of motorists (driving, of course, with blacked-out head-lights) who disobeyed; or perhaps misinterpreted, the Volunteers' signals to stop and were shot dead.[2] The nation, so strangely and for so long neglectful of the danger of a seaborne invasion, cannot be accused of underestimating the menace (as soon as it realised that such a thing existed) of airborne attack.

It is of some interest to establish how great, in actual fact, this menace was.

The Russian Army was the first in the world to train and equip troops for airborne operations; and in 1935, during autumn manoeuv-res in the Ukraine, foreign military attachés witnessed, much to their surprise, a parachute-drop in approximately battalion strength. The Red Army, whose battle honours had been largely won fighting against its own countrymen, had not at that time a high reputation; and the only nation to follow the Russian lead was Germany.

The Germans formed two battalions of parachute troops, one belonging to the Luftwaffe, the other to the Army. The role of the Luftwaffe unit, as originally conceived, was to dot the i's and cross the t's after a bombing attack; it was recognised that, with the small bombs and rudimentary bomb-sights then in service, attacks on industrial plants and other installations would be hit-or-miss affairs, and it was for a time envisaged that parachute troops could usefully be dropped as saboteurs to complete the destruction of the target's vitals.

In July 1938 both battalions were placed under the command of Student, a Luftwaffe officer. He was told that they were to form the

[1] Including, at first, the police. Volunteers, especially in rural areas, were not behindhand in exercising their right to treat the local constable as a suspect; and the police, who had taken on a number of additional responsibilities in connection with the enrolment and equipping of the LDV's, felt themselves ill requited for their pains. Eventually a compromise was reached. The LDV was still empowered to compel a police officer to prove his identity, but the police officer was given the same powers in respect of the LDV. On paper this Gilbertian formula was calculated to increase friction between the two forces, but in practice it seldom failed to create a ridiculous situation and thus had an emollient effect. (Graves.)

[2] On the night of 2/3 June four people were killed in four separate incidents of this sort.

nucleus of 7 *Flieger-Division*[1] which was to carry out a landing in rear of the powerful fortifications protecting Czechoslovakia's frontiers in the Sudetenland. In October of the same year, after the Munich Agreement had postponed war at Czechoslovakia's expense, the operation was done as an exercise. It took place near Freudental. The two parachute battalions were reinforced by one regiment[2] of 22 Infantry Division, and the whole force was successfully landed in Junkers 52s before a small but influential military audience. Thereafter airborne operations were taken seriously by the German General Staff.

All armies, however, have a strong prejudice against what the British Army in those days called "gladiators". Picked troops are all very well, but they have to be picked from somewhere, and commanding officers take it amiss when their most promising young officers and NCOs are posted, or ask for a posting, to some new-fangled corps or unit with a supposedly glamorous role. Occupational handicaps of this nature acted as a brake on the expansion of the German airborne forces before the war; and controversy about whether they properly belonged to the Luftwaffe or to the Army was always tending to bedevil their destinies.

Their prestige had a set-back when they were not employed in Poland, a sparsely inhabited country which many considered well-suited to their capabilities. But in the Low Countries—and particularly at Eben Emael, one of the forts covering Liège, which was reduced by a small force landed in gliders on its flat roof—the airborne troops did much more than justify their existence.

In June 1940, however, when the British were anxiously preparing against a massive assault from the skies, the German airborne potential was still very small. The two parachute battalions had been expanded to five; but all five had been committed in *Operation Yellow* and had suffered heavy casualties.[3] Student himself had

---

[1] "Air Landing Division" is probably the translation nearest to the military terminology of the time.

[2] Equivalent to a British brigade, and normally comprising three battalions.

[3] Detachments from these units had also been employed in Norway and Denmark. Their casualties had been light, but much irreplaceable equipment had been expended.

been seriously wounded, and although Putzier, who succeeded him, had 22 Division under command as well as the parachute troops, the airborne forces available at this time probably amounted to 25,000 men at the outside, and of these not more than 6,000 or 7,000 were trained parachutists. Very few gliders, which had not hitherto found favour with the High Command, were in service; each carried only eight men besides the pilot. There was even a serious shortage of parachutes, and purchasing commissions were scouring France for supplies of silk.

The available numbers of transport aircraft (Junkers 52s, each carrying twenty men) and gliders were reported to OKH on 11 July as, respectively, 400 and 110. Five days later this total was stepped up to 1,000 aircraft and 150 gliders; only 75 per cent of the aircraft were said to be operational.

The German airborne potential must have increased to some extent in the weeks that followed, but it was sharply reduced by Hitler's decision in late August to earmark 270 aircraft and one regiment of airborne troops for possible intervention in Rumania. These forces did not revert to their original *Sea Lion* role until a very few days before the operation was cancelled. The figures suggest that if the parachute battalions had been able to capture and hold a landing ground, the Germans could, given good luck and minimum casualties to aircraft, have flown into south-eastern England a maximum assault force of 15,000 men,[1] whose most serious weakness would have been their lack of artillery and vehicles. These they would not have received until a port had been captured as a result either of their own operations or of a seaborne assault, or (more probably) of both.

It was fully realised in 7 *Flieger-Division* that to drop, at dawn on a Sunday morning, upon a neutral country still technically at peace was a very different matter from parachuting into England after Dunkirk; and in fact no projects for the independent employment of airborne forces against the islands were ever entertained by the Germans. In the final plan for *Operation Sea Lion* their role was a

[1] In 1941 a German airborne force just over twice this size narrowly succeeded in capturing Crete, which was held by a weak garrison with virtually no air support.

straightforward tactical one, with dropping-zones in the immediate vicinity of the bridgeheads.

So once again the expectations of the British were at fault. No parachutists descended on their jealously though inadequately guarded islands; nor, incidentally, were more than a handful of individuals prosecuted under the Treachery Act, 1940, during the war. They included four British subjects, only two of whom were residents of the United Kingdom.

CHAPTER SIX

The Mirages in Hitler's Mind
(1) Capitulation

> Shall we, too, bend the stubborn head,
>   In Freedom's temple born,
> Dress our pale cheek in timid smile,
> To hail a master in our isle,
>   Or brook a victor's scorn?
>
> Sir Walter Scott: *War-Song of the Edinburgh Volunteers.*

There is at this time a real possibility, I might almost say a probability, of a negotiated peace.

> From an anonymous talk transmitted by the New British Broadcasting Station
> on 9 July 1940

I see no reason why this war should go on.

> Adolf Hitler, in a speech to the Reichstag on 19 July 1940

IN war, as in other human affairs, it is a mistake not to be single-minded; and throughout the summer of 1940, as far as Great Britain was concerned, Hitler was trying to do two things at once. He planned for an invasion, but he never ceased to dream of a capitulation. In his own mind the dream always had priority over the plan. Invasion was a second-best, a "last resort". (On 11 July, before he was fully seized of the dangers and difficulties involved, Hitler endorsed this definition, by Raeder, of the project's status; a month later he repeated it—invasion was to be attempted "only as a last resort, if Britain cannot be made to sue for peace in any other way".) *Sea Lion* was always a poor relation.[1]

[1] Its status as such is illustrated by the fact that, at their 11 July conference referred to above, Hitler discussed with Raeder his forthcoming speech to the Reichstag (in which he was to offer the British an opportunity of coming to terms) *before* they broached the question of *Sea Lion*. Raeder thought the speech was an excellent idea, "because the contents would become known to the British public". He felt that it might prove even more persuasive if it was preceded by a violent bombing attack on an important British city.

"Dream" is perhaps too nebulous and indeterminate a word to apply to Hitler's conviction that the British would seek an accommodation and withdraw from the war. It was a conviction based on intuition rather than on reason (though at the outset it had, on paper, a great weight of probability behind it). It seems to have been little affected by the march of events or by the passage of time. The many neutral observers who shared this conviction in June— they included the United States Ambassadors in Paris (Bullitt) and London (Kennedy) both of whom were "bleakly defeatist"[1]—abandoned it, or held it less and less strongly, as the summer wore on and the British remained cheerfully defiant. Hitler was extraordinarily slow to reassess his dream in the light of changing circumstances. After the occupation of the Rhineland in 1936 he had said: "I go the way that Providence dictates with the assurance of a sleepwalker"; and in the summer of 1940 there was more than a hint of somnambulism about the manner in which he approached the British problem.

Hitler's knowledge of the French was not profound, but he had some understanding of them; when he guessed about the French, he often guessed right. His view of the British was clouded by a conflict in his personal attitude towards their nation and her achievements. On the one hand these moved him to admiration, often expressed in terms which—since the British were Anglo-Saxons like the Germans—had about them an almost proprietorial ring.[2] At other times the British inspired a venomous hatred, in which envy, the desire for revenge and resentment at the frequency with which they opposed his designs blended with other feelings—among them, perhaps, something approximating to a sense of social inferiority. He alternately wanted them on his side and at his feet; and in his policy after the Fall of France these two strains of purpose coupled to breed a mongrel strategy.

[1] Robert E. Sherwood: *The White House Papers of Harry L. Hopkins*. New York, 1948.

[2] Cf., among much other testimony: "I recall an interview with him in 1943 when, on my appraising the military achievements of the English, Hitler threw back his shoulders, looked me squarely in the eye and commented: 'Of course, they are a Germanic people too!'" (*The Memoirs of Field Marshal Kesselring*. London, 1953.)

With France prostrate, it appeared to Hitler—not altogether unreasonably—that there was nothing to keep Britain in the war. She had entered it ostensibly to succour Poland, in fact to thwart German plans for the domination of Europe. She had failed by a wide margin to achieve either object. She was no longer bound to the conflict by her honour; there was no one left to leave in the lurch. Hitler had let it be known that, if England gave in, nothing of importance would be demanded of her save the return of the former German colonies, and the comparatively lenient terms imposed on France were an earnest of Germany's magnanimity to her fallen foes. Logic, prudence, self-interest, even ordinary commonsense urged upon the British the course of least resistance and the claims of peace. Hitler, marking time at Kniebis, daily awaited a *démarche*.

So sanguine were his expectations that he did not, at this stage, put out through diplomatic channels and neutral intermediaries any of the feelers to which he later had some ineffective recourse. At the end of June and in early July he more than once postponed the meeting of the Reichstag at which he had hoped, with the whole great drama successfully concluded, to take his curtain-call before the German nation.[1] But presently he saw that all was not quite over bar the shouting, that there would have to be another act; he roughed out its plot in Directive No. 16; and three days later, on 19 July, he made, in the course of an harangue to the Reichstag which struck listeners as being unusually sober in tone, a vague, hectoring statement clearly intended to imply that he was ready for a peaceful settlement with Great Britain.

The speech, like all Hitler's speeches, was a very long one; it began at a late hour and what came to be referred to as his "peace offer" was reserved for the peroration. The olive branch was not at first sight easily recognisable as such. Coming at the end of a long tirade of boasts and threats, phrases like "Herr Churchill ought perhaps for once to believe me when I prophesy that a great empire will be destroyed—an empire which it was never my intention to destroy or even to harm" did not yield their pacific content as readily to

---

[1] One postponement, according to Halder, was due to information that a reshuffle of the British Cabinet impended. This was expected to produce a more accommodating attitude in London.

tired sub-editors working against time as they did, afterwards, to more leisurely and expert analysts.

"It almost causes me pain," ran one passage, "to feel that I should have been selected by fate to deal the final blow to the structure which these men [Churchill and his colleagues] have already set tottering." Delivered with the emotional sincerity and the almost hypnotic compulsion of which Hitler on the rostrum was a master, these words were more than capable of producing upon a packed German audience, elevated by the sense of triumph and a great occasion, the impression of a generous, sensitive soul recoiling from a dreadful duty. The British, reading them in cold print, merely found them funny.

In all these circumstances—what with the late hour at which the "peace offer" reached the offices of London newspapers whose early editions (containing the first parts of the speech) had already gone to press, what with the *de haut en bas* and involved manner in which it was worded, and what with the low opinion the British people had formed of Hitler and the high opinion they now held of themselves—it is hardly surprising that the gesture which he had been meditating since France fell appeared, in the London press on 20 July, to have gone amiss. "Hitler's Threats to Britain" was the headline under which *The Times* printed extracts from his address. The dove, publicly released after so much thought and with so much condescension, was mistaken for another of his hawks.

Nor were the reactions of the British when they had had time to digest Hitler's message of hope any more encouraging. On 21 July the German press and radio were describing the comments made on Hitler's speech by their opposite numbers in Britain (who lacked the statutory guidance of a Propaganda Ministry) as a mixture of "insults, impudence and arrogance".

On the previous day it had crossed Churchill's mind that "it might be worth while meeting Hitler's speech by resolutions in both Houses [of Parliament]". The colleagues—Chamberlain and Attlee —to whom he referred this passing thought both agreed that "this would be making too much of the matter, upon which we were all of one mind".[1] In the end the British Foreign Secretary (Halifax)

[1] *Their Finest Hour*

expressed, in a broadcast on 22 July and in terms more measured than those used in the past three days by even the least ribald organs of the press, the basic British attitude to Hitler's *démarche*. "We shall not stop fighting", he said, "until freedom is secure." It was a point of view which Hitler, who was not prepared to stop fighting until exactly the opposite had happened, could hardly be expected to appreciate.

An entry in Ciano's diary, made after a meeting with Hitler on 20 July, gives the impression that the Fuehrer had, within a few hours of concluding his speech, swallowed and accepted the implications of its rebuff—that Mr Hyde had, with characteristic and dynamic celerity, replaced Dr Jekyll. "The reaction of the English press," Ciano wrote on the 20th, "has been such as to allow of no prospect of an understanding. Hitler is therefore preparing to strike the military blow against England."

This impression is not borne out by other evidence. Hitler's interest in "the military blow against England" had been of slow and rather reluctant growth; after 20 July it showed no tendency to quicken until, on 3 August, he travelled from the Berghof to Berlin to preside over the launching of his air offensive. When, because of bad weather, this had to be postponed for a week, Hitler did not take advantage of the enforced delay to visit the units of his naval and land forces upon whom, ultimately, the success of *Operation Sea Lion* depended; he returned to the Berghof. At no time was he moved to go and have a cursory look at the Channel; he hated, and feared, the sea.

From the apparatus of "the military blow", from the complex machinery which his orders had set in motion on 16 July, Hitler held himself aloof; but he still clung with a wistful obstinacy to his dreams of peace with England. London's initial reactions to his Reichstag speech were known in Berlin, through the medium of the BBC's late news bulletins, on the night it was delivered[1]; and

---

[1] "The announcer heaped ridicule on Hitler's every utterance," the American correspondent William Shirer recorded in his diary that night. He had gone to the *Rundfunkhaus* to broadcast to America and witnessed the stupefaction of the Germans as they listened to the BBC. (W. L. Shirer: *A Berlin Diary*. London, 1941.)

for the next few days they were confirmed and amplified from a wide variety of sources. A *ballon d'essai* could hardly have been more summarily shot down. Yet Hitler showed a marked reluctance to take No for an answer.

Though his propaganda services bitterly reproached the British for their churlish rejection of the conqueror's outstretched hand, they revealed very clearly the hope that wiser counsels might prevail when the matter had been more deeply pondered. "The initiative is now with England", the German press was saying on 21 July; and it pointed out, with a hint of cajolery, that the Fuehrer had set no time-limit by which he required the British to take up their option on a reprieve. On the 23rd, after Halifax's broadcast of the night before, headlines such as "The Die is Cast" appeared to indicate that the German attitude had hardened; but more than one commentator chose to disregard the Foreign Secretary's categorical rejection of a compromise and indicated that the German Government were still waiting for an "official" reply.

They were, in fact, soliciting one through diplomatic channels, and various attempts to hawk the olive-branch round neutral capitals culminated on 3 August in a well-meant offer by the King of Sweden to act as a mediator. To this, and to the other tentatives which had preceded it, the British declined to pay the slightest attention.

As the files of barges converged through the waterways of Europe upon the Channel ports, as the great guns were trundled into their casemates on Cap Gris Nez, as the rubble from bombed houses was poured into craters on the pockmarked airfields of France and the Low Countries, the Supreme Commander of the German Armed Forces—like a snake-charmer who squats unobtrusively at the edge of the jungle playing a low, sweet, beguiling tune upon his pipe— waited for a telephone call from the Wilhelmstrasse. He could hardly have been less profitably employed.

On the night of 1/2 August an odd thing happened. Large numbers of leaflets, headed "A Last Appeal to Reason" and containing an English translation of the Reichstag "peace offer", were dropped by German aircraft in various parts of England.

The British, who in these months were easily moved to hilarity, treated the affair as a joke, albeit an obscure one. Newspapers carried pictures of beaming housewives studying the Fuehrer's cloudy proposals, and in some places the leaflets were auctioned and a few pennies or shillings raised for the Red Cross. But nobody could see the point of the whole thing. What was the sense of diverting even one aircraft from offensive operations in order to distribute among the islanders copies of a speech, made nearly a fortnight before, which, as the Germans well knew, had been widely reported in and commented on by the British press and radio? Hitler's reputation for sagacity, which had once stood so high, suffered a further small decline.

In war it is natural, but seldom wise, to assume that the enemy's every action is the expression of a deep-laid design, to whose execution all his resources are dedicated in perfect harmony. Since navies, armies and air forces are like other large organisations composed of individuals and subdivided into departments (or their equivalents) whose relations with each other are often bedevilled by jealousy, secretiveness and other human weaknesses and none of which is completely efficient, this assumption is likely to prove erroneous; and it could simply have been as a result of muddles or misunderstandings that the first pamphlet-dropping sorties were made by the Luftwaffe.

If this had been the case, however, further operations of this type would hardly have taken place, as they did, on three or four other nights in the same week; for the arrival of the leaflets received wide publicity in Britain, and if the whole thing had been due to a failure in staff duties at the headquarters of *Luftflotten* 2 or 3, the aircraft involved would have been recalled to some more lethal duty at a time when Goering was about to throw every available machine into the decisive phase of his operations.

It seems therefore certain that the leaflet-dropping, pointless though it was, was a stroke of policy at the highest level. The episode is symptomatic both of the tenacity and of the ineptitude with which Hitler continued to pursue his dream of peace; and it raises, by its sheer futility, this question: Was there, behind Hitler's almost unwavering belief that the British would come to their senses and treat for terms, some specific delusion, some fertile plot of misconceptions in which his chimerical hopes took root and flourished?

Hitler, though capable of folly, was never called a fool. Bullock, describing the disappointment in Berlin at the contumely with which the British received his "peace offer", finds it "doubtful whether Hitler himself expected anything else"; and it does indeed seem scarcely credible that so shrewd an opportunist should have failed so signally to assess the temper of his adversary. To do so involved ignoring or discounting virtually all the available evidence about the attitude of the British which had been accumulating since Dunkirk—the statements of Churchill and other leaders, the tone of the debates in both Houses of Parliament, the reports of neutral observers in the United Kingdom, the unmistakable jingoism of the British press and the BBC, and finally the ruthless preventive action taken against the French fleet at Oran. It would have been venial enough to indulge, for a week or two in June, in wishful thinking; but Hitler's conviction that the British would somehow eliminate themselves from the war survived long after it had conspicuously ceased to bear any relation to existing possibilities; and when he was at last forced to discard it, it was replaced by the kindred hope— more rational but not less groundless—that the British would crack under the stress of bombardment from the air.

Why did Hitler continue for so long to pursue what less astute and less well-informed men had no difficulty in recognising as a mirage? A possible answer, which will be examined in a later chapter, is that when he looked towards the British Isles he saw not one mirage, but two.

CHAPTER SEVEN

John Bull at Bay

I have, myself, full confidence that if all do their duty, if nothing is neglected, and if the best arrangements are made, as they are being made, we shall prove ourselves once again able to defend our island home, to ride out the storm of war, and to outlive the menace of tyranny, if necessary for years, if necessary alone. At any rate, that is what we are going to try to do.

Winston Churchill in the House of Commons, 4 June 1940.

Algernon. "Well, I can't eat muffins in an *agitated* manner."

Oscar Wilde: *The Importance of Being Earnest*

For the British their predicament retained to the end a story-book quality. Try as they would, they never quite succeeded in taking a realistic view of the prospect before them. They paid lip-service to reality. They took the precautions which the Government advised, made the sacrifices which it required of them and worked like men possessed. They studied fragmentary and discouraging reports of German tactics; they dug trenches, cleared fields of fire, coined complicated passwords, doled out their slender stocks of ammunition, selected sites for mass graves. But both in the early days (when as their leader—himself a story-book character—was later to admit: "Never has a great nation been so naked before her foes") and afterwards when they knew that they could at least give a good account of themselves, they found it impossible, however steadfastly they gazed into the future, to fix in a satisfactory focus the terrible contingencies which invasion was expected to bring forth.

It was easy to imagine what bombing would be like; Abyssinia, Spain, China, Poland, Norway, France—for five years eyewitnesses and photographers had prepared their minds for the hazards of this impersonal form of attack. Invasion was a different matter. Would tanks, one day, come nosing through the allotments? Would tracer bullets flick across the recreation ground? Would field-grey figures carrying stick-grenades and flame-throwers work their way along the hedges towards the flimsy pill-box opposite the Nag's Head?

Reason, and their leaders, told the British that these things were very likely to occur; but the mental pictures which they formed of them, though highly coloured, were somehow not really alarming. They retained an affinity with patriotic melodrama; they were illustrations to a stirring tale of adventure rather than images of a dreadful reality. The British contemplated them with a morbid relish, but without complete conviction.

This attitude was natural rather than creditable. The outlook of all human communities is influenced by precedent; and in Great Britain, a small, old, insular community with a marked continuity of tradition, this influence is strong. There can be little doubt that in their dismaying quandary the British derived, subconsciously, much strength from the fact that no recent precedents for the successful invasion of their country existed.

With the exception of Switzerland, whose frontiers had been inviolate for 140 years, all Britain's European neighbours had suffered in modern times the incursion of a conquering army into at least a part of their territories; several of them had undergone this cruel experience more than once within living memory. Britain alone had escaped it for the best part of a thousand years.

Nations tend to remember victories and to forget defeats; with individuals it is often the other way round. Victories are won by the armed forces, splendid actors upon a distant stage; but defeat comes to everybody's doorstep, and in districts which have been repeatedly fought over and occupied by force its lessons weave themselves into something between a folklore, a tradition and a drill. There exists a kind of protocol of disaster. In the back of men's minds (but nearer to the forefront of women's) the lessons of a "last time" linger. What to hide, where to hide it: how much to tell the children: where to go. . . . This store of hard experience, handed down from generation to generation, does not directly promote defeatism. In a brave people it has initially the opposite effect; for to them conquest looms, not as a fearful abstract contingency but as an experience which, although they have survived it in the past, they must at all costs prevent from recurring.

Past tragedies and humiliations may have tempered the will to resist, but they have also taught the value of timely precautions in case resistance should fail. When war threatens some frontier-region with long experience of its ravages, two different processes are simultaneously set in motion, two not easily compatible motives govern the actions and outlook of the population as a whole. The young men flock to the colours, the old men take down muskets from the wall; but even before they have left to defend their rarely defensible land-frontiers, their families and indeed the whole community to which they belong are, as unobtrusively but as automatically as circus-hands who stretch the safety-net under acrobats on the trapeze, doing all they can to minimise in advance the effects of disaster. The community's war-effort is not half-hearted; both halves of its heart beat with equal vigour. But they beat to different purposes; and only very rarely in modern times has a European land-frontier been successfully defended against a superior foe.[1]

For the British there had been no "last time". To military defeat on foreign fields they were so inured that, when in June 1940 they began to realise what they were in for, the extrusion in swift succession of their expeditionary forces from Norway and from France seemed to play almost no part in the thoughts and conversation of ordinary men and women. The population had been stunned by both reverses; both—and above all the loss in France of virtually the whole of the nation's armoury for its land forces—directly affected their chances of resisting invasion; both had occurred within the last six weeks. Yet these defeats seemed now to have no bearing on the existing situation. It is true that in the Army many post-mortems were held, and that from them emerged

[1] The exploits of the Greeks, who, with limited support from the RAF, stemmed and threw back the Italian invasion of their Albanian frontier between October 1940 and April 1941, offer on paper a striking modern exception to this rule. But it should be remembered (a) that the Italian army and air force hardly constituted, save in the numerical sense, a "superior foe"; (b) that the mountainous regions through which, at the wrong time of year, Mussolini ordered them to advance had nothing in common with the debatable, often-ravaged territories, some of whose psychological reactions to invasion have been analysed above; and (c) that when a "superior foe", in the shape of the Luftwaffe, did intervene, the Greek armies on the Albanian front were obliged to capitulate within a matter of days.

verdicts which helped to shape the improvised policies governing training and equipment. But to the ordinary citizen the two spectacular disasters which his country had suffered overseas seemed almost irrelevant to her present plight. They appeared to belong to another chapter, perhaps even to another volume, of her history. And, as it turned out, they did.

The absence of precedents made it difficult for fearless realists and faint-hearted pessimists alike to assimilate the idea of invasion. A man in the grip of a nightmare often receives from some corner of his distracted mind indistinct, intermittent assurances that it is all a dream, that presently he will wake up and all will be well. The British were painfully aware that their plight was not all a dream. Fantastic though the situation was, there were no grounds for hoping that the omnisubjugant German armies across the Channel would prove to be some kind of an hallucination; and accordingly, with a vigour which helped to sublimate an inner sense of bewilderment and incredulity, the British proceeded to put their islands in a posture of defence as best they could.

Yet they retained—largely because there had been no "last time" —that sense of privilege, of ultimate immunity, which mitigates the horrors of a nightmare. They could not have analysed it, any more than the dreamer can. Across the Channel their would-be extirpators had a number of reasons for betting against invasion; any Britons who betted against it were, as their leaders lost few opportunities of reminding them, backing an outsider. In general, among all the people, the idea that the Germans would not only attack, but attack with unexampled fury, cunning and barbarity, was accepted almost as an axiom; yet in the back of their mind there lurked an unspoken disbelief. They were stubborn, angry, and for the most part brave; but below these qualities, and reinforcing them, resided the innocence, not of the child or even the fool, but of the simpleton. Like bumpkins admitted for the first time to the hall of some great, historic mansion, they were awed and impressed. But they found it difficult to relate what they newly glimpsed to what they had known for generations. And every now and then—as, half-heard and half-imagined, the bugles of a relief expedition are brought by a chance breeze to the ears of a beleaguered garrison—there came to many Britons the fugitive intimation that the nightmare of invasion would prove, in the end, to be only a bad dream.

It is possible to reconstruct, from a study of the official edicts and exhortations issued by the authorities to the public, a composite effigy of the model British citizen in the summer of 1940. He (or she) carried at all times a gas-mask slung from the shoulder in a rectangular canvas container; and for a quarter of an hour every day he donned the gas-mask in order to accustom himself to the inconveniences which its use imposed. He had about him a number of essential documents. First there was his National Registration Identity Card. On this were recorded his number on the National Register (which ran into six or seven digits), his name and address and his signature; more than half the card was taken up by five vacant spaces headed "*Removed to (Full Postal Address)*", reasonably ample provision thus being made for families who, having been evacuated in 1939 from a "Danger" Area to a coastal "Safety" Area, were re-evacuated in 1940 when their new home became a "Protected" Area, were then by ill luck bombed out, and might expect further nomadism when the invasion came. On every citizen's identity card was printed the warning that if he made any alteration on it, failed to carry it, or omitted to report its loss he could be punished by a fine or by imprisonment or both.[1] Inside his identity card was (or should have been, after an appeal by the authorities on 18 July) a slip of paper giving the name and address of his next of kin; this was to facilitate matters if he became a casualty in an air-raid.

The model citizen also carried his ration-book and his petrol coupons and—if he worked in a factory or other large organisation—a security pass which entitled him to enter its premises. The wings and bumpers of his car were painted white, its headlights were shrouded in plastic visors, and the wireless set (if any) had been

[1] During the invasion scare in September a battalion of the Dumbartonshire Home Guard, called out to man the road-blocks in its area, reported that between 2130 hours and 0930 hours the next day no less than 1,835 of the citizens passing through its picquets were without identity cards.

removed from its dashboard; if he left it unattended he opened the bonnet and removed the rotor arm.[1]

The windows of his house were crisscrossed with strips of sticky paper to minimise the effects of blast. Buckets of sand and water stood ready in the principal rooms, and the attics had been emptied of combustible junk. He was scrupulous not to hoard food, but always had on hand enough reserves to keep his household going if its occupants should be cut off by the flood-tide of invasion. He had handed over his sporting weapons and binoculars, via the police, to the Home Guard, and his aluminium utensils to the Ministry of Aircraft Production; he had surrendered (on 5 July) all fireworks "capable of being used for giving visible signals to the enemy", and on the following day had brought forcefully to the attention of his children an order, made under the Defence Regulations, forbidding "any person, other than a servant of his Majesty", to fly a kite or a balloon. His air-raid shelter was a model of amenity and hygiene, and around it, in his garden, he heeded the posters' clarion call to "Dig for Victory".

He used the telephone only in cases of dire necessity, never retailed rumours about the progress of hostilities, and was careful not to shoot carrier pigeons. He carried on as usual, worked as he had never worked before, and, while firmly discounting all claims made by the enemy about his military potential, never for a moment underestimated the might of the Nazi war machine.[2]

The reader will scarcely need to be told that this paragon did not, in his totality, exist.

We have noted already the nation's obsession, in the early stages, with the related dangers of airborne attack and treachery. Reports from France and the Low Countries drew attention sharply

[1] Prosecutions on a charge of "failing to secure a motor car" were frequent. On 20 August, for committing this offence in the West End of London, a man was fined £50. (*The Times*, 21 August 1940.)

[2] Cf. GHQ Home Forces Operation Instruction No. 5 of 27 June 1940: "It is not unlikely that the German High Command may even envisage the possibility of obtaining swift and decisive victory by an assault so comprehensive, and sustained, as will by its severity rapidly crush all practical possibility of resistance, even though morale may not be broken."

to another hazard which the latest German methods of warfare were liable to produce. In that theatre of war unwieldy, pathetic columns of civilian refugees clogged the roads, seriously hampering the movements of the Allied forces and spreading alarm and despondency far afield; the fears which had set them on the move were often converted into panic by the Luftwaffe's low-flying attacks. It was resolved that, when the onslaught on England was launched, nothing of this kind must be allowed to occur; and "Stay Put" (a later modification to "Stand Firm" was almost certainly inspired from the summit) became a watchword on which was based all official guidance to civilians about invasion.

The guidance was at first couched in terms which reflect the flurry and inexperience of those early days. Orders dealing with anti-invasion precautions could not, for obvious reasons, be broadcast to the population over the wireless, and a series of leaflets and folders were hastily printed. One of the first, issued by the Ministry of Information and headed *How shall I Prepare to Stay Put?*, has an almost Biblical ring. "Make ready your air-raid shelter", the citizen was enjoined. "If you have no shelter, prepare one. If you can have a trench ready in your garden or field, so much the better, especially if you live where there is likely to be danger from shell-fire." No advice was or indeed could be given as to which localities might find themselves in this last, unenviable category. Meanwhile a manifesto from the Ministry of Transport laid down various methods of disabling private cars which were in danger of falling into the enemy's hands; one suggestion was that "as an emergency measure the tank can be punctured at its lowest part, e.g. by a large nail".

"Farmers!" exclaimed a Ministry of Agriculture notice belonging to the same vintage. "Unless military action in the immediate neighbourhood makes it impossible, farmers and farm-workers must go on ploughing, sowing, cultivating, hoeing and harvesting as though no invasion was occurring." This document was taken in some rural quarters to be the work of Fifth Columnists. Who else, it was argued, would seek to confuse men's minds by suggesting that you cultivated after you had sown? Who else would have tried, by pointedly ignoring their existence, to disaffect the stockmen and

DANGER of INVASION

Last year all who could be spared from this town were asked to leave, not only for their own safety, but so as to ease the work of the Armed Forces in repelling an invasion.

The danger of invasion has increased and the Government requests all who can be spared, and have somewhere to go, to leave without delay.

This applies particularly to :—

SCHOOL CHILDREN
MOTHERS WITH YOUNG CHILDREN
AGED AND INFIRM PERSONS
PERSONS LIVING ON PENSIONS
PERSONS WITHOUT OCCUPATION
OR IN RETIREMENT

If you are one of these, you should arrange to go to some other part of the country. You should not go to the coastal area of East Anglia, Kent or Sussex.

School children can be registered to join school parties in the reception areas, and billets will be found for them.

If you are in need of help you can have your railway fare paid and a billeting allowance paid to any relative or friend with whom you stay.

If you are going, go quickly.

Take your
NATIONAL REGISTRATION IDENTITY CARD
RATION BOOK
GAS MASK

ALSO any bank book, pension payment order book, insurance cards, unemployment book, military registration documents, passport, insurance policies, securities and any ready money.

If your house will be left unoccupied, turn off gas, electricity and water supplies and make provision for animals and birds. Lock your house securely. Blinds should be left up, and if there is a telephone line, ask the telephone exchange to disconnect it.

Apply at the Local Council Offices for further information.

Private Car and Motor Cycle owners who have not licensed their vehicles and have no petrol coupons may be allowed to use their cars unlicensed for one journey only and may apply to the Police for petrol coupons to enable them to secure sufficient petrol to journey to their destination.

ESSENTIAL WORKERS MUST STAY
particularly the following classes :—

Members of the Home Guard
Observer Corps
Coastguards, Coast Watchers and Lifeboat Crews
Police and Special Constabulary
Fire Brigade and Auxiliary Fire Service
A.R.P. and Casualty Services
Members of Local Authorities and their officials and employees
Workers on the land
Persons engaged on war work, and other essential services
Persons employed by contractors on defence work
Employees of water, sewerage, gas & electricity undertakings
Persons engaged in the supply and distribution of food
Workers on export trades
Doctors, Nurses and Chemists
Ministers of Religion
Government Employees
Employees of banks
Employees of transport undertakings,
namely railways, docks, canals, ferries,
and road transport (both passenger and goods).

When invasion is upon us it may be necessary to evacuate the remaining population of this and certain other towns. Evacuation would then be compulsory at short notice, in crowded trains, with scanty luggage, to destinations chosen by the Government. If you are not among the essential workers mentioned above, it is better to go now while the going is good.

AUCKLAND GEDDES,
REGIONAL COMMISSIONER FOR CIVIL DEFENCE,
TUNBRIDGE WELLS,
MARCH, 1941.

These clear and detailed instructions, posted in March 1941 in many coastal towns, show a marked improvement over their prototypes of the previous summer. (See opposite page.)

the shepherds? In practice these early and almost meaningless directives followed the well-meant *paperasserie* of the Phoney War period into the waste-paper basket. They made little impact on the nation's mind, and are quoted only as typical by-products of the bustle and confusion in Whitehall when invasion suddenly exchanged the status of an unfancied outsider for that of an odds-on favourite.

This period—the end of May and the beginning of June—was one of carefree improvisation as far as most civilians were concerned. It was as though the whole country had been invited to a fancy-dress ball and everybody was asking everybody else "What are you going as?" A latent incredulity, and the fact that almost everybody —men and women—had more than enough to do already,[1] combined to give problems connected with invasion (like those connected with a fancy-dress ball) the status of engrossing digressions from the main business of life.

What may be called the Swiss Family Robinson period, during which households and small communities made, or neglected, their own arrangements did not last long. Gradually the problems most likely to arise when the invaders came were brought into some sort of perspective; but it was easier to see what might have to be done than to allot responsibility for doing it. The Army (and in the ports the Royal Navy as well), the ground-staffs of the Royal Air Force, the Home Guard, the police, the Civil Defence services, the Regional Commissioners, the county and borough councils, to say nothing of the various government departments—how did the duties of all these dovetail into each other?

It was (to take one tiny but typical example) widely believed that the best way to render petrol not only useless but harmful to the user's vehicles was to put sugar in it. But in a village or a street where there was a filling station who was responsible for ordering this to be done, and who for doing it? Who, on whose recommendation, would authorise the issue of a "supplementary" sugar ration to the doer, and who would ensure that this prized commodity was

[1] It is surprising that there should, throughout the summer, have been something like 1,000,000 unemployed. The total in early September was 800,000, of whom 300,000 were women.

not used for normal gastronomic purposes? The defence of the island was found to bristle with dilemmas of this sort.

As more and more cooks converged upon the broth, the cry was everywhere for leadership, for decisions. On 22 May the Emergency Powers (Defence) Act had required all persons "to place themselves, their services and their property at the disposal of His Majesty"; and the people, who through their elected representatives had made this far-reaching surrender of their rights with alacrity, now longed to be told what to do. "Most of the grumbling", observed *The Times* on 1 July, "is about insufficient direction." In the same issue a newspaper proprietor inserted, as a half-page advertisement, an exhortation to civil servants; its burden was "This is the time for initiative". But although numerous small follies and blunders were committed, and frustration, like a childish epidemic, was always breaking out in one section or another of the community—the intellectuals, if not the principal sufferers, were the most articulate [1]—it can fairly be said that the British, in improvising measures which affected drastically the lives of all to meet a mortal danger whose exact nature could not be foreseen, put forth much resource and ingenuity, and showed a good spirit.

At a later stage all purely local civilian responsibilities were made the concern of "Invasion Committees", each of which looked after the interests of its own district. These committees were required, among other things, to prepare "War Books" which were to be destroyed "should hasty evacuation become necessary". The War Books were compiled in accordance with a standard pro-forma issued by the Ministry of Home Security. The War Book of Painswick in Gloucestershire survives in the Imperial War Museum, and although it belongs to a period later than the summer of 1940—the Invasion Committees were not dissolved until 1944—it would be uncharitable to deny it a place in these pages.

Painswick is a small place. Its population in 1940 was 1800; with it, for anti-invasion purposes, were grouped the still smaller villages of Pitchcombe (340) and Edge (180). The diligence with which the local Invasion Committee followed the procedure laid down by the

[1] See the *New Statesman and Nation*, *passim*.

pro-forma strengthens an impression that bureaucracy had drawn up this document with centres more populous than Edge and Pitch-combe in their minds.

In Part 22, for instance, details of "Sites earmarked for Mass Graves" had to be filled in; the Painswick Invasion Committee thought that the churchyards, where there was still a good deal of room, would probably be the best place for these. Part 9, envisaging a total breakdown of communications, asked for information about "Other Means of conveying Instructions and Information to the Public"; Painswick decided to record that "The Information Officer has a *Megaphone*".

Finally, Parts 18 and 19 required particulars of "Emergency Transport, Tools, Plant, etc." Painswick made a confident start with:

Horses	11
Wheelbarrows	16

But thereafter their determination not to overlook anything which might prove of service to their country in her hour of need introduced into their list something of the dream-like inconsequence of a jumble-sale. It continued:

Fish-kettles	1
Tea	7½ lbs.
Sugar	3 lbs.
Milk	3 Tins
Shotguns	7
Revolvers	1
Ammunition	1 [*sic*]
Bedpans	6
Scissors (large)	10
Hotwater bottles	13

The corresponding list for (say) Sheffield no doubt read differently.

On 17 May the United States Embassy advised all American citizens in Great Britain (they were believed, according to *The Times*, to number some 4,000) to return home by way of Eire as soon as possible; those unable to do so were urged to "seek accommodation in uncongested areas, as far as possible from metropolitan centres and points which might be considered strategical from a military point of view". A sterner warning on 7 June "stressed" (according to the BBC's news bulletins on that day) "that this may be the last opportunity for Americans to get home until after the war". Most heeded these warnings, but many elected to stay put, and in early June the 1st American Squadron of the Home Guard was formed in London. It was commanded by General Wade H. Hayes, had an average strength of 60–70, and wore British Home Guard uniforms (when these became available) with a red eagle shoulder-flash.[1]

America's estimate of Britain's chances of survival was not at this time high, but it might have been lower than it was. *The Times* of 12 September 1940 published the following particulars of a Gallup poll in which, at various stages of the first year of war, American voters had been asked which side they expected to win:

	Great Britain	Germany	Don't Know
	%	%	%
September 1939	82	7	11
May 1940 (after Norway)	55	17	26
June 1940	32	33	35
At the Fall of France	32	35	33
September 1940	43	17	40

These were the opinions, or the guesses, of private citizens. A good deal of evidence suggests that in Washington that summer the totals in the first column, and possibly also in the third, would have been rather lower.[2]

[1] The mustering of this unit caused alarm in the Foreign Office. If the citizens of one neutral Power were allowed to form an armed contingent, it would be difficult to withhold this right from other Powers who might claim it; and there was, among others, a sizeable Japanese community in the United Kingdom. The American Ambassador (Kennedy) strongly disapproved of the whole business, on the grounds—as he told an officer of the Squadron—that "it might lead to all United States citizens being shot as *francs-tireurs* when the Germans occupied London".

[2] Cf. *The Secret Diary of Harold L. Ickes*, Vol. III (New York, 1955). An entry describing a meeting of the United States Cabinet on 6 September records: "Cordell Hull reported to the Cabinet that England was undergoing a terrific

The British were not merely making the best of things when, after the Fall of France, they professed themselves well satisfied to stand alone.[1] The illogical and indeed foolish conviction that they were somehow better off without allies prevailed throughout the country. Their isolation seemed to them to simplify the issues, and phrases like "we shall get on better by ourselves" were in frequent use. This attitude was not based, even remotely, on reason; nobody attempted to demonstrate why, if the defeat of France simplified the issues for Britain, it did not simplify them to a much greater extent for Germany. Had they been closely analysed at the time, the nation's reactions might well have been proved an alloy in which much was base; conceit, stupidity, xenophobia, fecklessness and wishful thinking—these, among other flaws, might have been found in the gleaming brass of its self-confidence. The historian can only record that the brass did gleam, and that the British, when their last ally was pole-axed on their doorstep, became both gayer and more serene than they had been at any time since the overture to Munich struck up in 1937.[2]

---

attack. As a matter of fact it has been getting worse and worse over there. . . . It was actually claimed in some quarters that England would be suing for peace before last week came to an end."

[1] To say that Great Britain "stood alone" after the Fall of France is inaccurate. It overlooks a useful Imperial contribution to the defence of the islands. During the summer of 1940 this was made up as follows:

From Canada: One infantry division plus various ancillary units arrived in the spring. A second infantry division completed its concentration in England during September.

From Australia: Elements of one infantry division equivalent (in numbers but not in equipment) to a strong brigade group arrived during June.

From New Zealand: 7,000 men, mustered in two numerically weak infantry brigades and an improvised covering force, arrived during June.

From India: A number of mule transport companies were evacuated with the BEF from St Nazaire in June.

From Newfoundland: One artillery unit, about 1,000 strong, arrived during June, and several pioneer companies specialising in forestry work had spent most of the winter in the United Kingdom.

Other forces from the Dominions and Colonies were serving in the Middle East and elsewhere.

The strengths of Allied contingents in the U.K. (land forces only) are given in the footnote to p. 65.

[2] "The whole tenor of life had altered and had become simpler and in a way much easier. There was more than a touch of the address before Agincourt in the

The threats—of invasion, of bombing, of treachery, of chemical and bacterial warfare and of those newer weapons at which Hitler was understood to have hinted—loomed large, terrible and imprecise; "never before", as the *Spectator* put it on 28 June, "has it been possible to attack human self-possession from so many directions at once". Although the British for the most part retained their *sangfroid*, there was one context in which *sangfroid* would have been unnatural. A battlefield was no place for children; and an inter-departmental committee was set up to study the possibilities of evacuating them overseas.

The Lord Privy Seal (Attlee) told the House of Commons on 19 June that the Government had adopted the committee's report and "considered the establishment of the necessary machinery for the operation of the scheme to be a matter of the utmost urgency". The Dominions and America were only too ready to play their parts. Throughout the country families faced a cruel dilemma.

At first the Government made it clear that they were in favour of the scheme [1] and wished as many children as possible to leave the country; but they were, according to *The Times* of 3 October 1940, "rather taken by surprise by the number of parents wishing to avail themselves of the scheme". It is difficult to see why the Government should have been surprised. 200,000 applications were received before the Children's Overseas Reception Board announced, early in July, that they could accept no more for the time being; but this represented only an infinitesimal proportion of the children aged between five and fifteen whose parents could have put them down for evacuation. The truth of the matter seems to have been that many people brought their early fears into focus before the machinery of evacuation had begun to work; and allowance, too,

---

air, a secret satisfaction that if it was coming we were to be the chosen, we few, we happy few. . . . All this looks childish written down but it was a direct, childish time, quite different from but more entirely satisfying than any other piece of life which I at least have ever experienced." (Margery Allingham: *The Oaken Heart*. London, 1941.)

[1] To judge by a personal minute which he addressed to the Home Secretary on 18 July, Churchill did not share his colleagues' liking for the project: "I certainly do not propose to send a message by the senior child to Mr Mackenzie King, or by the junior child either. If I sent any message by anyone, it would be that I entirely deprecate any stampede from this country at the present time."

must be made for the growth of confidence as the change in leadership (from Chamberlain to Churchill) made itself felt. To say that
the British people now "passionately attached themselves to the
war" [1] is perhaps to overstate the case; but there was enough hope,
as well as enough determination, in the islands to strengthen decisively the case for keeping the children at home. Some of the older
children felt strongly that there was something shameful and unbecoming about evacuation. One Eton boy, whose father insisted
on sending him out of the country, slipped off the ship at Liverpool
and made his way back to Eton; another, unwilling to admit the
true reason for his departure, gave it out to his friends that he had
been expelled. [2]

In the event the exodus was a trickle rather than a stampede. Less
than 5,000 children between the ages of five and fifteen sailed for the
Dominions, less than 2,000 for the United States; 2,666 of these left
under the official scheme before it was suspended. The American
Government approached the German Government with a request
that the ships carrying the children should be given safe-conduct.
It was rejected; an OKW document records the decision that
"Germany must most decidedly reject every request referring to this
matter. . . . It is entirely contrary to our interests if the power of
resistance of the British people is strengthened by the evacuation of
refugees and children". This was a harsh but hardly an improper
military decision; later in the war the Allies, when investing
German garrisons cut off on the Channel coast, felt bound on more
than one occasion to refuse requests that French civilians should be
allowed to leave the towns.

Tragedy, as the parents well knew, had always threatened the
evacuation; and tragedy brought it to an end. Soon after all the
320 children on board had been rescued from one torpedoed ship,
the *City of Benares* was sunk by a U-boat on 17 September.
260 lives were lost, and of the 90 children she was carrying only
11 were saved. All further government-sponsored evacuation was
stopped on 2 October, and the American voluntary organisations,
which had sent nearly 1,000 children across the Atlantic, suspended

---

[1] Sir W. K. Hancock and M. M. Gowing: *British War Economy*. London, 1949.
[2] B. J. W. Hill: *Eton Medley*. London, 1948.

their activities a week later. Judging by the accounts of survivors, the children on the *City of Benares* met their fate with a singular heroism.

Earlier in the summer, at about the time of the Fall of France, the Government had taken the momentous decision to send out of the country all the gold in the banks. With it, in crates, went the nation's entire holding of foreign securities; it took seventy miles of tape to tie up the innumerable separate parcels.[1] The first shipment left for Canada in the cruiser *Emerald* on 24 June. Further consignments followed, some in warships, others in fast merchantmen. Special trains, heavily guarded, met the ships, and their cargoes—so valuable that the question of insuring them did not even arise—were taken to capacious vaults in Montreal. None of the ships was torpedoed or even attacked. The biggest and boldest financial transaction in history remained a well-kept secret; and by August gold and securities to the estimated value of seven billion dollars had been carried across the Atlantic. This vast treasure was known for security purposes as "fish".

Meanwhile children were being moved out of London and other large cities, as well as from the south and east coasts. At the outbreak of war in the previous year nearly 1,500,000 men, women and children had been evacuated from the towns under official arrangements, while large numbers (estimated by an official historian[2] at two million) had left of their own accord. Most of the former, and many if not most of the latter, had drifted back during the period of the Phoney War. But now that the crisis had come, the townspeople (influenced, perhaps, by memories of the uncongenial rusticity of the "reception areas") showed a marked reluctance to take evasive action, or even to send their children away. Another official historian records that "during July and August, when the Battle of Britain was being fought and daylight raids were made on many towns, there was no significant demand for the evacuation of children to safer areas"; indeed, "resistance to evacuation steadily

[1] Leland Stowe: "The Secret Voyage of Britain's Treasure." *Readers' Digest*, November, 1955.

[2] R. M. Titmuss: *Problems of Social Policy*. London, 1950.

hardened as Londoners became familiar with air-raids and shelter life".[1]

Hotel advertisements of the period serve as a sad, genteel reminder of the sanctuaries which many elderly people of the more prosperous sort felt obliged, or were prevailed upon, to seek. Though they were sometimes uncharitably called "funk-holes", these hotels seem to have been debarred by some unwritten code from suggesting that people might like to come and stay in them for reasons of prudence. "For Quietude" was the nearest one hotel, deep in the West Country, came to defining the principal amenity it had to offer; but perhaps the Aviemore Hotel in Inverness-shire carried euphemism further than any of its rivals. "To-day, more than ever," ran its advertisement,[2] "Aviemore will come as a haven of peace and rest. Here, among the tonic air of the pinewoods, you will find a sanctuary far removed from the rush and nerve-strain of the outer world."

On 13 June a ban on the ringing of church bells was announced; henceforth they would be rung only by the military or the police to give warning that an attack by airborne forces was in progress. This arrangement had, in addition to the story-book quality so characteristic of the period, an agreeably traditional flavour; but it was viewed with concern by the *Ringing World*, an organ devoted to the interests of campanology. The ban was seen as "a stunning blow to ringing, from which, even when the war is over, it will take a long time to recover" and correspondents pointed out, with justice, that a novice handling a bell-rope for the first time would be lucky if, after repeated tugs, he produced "one very half-hearted boom"—unless indeed the bell had been left "set", in which case he ran a risk of serious injury.

On the night of the great invasion scare (7 September)[3] the church bells were rung over wide areas of southern and eastern England, and two days later a similar false alarm set them pealing in five Scottish towns. Otherwise they remained silent, and as time

[1] O'Brien.
[2] In the *Spectator* of 21 June 1940.
[3] See Chapter 19.

went on people began to miss them and to doubt whether—however congruous to patriotic melodrama—their use as a method of sounding the alarm was entirely practical.

These doubts were ably summarised in a Parliamentary question put to the Secretary of State for War on 13 May 1942 by A. P. Herbert. He asked:

What form of enemy incursion was to be signalled by the ringing of church bells; whether the Secretary of State was aware that the church bells were greatly missed by the people in the meantime; that they were not the most effective available signal; that the church was the only public building which was never on the telephone; that the use of church bells for any military purpose might legitimately be taken as a technical justification for any enemy action against any church; and whether he would arrange for some other form of signal to be devised and adopted, as he would have to do if the churches were destroyed.

The authorities remained unmoved by these considerations. It was not until nearly a year later—on 4 April 1943—that Churchill admitted in the House of Commons that the bells had become "redundant" as a warning system. "For myself," he added, "I cannot help feeling that anything like a serious invasion would be bound to leak out." There was much laughter, and soon the familiar chimes rippled once more across the tranquil Sunday landscape. In Germany, whose ruler had no use for "the Jewish Christ-creed with its effeminate pity-ethics",[1] most of the church bells had by this time been melted down and made into munitions.

One of the nation's first reactions to the threat of invasion was an access of that Puritanism which is never far below the surface in England. Under the heading "Are We At War?" *The Times* published numerous letters—whose counterparts appeared in other newspapers—asking whether it was right that greyhound-racing, horse-racing and other sporting fixtures should continue to take place, or that the unpatriotic idlers who attended them should be allowed to deplete the nation's petrol stocks in the process. A similar concern was expressed in Parliament.

[1] Rauschning: *Hitler Speaks*. London, 1939.

At first the case against all forms of organised recreation seemed unanswerable; but then it began to be realised that, although there might be a few unpatriotic idlers here and there, the great bulk of the pleasure-seekers were either men and women who were working extremely hard or else Servicemen on leave, and that both classes had a right to some enjoyment in their brief periods of leisure. Although horse-racing was stopped "until further notice" on 19 June, most other forms of sport and entertainment went on. It may have been in an attempt to make capital out of this small controversy that the German radio reported on 9 July that a "revolt against plutocratic cricketers" had taken place throughout the country; "the people", it was said, "tried to destroy the playing grounds at night, and this led to a state of war between the population and the English sports clubs".[1]

In fact several of the Englishman's sports and pastimes were affected, though not in so drastic a way, by his country's predicament, especially when the bombing started. Air-raids, *The Times* Bridge Correspondent reported on 3 September, were "having a serious effect on bridge"; but the situation had its brighter side, for "a reader in Yorkshire tells of a recent occasion when the enemy interfered with his bridge at an extraordinarily interesting stage of the game", and a *post mortem* held on the unplayed cards next morning yielded much stimulating food for thought.

Daylight raids were a menace to cricket. "Interruptions such as occur these days", *The Times* Cricket Correspondent complained, "make it quite impossible for a captain to declare his innings closed at a moment even approximate to that which normally would allow of a reasonably close finish"; and he instanced a match in which the Buccaneers (268 for 9 declared) had been cheated of a probable victory over a British Empire XI (141 for 6) when an air-raid stopped play with an hour still left to go.

Foxhunting was not directly affected,[2] but it is perhaps worth recording that, when a bomb scored a direct hit on the kennels of

---

[1] *The Times*, 10 July 1940. To give German propaganda its due, this broadcast was probably intended for listeners—in Spain, the Balkans or elsewhere—in whom it would not have aroused mirth and might not have aroused scepticism.

[2] The season does not open till 1 November.

the East Kent Hunt in August, the hounds, though blown far afield by the explosion, were all recovered, unhurt, in the course of the next two days.

The Government's decision to advance the opening of the grouse-shooting season from the traditional Twelfth to the 5th of August was not well received by northern landowners and seems in practice to have been largely ignored. In a letter to *The Times* one Scottish peer wrote: "I am inclined to ask whether this bright idea emanates from the same brilliant brains as those responsible for the huge waste of paper circularising instructions to the Agricultural Executive Committees to put a stop to all hand-rearing of pheasants in July." His point, a valid one, was that by July the young pheasants had already been reared and it was too late to stop any waste of foodstuffs involved in the process. (The pheasant season was also put forward from 1 October to 22 September.)

When the air-raids started, the London Zoo had its fair share of bombs but casualties to the animals were remarkably light. The possibility of escapes was not overlooked. Within a few hours of the declaration of war all poisonous snakes, spiders and scorpions had been destroyed in accordance with a decision taken several months earlier. When the bombing started the lions, tigers, polar bears and full-grown apes were shut up every night in their sleeping dens. It was considered unlikely that the same stick of bombs would make breaches both in these well-built chambers and in the iron bars of their outer cages; but against this contingency the Zoo's Air Raid Precautions staff maintained a small reserve of trained riflemen.

Apart from three humming birds, a bird of paradise and a crane (the last two were recaptured), the only notable escape was that of a Grevy zebra. This valuable animal was pursued round Regent's Park by the secretary of the Royal Zoological Society and half a dozen keepers, and eventually rounded up. Monkey Hill, like the Zebra House, received a direct hit, but the morale of the monkeys remained unaffected. Indeed, all the animals stood up well under fire, supporting their ordeal with almost as much equanimity as the keeper who, after a shower of incendiaries had fallen on the Gardens, was heard to say that "it only needed a bit of music to make it seem like fairyland".[1]

As the attack on London developed, the world of entertainment contracted to a microcosm. The little Windmill Theatre, off Shaftesbury Avenue, gallantly continued to provide the public with solace and distraction; feminine nudity was its standard recipe and "We Never Closed" its boast. In September all the other theatres had to close; but before the end of the month two had reopened. "In this battered city of London," wrote Ivor Brown,[2] "when playgoing seemed to be as dead as under Cromwell, two theatres did open, one at noon, one in the afternoons. And both played Shakespeare." Donald Wolfit launched the experiment of playing "lunchtime Shakespeare" to audiences who munched their sandwiches and listened for an hour to deathless words while death quartered the skies above them. Midday concerts were given in the National Gallery and midday ballet at the Arts Theatre Club; and these iron rations of its normal pleasures helped to sustain the spirit of the mauled capital.

Any attempt to recapture from contemporary evidence the atmosphere of the period, and the mood of the nation, must necessarily be empirical. Between May and September, between the "miracle" of Dunkirk and the sudden, seemingly inexhaustible fury of the German onslaught on London, many preoccupations and several important illusions overlapped each other in a matter of weeks. Yet here and there small things were done or said or written which seem to throw some light on what men and women felt at the time.

"Dreadful confusion everywhere!" Like ships' logs, the war diaries of Army units and formations are normally laconic records of the chief events of the day; this entry in the war diary of 136 Brigade for 14 May is hardly in the tradition but probably near the truth. "The 'flap' continues", the Brigade Intelligence Officer noted two days later, as they carried out a hasty and ill-organised move towards the south coast. These unsoldierly *aperçus* must subsequently have caught the eye of some steadier, more conventional

[1] Julian Huxley: "Air Raids and the Zoo". The *Spectator*, November 1940.
[2] In the *Observer* of 29 September 1940.

officer; "flap" was crossed out, and "tension" substituted for it. Neither word seems inappropriate to a situation in which, on 27 May, a neighbouring brigade was ordered to remove the detonators from the explosive charges placed under Eastbourne Pier, upon which it was now expected that survivors from the British Expeditionary Force, and not the Germans, would be the first to land.

Throughout the period there was a tendency for suspicion and credulity to go hand in hand. During May and June scarcely a day passed without someone, somewhere, reporting that he or she had seen parachutists landing; and on 10 July the Ministry of Information, in view of a crop of rumours "often accompanied by vivid and precise details", found it expedient to state officially that no enemy had as yet descended upon the kingdom.

Perhaps the most notable false alarm occurred near Nettlebed in Oxfordshire. Here, on 1 July, the Observer Corps reported the transit of an unidentified aircraft from which a parachute appeared to fall. The parachute was probably a hank of hay, lifted off a rick by a spiral eddy of air on a hot day; but a detachment of Canadian troops, hastening to the spot, came on a young man with a furtive manner and an accent unfamiliar to them. When questioned, he gave an address in Reading which was quickly proved by the police to be a false one; and when taxed with being a German agent who had just landed by parachute he confessed that that was exactly what he was.

He was found to be in possession of a map of Wales, subdivided by boundaries bearing no relation to those of the existing counties (they were in fact the boundaries of the "cantreds" which failed to survive the conquest of Wales by Edward I). He gave detailed descriptions of several other spies who had been dropped from the same aircraft; these were immediately circulated throughout the kingdom. He also revealed the identity of the chief German agent in Oxfordshire, to whom he had been ordered to report. This man—a hitherto respected farmer in the Witney district, and a tenant of the Duke of Marlborough—was immediately made captive by Canadian forces from Oxford.

At GHQ Home Forces, then quaintly housed in the Army School of Music at Kneller Hall, Twickenham, the arrests created a lively interest, and the Commander-in-Chief (Ironside), who was an excellent linguist, decided to take a hand in the interrogation. He drove swiftly to Oxford, but his fluent German was wasted on the farmer, who was entirely innocent and who later recovered substantial damages from the Army Council for the indignities to which he had been subjected.

Investigation revealed that the "parachutist" was a parson's son who had deserted from an anti-aircraft unit in Wales; the farmer, for whom he had worked for a short time before the war, was the only person in that part of the country whose name he knew and he had confessed to being a spy partly because it seemed to be expected of him and partly because it offered the only readily available alternative to revealing his true identity and being court-martialled for desertion. He was sentenced to two years' imprisonment. Thus ended an episode which gave to all concerned in it (except the farmer, his family, and their accuser) much pleasurable though unnecessary excitement.

It was a little later that British land forces (other than anti-aircraft and coastal artillery) went into action on British soil for the first time since 1797, when a small French force, landed at Fishguard, surrendered without firing a shot. The crew of a Junkers 88 which had made a forced landing on Graveney Marsh in Kent opened fire on men of the London Irish Rifles as they closed in on the machine, and a short gun-fight took place before the Germans, two of whom were wounded in the action, surrendered. An officer, who was later awarded the George Medal for his coolness, entered the aircraft and dismantled two time-bombs with which it was equipped, and the bomber, which was of a type newly brought into service and thus a valuable prize, fell into the hands of the British intact.

The war diary of 45 Division, the only more or less complete field formation in south-east England at the time of Dunkirk, is filled with reports, mainly from Home Guard or civilian sources, of parachutists, mysterious lights and unexplained explosions. An entry on 21 May made a courageous attempt to correlate the first two types of phenomena: "A number of unaccountable lights continue to be observed. It is for consideration whether some of the lights reported are caused by enemy parachutists burning their parachutes. The fact that there is no record of a parachute being found lends colour to this theory."

A month later the staff of the same Division had their suspicions aroused by the heaps of lime dotted about the farmland in their area. Not only did these heaps seem unnecessarily large, but they were reported to glow at night, and thus to become visible from the air; they were believed to "point to" a railway junction.

In late September or early October 1939 a British officer attached to one of the French armies had noticed, while enemy aircraft were overhead, small quantities of a white, filmy substance floating to the ground. Specimens were collected by the French and taken away to be analysed. Though he never heard the results of the analysis, the officer included an account of the incident in one of his reports.

In the following year, when the danger of invasion was first appreciated in Britain, the General Staff ordered a review to be made of all possible clues, from whatever source, to the nature of the new and secret weapons which the Germans were expected to use.[1] In the process somebody came across the nine-month-old report from France, and the unidentified white substance floating down from the sky was thought worth mentioning along with other chimaeras, such as the discharge of gas from huge submersible tanks towed across the sea under water. It may have been for this reason that in early October an official warning was issued that the nebulous jetsam had made its appearance and, since it was liable to prove poisonous, should on no account be touched. It was in point of fact gossamer, which at this season of the year is discharged by spiders while mating in mid-air.

[1] "We are assured", the Prime Minister told the House of Commons on 4 June, "that novel methods will be adopted, and when we see the originality of malice, the ingenuity of aggression, which our enemy displays, we may certainly prepare ourselves for every kind of novel stratagem and every kind of brutal and treacherous manoeuvre. I think that no idea is so outlandish that it should not be considered and viewed with a searching but at the same time, I hope, a steady eye." Textual criticism can hardly be applied too nicely to a parliamentary speech; but in the first of the two sentences here quoted, "we may certainly"—deputising for "we must"—strikes that note of reservation, symptomatic of an ultimate disbelief, which characterised so many of Churchill's written and spoken references to the danger of invasion.

In one strange case credulity found itself allied not with fear but with hope. At the beginning of September a rumour spread swiftly through the country that large numbers of dead German soldiers had been washed up on the south coast. In many accounts the corpses were said to be burnt or charred, and it was widely believed that the RAF had somehow "set the sea on fire" at the very moment when an invasion was being launched.[1] "The Channel is white with dead" was a phrase in common use to describe a grim but satisfactory spectacle; and although watchers on the south coast could see for themselves that the statement was quite untrue as far as their own sector was concerned, the rumour ran as strongly there as in other parts of the country. No corpses had come ashore *here*, the enquirer would be told at A.; but further along the coast at B. the Sappers had been called in to clear the harbour. From B. he would be re-directed to C., where (it was said) a large part of the civilian population had been evacuated because of the stench. A characteristic (and from a psychoanalytical standpoint perhaps a significant) feature of the rumour was that the corpses were always supposed to have arrived not on deserted stretches of the coast, but in harbours, on municipal seafronts, and at other places where they were a public nuisance.

Churchill afterwards gave this account of the rumour and its origins:

During August the corpses of about forty German soldiers were washed up at scattered points along the coast between the Isle of Wight and Cornwall. The Germans had been practising embarkations in the barges along the French coast. Some of these barges put out to sea in order to escape British bombing and were sunk, either by bombing or bad weather. This was the source of a widespread rumour that the Germans had attempted an invasion and had suffered very heavy losses either by drowning or by being burnt in patches of sea covered with flaming oil. We took no steps to contradict such tales, which spread freely through

[1] Cf. "One particular series of raids was especially damaging. It is believed to have caught the German soldiers and sailors just at the moment when a kind of dress rehearsal was being staged and to have resulted in the killing and wounding of thousands of the troops embarked. . . . About this time some bodies of uniformed Germans continued to be washed up on our shores for some days after that date." (J. M. Spaight: *The Battle of Britain*. London, 1941.)

the occupied countries in a wildly exaggerated form and gave much encouragement to the oppressed populations.[1]

In fact the whole business was much odder than would appear from Churchill's narrative, for his first sentence—which gives the rumour some foundation in fact—has no such foundation itself. The recovery from the sea of forty dead German soldiers would have had at least four consequences which would still be traceable to-day. It would have been reported in the war diaries of the Army formations in whose sectors they were washed up; the casualties would have been notified to the German Government through the International Red Cross in the same way as casualties to air-crews or prisoners of war in British territory; the pay-books and other personal documents of the dead men would have been studied and commented on by M.I.14; and particulars of the West Country churchyards or cemeteries where the bodies were buried would have been recorded by the Imperial War Graves Commission.

None of these consequences ensued. To reach the coast "between the Isle of Wight and Cornwall" the forty corpses, assuming that they started from the nearest German embarkation area (Le Havre), would have had to drift a minimum distance of over a hundred miles in a north-westerly direction; and they must, with respect, be written off as not less imaginary than their countless fellow-victims who were said at the time to be whitening the whole Channel.[2]

It is clear, in retrospect, that a rumour which swept first the United Kingdom, and then much of the rest of mankind, was wholly spontaneous, wholly baseless and wholly inexplicable. No version of the supposed facts was published in the British or even in the American press at the time; but the tale, launched into the whispering gallery of a curious and uneasy world, was of some small assistance to the British cause.

Wireless broadcasting had played no part in the First World War; in the second its importance was considerable. Since the outbreak

---

[1] *Their Finest Hour.*

[2] Although "the Channel is white with dead" has a vivid, eye-witness ring about it, corpses clad in field-grey would not in practice have inspired its use, particularly if they had been scorched or charred.

of hostilities German broadcasts in English to the United Kingdom had been dominated by the radio personality of William Joyce, an under-sized, harsh-voiced ex-member of the British Union of Fascists in his middle thirties, who was hanged for treason after the war. Under the sobriquet of "Lord Haw Haw", bestowed on him by the radio critic of the *Daily Express*, he became something of a national institution, and a revue called *Haw Haw!*, described as a "new laughter show", had a successful run at the Holborn Empire during the summer of 1940.

No attempt was made to jam the German broadcasts, particulars of whose times, wave-lengths and so on continued, as in peacetime, to be printed in *The Times* and elsewhere along with the details of the BBC's programmes. But during the Phoney War some concern had been felt in official circles about the influence exerted in this medium by the German Propaganda Ministry, and in March 1940 the BBC produced a confidential document entitled *Hamburg Broadcast Propaganda: A summary of the results of an inquiry into the extent and effect of its impact on the British public during midwinter 1939/40*.

This report showed that "at the end of January, out of every six adults in the population, one was a regular listener to Hamburg, three were occasional listeners, and two never listened. (At that time four out of every six people were listening regularly to the BBC news.)" Listeners to Hamburg were relatively more numerous among people of intelligence and education; 30 per cent, for instance, of *The Times*'s readers listened, against 16 per cent of the readers of the *Daily Mirror* and the *Daily Sketch*. This was during a static war, when "as yet widespread hatred of the enemy does not exist". Joyce's grating and arrogant voice was a source of irritation; but "it seems likely [the BBC thought] that, by pure accident, Lord Haw Haw has secured some degree of immunity from the full force of British anger. For this he must thank his voice and manner which are so sinister, and so patently insincere, that they have given him the necessary degree of unreality." The report compared the licence extended by listeners to his insults and extravagances with that extended to the chronic impudence of a ventriloquist's dummy.

Interest in the Hamburg broadcasts, which had been waning when the report was completed, seems to have temporarily revived after Dunkirk. Although, however, the Germans spiced their propaganda with short lists of the names of British prisoners of war,[1] Haw Haw had by now become (especially to women) an object of odium rather than of curiosity, and in the new temper of the country he stiffened rather than diluted the nation's will to fight.

One odd legend, however, sprang up in connection with Haw Haw. This was that on various occasions his broadcasts had revealed an uncannily accurate knowledge of some local condition or phenomenon of which the Germans could have been informed only by their secret agents; the most widely quoted allegation was that Haw Haw had mentioned the exact time at which the church clock at So-and-So had stopped, but stories were also current that he had prophesied the bombing of a town or village shortly before it occurred. These rumours were as baseless as those about the German corpses in the Channel. It is just possible that they were initiated in the first place by German agents or German sympathisers; but if they were it would have been reasonable to expect to find their echoes or their counterparts in the traffic of the German "black" radio,[2] which contains no trace of this gambit. The most probable explanation is that they were a natural by-product of the human imagination and the human ego, interacting upon each other under stress.

To the BBC's broadcasts, and particularly to its news bulletins, the British listened as they had never listened before. "The News" —normally the 9 p.m. bulletin—became in most households an institution almost as sacrosanct as family prayers had once been. Although there were now six news bulletins every day, whose content—until the Battle of Britain started—could not be expected to vary very much, few citizens shared the view, expressed in a

[1] The fate of the tens of thousands of members of the BEF who did not return from Dunkirk remained in many cases uncertain for cruelly protracted periods. Throughout the summer *The Times* published, alongside the "Agony Column" on its front page, a list of enquiries about officers and other ranks headed "Information Wanted". In June this occupied a whole column, but as time went on and casualties were notified through the International Red Cross it grew gradually shorter and finally disappeared.

[2] See Chapter 8.

letter published in the *Spectator* of 12 July, that so many bulletins were bad for the nerves.[1] Soon after Dunkirk the BBC's announcers abandoned their hitherto unbroken tradition of anonymity, each giving his name before he read the bulletin. This precaution was taken lest a *coup de main* by Fifth Columnists or airborne troops should gain for the enemy control of the microphones in Broadcasting House and thus enable him to broadcast tendentious or misleading matter without listeners being any the wiser. The innovation was popular with the public, lending as it did a personal touch to the ritual of "The News". The announcers did not revert to anonymity until 4 May 1945.

Before the summer of 1939 Great Britain had established a comfortable lead over the rest of the world in the development of television, and more than 20,000 households owned television sets. On the outbreak of war the BBC's television services—like its weather forecasts, though for more technical reasons—were suspended. Broadcasting House received a direct hit during an air raid on 16 October 1940, seven members of the staff being killed. The announcers who were reading news-bulletins at the time—both on the Home Service and in German to Germany—continued to do so with commendable imperturbability, and listeners were not aware until later that anything was amiss.

There was one matter which troubled the conscience of the British people increasingly as the summer wore on. It is possible that the official archives may contain material vindicating the Government's policy towards enemy aliens, but this does not seem likely. What is certain is that all male Germans, Austrians and (after 11 June) Italians between the ages of sixteen and sixty[2] were interned, and that the circumstances under which they were detained aroused, on a number of counts, a growing volume of public indignation.

The history of what by mid-July it seemed quite natural for a sober journal like the *Spectator* to call "The Internment Scandal" went back to the beginning of the war, when some 2000 suspects

[1] "Let us have [instead] lectures on our historical and gallant fights for freedom and also a few calming nature talks", urged the writer, a retired colonel resident in Great Snoring.

[2] Later raised to seventy.

were rounded up and interned. 120 Aliens' Tribunals were then set up, and nearly 74,000 cases were investigated, including those of 55,000 political refugees. Of all these 600 were interned, 6800 were placed in Category B ("absolute reliability uncertain") and the remainder were given certificates of reliability.

In the following year the news first from Norway and then from the Low Countries generated fears, which were not far removed from panic, about the Fifth Column. On 10 May all male aliens living in the coastal areas most liable to invasion were interned. On 16 May all males in the B category, wherever they lived, were taken, and a few days later females in this category, with their children, were transported to the Isle of Man. At this stage the Press and public were demanding still more drastic precautions,[1] and on 21 June all the remaining enemy aliens (more than 50,000 of whom were Jewish refugees) were taken into custody. Some 8,000 were shipped to Canada and Australia, and many, including individuals of unquestioned probity and considerable distinction, lost their lives when the *Arandora Star* was torpedoed early in July.

By this time public opinion had begun to turn sharply against the Government's policy, and particularly against the callous way in which it was often carried out. News of suicides among the refugees, of the break-up of families, of the sequestration of scientists who were doing valuable work for the nation—a whole avalanche of dirty linen came tumbling into the centre of public life. In Parliament and in the newspapers harrowing stories, all too well authenticated, were told of individual tragedies brought on by the hurried, impersonal implementation of mass-internment; and gradually the blunders and the petty inhumanities were purged from the system, the right of appeal was restored to internees and the whole ugly business was, save by its victims, largely forgotten.

That it was an ugly business, and that it came to be recognised as such by the mass of the British people, there can be no doubt; even the neutral correspondents stationed in London felt impelled to

[1] Cf. the *Daily Herald* (headline), 17 May 1940: "COUNTRY SAVED FROM FIFTH COLUMN STAB."

The Times, 18 May 1940: "The main criticism, showing itself in numerous letters from readers, seems to be that it is probably unwise not to intern female enemy aliens."

make a corporate protest. Given the circumstances—and the illusions —prevailing at the time, could it have been anything else? In May 1940 the British Government had excellent reasons—or reasons which seemed excellent then, which is the same thing—for taking prompt and far-reaching precautions against the Fifth Column. Since it lacked both the time and the machinery for effectively discriminating (or in most cases re-discriminating) between one alien and another, it was in duty bound to intern the lot; in face of so grave and yet so elusive a danger as enemy-organised treachery, no margin of risk could be accepted. It was not a Government spokesman, but an Independent Member of Parliament (K. Pickthorn), who, speaking in a debate on the subject on 22 August, said:

If an archangel appeared before all the members of the War Cabinet at once and said, "There is one red-headed man in England who, unless care is taken, will do something to injure the State", I think it would be the duty of the War Cabinet to see that all red-headed men were interned. I should say it was their duty to do this at whatever cost to human misery, or at whatever risk to what is called British prestige.

It is difficult even now, and was impossible then, to dispute the thesis thus fancifully put forward. Where the Government failed was, not in adopting a harsh policy, but in failing to humanise as far as possible the methods by which the policy was carried out. Yet these were bound to be rough and ready. No adequate accommodation was ready for the internees. Since it was assumed that some were dangerous and perhaps desperate men, they had to be rounded up brusquely and without warning. Administrative staffs to look after them had to be improvised. Documentation was a slow and cumbrous process; by September no fewer than 750,000 files were circulating round the regional sections of the Aliens Branch of the Home Office, which had never had anything corresponding to regional sections before. There was, in short, bound to be a great muddle and much hardship.

It is however difficult for the historian to dissent from the verdict of public opinion at the time (once it had got over its spy-fever[1]). This was that a grave and in some cases an irreparable wrong

[1] This hateful malady led to "a little misguided stone-throwing by members of the public" when a batch of a thousand women and children were sent from London to the Isle of Man. (*News Chronicle*, 31 May 1940.)

was done to a large number of innocent and helpless people, not one of whom was ever proved to have harboured malignant designs upon the State in which most had sought asylum from persecution.

It would be possible to write almost indefinitely of the many things, large and small, which combined in the summer of 1940 to give life in the United Kingdom a flavour which distinguished that brief period from all the rest of British history. To save man-power, juries were reduced from twelve to seven (except in cases of murder, treason and other serious crimes). Stationers sold large cards, for display in the home, on which was printed: "We are not interested in the possibilities of defeat. They do not exist." "Because their second daughter was born as an all-clear siren was sounding, Mr and Mrs R. English propose to name her Sireen."[1] Fashion marched to the sound of the guns; among the autumn models for everyday wear, *The Times* informed its feminine readers on 26 August, was "the battle-dress siren suit in washable corduroy with a skirt to match".[2] To the same paper, a few days earlier, a reader had written in the hope of putting the mounting air-raid casualties in their true perspective; "to kill one in every ten people in the British Isles [he pointed out] the enemy must kill one thousand people every day for thirteen and a half years." The mathematical odds against sudden death might be long, but one member of the Royal Academy thought it worth advertising his willingness to execute "life-size portraits, DONE QUICKLY", for a fee of five guineas.

On the battlefield a display of *sangfroid*, conscious or unconscious, distracts attention from the suffering and sacrifices which are its

[1] The *Evening Standard*, 30 August 1940. "Sireen", or something like it, was a normal pronunciation. Cf. V. Sackville-West in the *New Statesman and Nation*, 4 August 1940: "Among the many wonderments provoked by this war, I wonder why so many people pronounce siren as cyrene?"

[2] In the world of fashion heroic efforts were made to rise to the occasion, and leading houses advertised (though not for long) ladies' hats "reinforced with a lightweight steel cap" and an "anti-concussion bandeau of aerated rubber" which, besides being extremely *chic*, "affords protection to the sensitive portions of brain and ear-drums". The ladies totally rejected these attempts to dilute the quest for elegance with the instinct of self-preservation; and the only semi-permanent sartorial legacy of the period was the habit, hitherto largely confined to the peasantry of Ireland and Eastern Europe, of wearing head-scarves. This was basically due to the effects of clothes rationing.

background. Evidence that the British, in this crisis, bore themselves well should not be taken as proof that they had little to bear. Apart from the fact, of which they were too preoccupied or too proud to take cognisance, that there was no light at the end of the tunnel, no discernible pebble in the brook with which Goliath might be suddenly felled, all of them had already suffered loss. The loss might be expressed in terms of bereavement or of separation: of a career interrupted, a house requisitioned, a scholarship forgone: of an oak-grove felled, a flower-bed incorporated in the foundations of a pill-box, a trawler converted into a minesweeper: of anything from tragedy to inconvenience. But all had already lost something, and all, as the piles of rubble and the lists of casualties began to mount, knew very well that they were going to lose more: perhaps everything.

This knowledge was universal throughout the community. Why, then, were spirits so high in Britain in the summer of 1940? Since at the time no one bothered to enquire scientifically into this phenomenon, no considered explanation survives; but it seems possible that a Fourth Leader in *The Times* of 3 July 1940[1] came near to the truth. "We have almost ceased to look forward", the writer suggested; holidays, peace, victory were no longer on the agenda. He went on: "The days of looking forward used to pass slowly and heavily because they had merely to be lived through, for the sake of others to come, but now the days are all lived for their own sake."

More sapient diagnoses might well prove wider of the mark.

[1] Fourth Leaders have normally a more frivolous character than those which precede them on the leader page.

CHAPTER EIGHT

The Mirages in Hitler's Mind
(2) Disintegration

Napoleon's own judgment was founded, to a great extent, on most utter fallacies about the dispositions of the mass of the English people towards himself, and towards their fellow-countrymen. . . . Much more of this gibberish (as Sir Walter Scott rightly calls it) may be found in his conversations; and it proves how little he foresaw the determined and unanimous resistance which he would have encountered from the English nation.

E. S. Creasy: *The Invasions and Projected Invasions of England, from the Saxon Times: with Remarks on the Present Emergencies.* 1852

But he had other matters on hand which he judged (God knows how erroneously) to be more important.

Robert Louis Stevenson and Lloyd Osbourne:
The Wrong Box

German broadcasts in English were interspersed with code messages instructing listeners to prevent invasion taking place by means of an open revolt.

From a report on Enemy Broadcasts by the BBC Monitoring Service,
August 1940

HITLER had always been fascinated by the idea of a bloodless victory, brought about by trickery, subversion and the sapping of his enemy's morale. In 1932, while discussing with cronies the attractions of bacterial warfare, he had digressed to prophesy that "Our real wars will in fact all be fought before military operations begin. I can quite imagine that we might control Britain in this way. Or America." [1]

Will America again intervene in European affairs? they asked him. Hitler did not seem greatly to care if she did. "There are new weapons", he said, "which are effective in such cases. America is permanently on the brink of revolution. [2] It will be a simple matter

[1] Rauschning.
[2] This was said at a time when the United States was in the throes of a major economic crisis.

for me to produce unrest and revolt in the United States, so that these gentry will have their hands full of their own affairs. . . . Our strategy is to destroy the enemy from within, to conquer him through himself."

To this theme he returned again and again. "What is the object of war? To make the enemy capitulate. If he does, I have the prospect of wiping him out. Why should I demolish him by military means if I can do so better and more cheaply in other ways?" The formula had worked with Austria and Czechoslovakia; it had contributed greatly to the overthrow of France. A good deal of evidence —hitherto neglected—supports the view that until the last moment Hitler was relying on it to bring about the disintegration of British resistance.

On 6 July Hitler returned to Berlin from a honeymoon with victory at Kniebis. During his ten days in the Black Forest he had virtually ceased to make war or even to exercise command. Every morning he drove off on a sight-seeing tour. With two comrades of the First World War—one of them Max Amann, in those days a power in the Battalion Orderly Room, in these the wealthy controller of the Party's publishing interests—he spent a long week-end visiting the battlefields on which, as a company runner in the 16th Bavarian Reserve Infantry Regiment, he had won two Iron Crosses and a corporal's stripes[1]; he examined the damage done by bombardment to the forts of the Maginot Line; he studied the monuments of Strasbourg, where he had never been before. In the evenings he returned to the pastoral surroundings of the Supreme Command Headquarters.

Here, during the day, military affairs stagnated. The handful of officers through whom the most powerful military machine in history was controlled had nothing whatever to do. Hitler had suggested that they should spend money freely in the two little country inns where they were quartered, so that the landlords should not lose by the exigencies of war; and much *Erdbeerbowle*— an iced punch with wild strawberries in it—was drunk. In the evenings Hitler was busy with the first draft of the speech which he was to deliver to the Reichstag, after various postponements, on 19 July.

[1] Bullock.

He had more time for Hewel, the Foreign Office representative at OKW, than for Jodl, hovering in the background with a lengthening list of urgent military matters awaiting decision. Greiner, who was at Kniebis, describes the situation thus: "Initially Hitler treated the suggestions put up to him by his military staff at *Tannenberg* with great reserve, and when on 2 July he finally sanctioned the collection of intelligence data and the formulation of plans for a landing operation 'as one of the contingencies that may arise', he firmly laid down that no material preparations were to be made for the time being."[1]

Hitler lived in a dream at Kniebis. Before going there he had received from a Swedish source intimations that London was disposed to negotiate; and it may have been because he accepted these as reliable that he told von Brauchitsch on 23 June that Britain was "coming down a peg". It was not until 6 July, when he left the Black Forest for Berlin, that he awoke from his dream.

His return had all the trappings of a triumph. Flowers strewed the streets. When Hitler and his three commanders-in-chief appeared on the Chancery balcony, a massed choir of the *Bund Deutscher Mädchen* broke into the strains of *Wir fahren gegen Engelland*.

> Our flag waves as we march along.
> It is an emblem of the power of our Reich,
> And we can no longer endure
> That the Englishman should laugh at it.
> So give me thy hand, thy fair white hand,
> Ere we sail away to conquer Eng-el-land![2]

All this was doubtless gratifying. But in Berlin there was no news of overtures from the British, no signs of a response, however cautious, to the German peace-feelers; and the drastic action taken by the Royal Navy against the French Fleet at Oran on 3 July hardly suggested a trend towards compromise in London. Hitler had

---

[1] Helmuth Greiner: *Die Oberste Wehrmacht Fuehrung*. Wiesbaden, 1951.

[2] In war the enemy's patriotic songs always seem ridiculous. This one was a perfectly worthy representative of its genre, and British readers in whom it raises an indulgent smile should remember that in 1939 the BEF crossed to France to the strains of:

> We'll hang out our washing on the Siegfried Line—
> If the Siegfried Line's still there.

wasted ten valuable days. Their only by-product—the draft of his Reichstag speech—had now to be revised.

A fortnight later Hitler's "peace offer" had been made and contemptuously rejected. By now the comforting illusions he had entertained at Kniebis had grown threadbare; but still he refused to discard them. Every day brought fresh evidence that the British Government were utterly determined to go on fighting and that no accommodation with them was possible. Yet Hitler continued to hope for—what? What did he mean when, in mid-August, he told Raeder that invasion would be tried "only as a last resort, *if Britain cannot be made to sue for peace in any other way*"? All through the short history of *Operation Sea Lion* some unspecified fancy at the back of the Fuehrer's mind flits like a will-o'-the-wisp. Von Brauchitsch's *Instructions for the Preparation of Operation Sea Lion*, issued to OKH on 30 August, laid down that "the order for execution *depends on the political situation*". A week later Raeder told a conference of his staff that "the Fuehrer's decision to land in England is still by no means settled, as he is *firmly convinced* that England's defeat will be achieved even without the landing".[1] Finally, in mid-September, the rumour ran round OKW that Hitler "seriously expected" the outbreak of a revolution in England.

The trail thus faintly blazed will lead us to one specific and curious event, which may perhaps fall more easily into perspective if it is described before, rather than after, its exceedingly complex antecedents.

On the night of 13/14 August an unknown number of German aircraft dropped a miscellany of objects at various places in the English Midlands and the Lowlands of Scotland. The objects included parachutes, wireless transmitters, small quantities of high explosive, maps, photographs, lists of addresses of prominent people, and instructions to imaginary agents defining their role when the invaders came; these instructions combined with other clues to simulate a threat to the east coast. On 16 August Greiner noted in

---

[1] It is possible to argue that both von Brauchitsch and Raeder were referring by implication to the results expected from the German air offensive. But this was by then well under way and had shown no signs of ending the conflict or of decisively altering the situation. It is in any case difficult to see why, if that was what both meant, neither of them said it.

the OKW war diary: "We dropped pack assemblies in order to feign a parachute landing, which caused great excitement in the British Press." On that night further parachutes were dropped.

In fact the operation had a wider purpose than "to feign a parachute landing". The evidence with which it supplied the British was intended to point to three main conclusions:

(*a*) that invasion was imminent;
(*b*) that it would fall on the east coast;
(*c*) that a powerful and well-organised Fifth Column was in being throughout the country.

It was to the third of these conclusions that the greatest importance was attached by Hitler and the small handful of men who planned the ruse.

Superficially this attempt to simulate the successful landing by air of a strong, well-briefed party of agents and saboteurs resembles the pamphlet-dropping activities of the previous week. Both operations involved the diversion of aircraft from normal offensive missions at a time when every bomb-load was needed; both (and in particular the second, which was carried out on the second night of the delayed air offensive) could have taken place only on orders from the highest level. It is in fact known[1] that the objects used in the dummy parachute drop were submitted to Goering in the dining car of his special train, and that he more than once mentioned that Hitler had been "very pleased" with what was known as the *Abwurf Aktion* (dropping operation).

But there the resemblance between the two operations ends; for whereas the dropping of pamphlets was an aimless, isolated and ill-timed digression, the dropping of "pack assemblies" was a carefully planned development of German psychological warfare, to whose main strategy the ruse was linked closely and not without ingenuity. Its true status can be understood only if it is viewed against the background of the German "black" radio, to which it was intended to be an important ancillary.

[1] Testimony of General Schmid, at the time head of the Intelligence Branch of the Luftwaffe Staff.

During the Phoney War and throughout *Operation Yellow* the Germans had operated—with good results in their own estimation—a broadcast service called *La Voix de la Paix*; it purported to be run by Frenchmen from French territory and was an agent of alarm and defeatism. Its British counterpart was first heard in England on 25 February 1940, though internal evidence suggests that transmissions began five days earlier. It called itself the New British Broadcasting Station, used "The Bonnie, Bonnie Banks of Loch Lomond" as a signature tune and ended its transmissions with the National Anthem.

It was later joined by three other "black" stations. "Workers' Challenge" (first heard on 8 July) was anti-capitalist in tone and specialised in the coarser terms of abuse. "Caledonia" (first heard on 18 July[1]) had "Auld Lang Syne" as a signature tune, essayed a Scots accent with imperfect success and urged its listeners to seek, by violence if necessary, a separate peace for their down-trodden country. Finally there was the "Christian Peace Movement", which used "Blessed are the peace-makers" as its slogan and implored all men of good will to refrain from aiding the war effort. Reception from all four stations, and particularly from the last two, was poor; the Germans, however, had no means of knowing this.

A vivid picture presents itself to any reader of the monitored traffic of the New British Broadcasting Station—a picture of England as Hitler, in the summer of 1940, would have liked her to be. The broadcasts postulated the existence of a widespread and highly organised Fifth Column; cryptic messages to its members were at times transmitted in an easily breakable code by the main German broadcasting stations, and to these transmissions cross-reference was made by NBBS. Disunity, demoralisation, hatred of its leaders and a passionate yearning for peace were the distinguishing characteristics of this cloud-cuckooland. Everybody knew that not only Churchill and his friends but even Socialist Cabinet Ministers were being bribed by the Jews to continue the war. Sabotage was rife,

---

[1] The fact that both these stations, followed within a month by the third, were activated precisely at the time when Hitler first began to realise that his hopes of a negotiated peace were vain is possibly no more than a coincidence.

and so were foot-and-mouth disease, faked Treasury notes and tins of meat poisoned by German agents in the Argentine.

Terror was a staple ingredient of the interesting brew. A regular series of first-aid hints for use in air-raids provided a pretext for describing particularly gruesome and disgusting injuries, and listeners were urged to agitate for the provision of strait-jackets in the public shelters, since men and women would certainly go mad under the stress of bombing. Occasionally a Teutonic ingenuity was shown, as in the revelation that German airborne troops were being provided with "fog-pills", which enabled each soldier to conceal himself in a small cloud; since they now had dirigible parachutes, capable of staying aloft for as long as ten hours, they were not readily distinguishable from several common types of cloud formation. Some play was also made with an "electro-magnetic ray", said to have been used in the reduction of the fortress of Eben Emael, outside Liège; the Germans were aware that the method of its capture—by glider-borne troops landed on its roof—was still something of a mystery. Threats of chemical or bacterial warfare were never used.

Towards the end of August there was a marked change in NBBS policy, or at least in its political technique. Until then listeners had been urged to strive for peace by stealthy or pseudo-democratic tactics, such as chain-letters, demonstrations in Downing Street or hissing Churchill whenever he appeared on a news-reel. On 27 August the broadcasts went over to a campaign of envenomed rabble-rousing. "There is a danger that we may get slack in our work for peace", the announcer pointed out, and conjured the populace to horsewhip Churchill and his underlings and to burn their property. From then on the scripts seem almost to foam at the mouth, and there is what can only be described as a *personal* note of malice in the daily exhortations to "go forward gloriously in a campaign of frank terrorism for the good of Britain". Listeners were told to "use hard physical force" against "this shameless, indecent, rotten and demoralised ruling class"—break their windows in the blackout, make Black Lists, see that the warmongers go in constant fear of their lives.[1]

[1] "Of course you know the history of revolutions," Hitler had told Rauschning seven years earlier. "It is always the same. The ruling classes capitulate."

A few days later the broadcasters found it expedient to rebut allegations that they were Germans. "The fact that we are British must be clear from every word we broadcast." They suggested that the allegations had been made, not for the first time, in the hope that they would be provoked into showing their hand and thus allowing Scotland Yard to catch up with them.

The NBBS transmissions were closely linked with *Operation Sea Lion*. Their most obvious aim was to intimidate. Invasion was a certainty; every day's delay meant only that the attack, when it came, would be more terrible—"utterly inhuman" was one of the phrases used. To stay put, as the Government advised, would be fatal; all should take to the roads and make for north Wales and north-west Scotland, the only parts of the kingdom which offered any hope of sanctuary. These vague threats were stiffened with accounts of the new German weapons. Some of these—like the "fog-pills"—were flights of fancy; but at least two real weapons, one of which had not been developed while the other had been tried and found wanting, were described in general terms, though both must still have been on the secret list.

The first of these was the guided missile, known to the British as the V1, with which the Germans began to bombard London in 1944; on 22 August 1940 the NBBS prophesied the destruction of the capital by "aerial torpedoes carrying many tons of high explosive and guided by radio". The second was a high-speed landing-craft powered with an aircraft engine; craft of this type, compendiously known as *Truppentransporttragflachenschnellboote*, were in fact experimented with—Halder watched tests at Rangsdorf on 3 August—but proved unsatisfactory. NBBS mentioned them on 10 September. Both items suggest that the compilers of the NBBS broadcasts not only knew more about technical military secrets than would normally be the case in an offshoot of the Propaganda Ministry, but were also allowed greater latitude in divulging them.

General Hasso von Wedel, in 1940 head of the Propaganda Section of OKW, has given the following general account of the way in which NBBS was controlled:

OKW and the Ministry of Foreign Affairs had liaison staffs with the Propaganda Ministry and, in particular, with NBBS, for which that

Ministry was responsible; their job was to put over our [i.e. OKW's] material and to censor anything that had to be kept secret. Hitler himself frequently interfered, however, and when doing so he never referred to the competent authorities but dealt only with Dr Goebbels.[1]

Of particular interest are the German attempts to use NBBS for the purpose of strategical deception. These attempts were of an elementary character. On 27 June (before the *Sea Lion* plan had been formulated, or invasion decided upon) NBBS forecast that the Germans would attack at some twenty different points; those mentioned were all large centres of population and virtually the whole coast from Invergordon clockwise to Glasgow came under this shadowy threat. The German objectives were given as the "Scottish industrial region", the Black Country, South Wales, Glasgow and London. An attack on Ireland was sometimes referred to during this period.

On 6 August a more business-like note was struck. "A favourable tide is occurring now and will last till about Friday", NBBS lied; "the next will then be between the 2nd and the 9th of September." Ten days later the speaker (who, it must be remembered, was supposed to be no more than an exceptionally well-informed British patriot, broadcasting from somewhere in England) suspected that the intensified air-raids on south-east England foreshadowed surprise landings elsewhere, possibly in the north-east. These were obvious red herrings, but the intention behind them made sense; they represented a well-meant though oafish effort to mislead the British about the timing and objectives of the German attack.

It is less easy to construe the broad strategical hints which, from 23 August, represent not the abandonment but the reversal of this effort. On that date—the day after the VI project had been taken off the secret list and broadcast to its intended victims[2]—NBBS told its listeners that the shelling of Dover by long-range artillery from the French coast indicated a German intention to land in that area. On 1 September, after further bombardments, it pointed out that Dover was "already practically German territory". On 11 September it

---

[1] Private letter.
[2] In this cauldron of claptrap it aroused nobody's curiosity.

interpreted the Luftwaffe's sustained attacks on railway communications in "the London – Ramsgate – Folkestone area" as confirmation that this part of south-east England was the main German objective. These previews of the *Sea Lion* plan were interspersed with such urgent warnings as "Hitler may at any hour give the order", "He prepares to strike the final blow", "Invasion may come any day", "The time is fast approaching" and "I call upon our collaborators to make with us one last great effort to bring about peace".

This last appeal was broadcast on 10 September. On the 12th soft-pedalling had started ("financial collapse will arrive very suddenly"). It continued on the 13th ("even if invasion does not come for some time the air-raids will make life impossible"), and by 28 September the *diminuendo* had sunk to a distant mutter: "winter will provide no protection against invasion".

A curious arrogance underlay the NBBS broadcasts. The initial aim of propaganda is normally to create an influential minority of converts. NBBS began by pretending that this minority already existed; it was from the centre of a hard but steadily expanding core of peace-loving dissidents that it purported to address the British nation. Whether these tactics had (as seems probable) their origins in the twisted audacity of Goebbels's mind, or whether they were the product of wishful thinking at some other level near the summit, none can say; what is certain is that they were based on a delusion.

But when men adopt a course of action whose effects must remain for some time imponderable, they do not look for evidence that they were wrong to adopt it; they look for evidence that they were right.

Their broadcasts make it clear that the controllers of NBBS studied the British Press and radio very closely. They played on the fears and grievances which they found there[1]; and in their search for

---

[1] To quote a crude example: At the beginning of June the BBC reported on more than one occasion that motorists who failed to halt at road-blocks had been shot dead by trigger-happy Home Guards. Effective precautions were taken to prevent these mishaps recurring, but NBBS returned to the topic at intervals, and by 20 July their notional casualty list had risen to 219. Five weeks later it had topped the 400 mark.

themes of alarm and despondency they cannot have failed to notice numerous indications that the assumptions on which their propaganda campaign was based were correct.

The British Government, as we have seen, was not prepared to admit that the universal public demand for drastic action against Fifth Columnists was baseless or even over-emphatic. Was there any reason why the German Government should have appraised it more sceptically? What did Dr Goebbels, or even Hitler himself, make of "The Silent Column", an ill-defined movement or cause in which all British patriots were urged (by the Minister of Information, Duff Cooper, early in June) to enroll themselves so as to prevent the dissemination of defeatist talk? The Silent Column produced a corps of honorary vigilantes, popularly known as "Cooper's Snoopers", on whose evidence a number of citizens were convicted in the courts of speaking in disparaging terms of the prospects before their country. It is true that on 22 July the Prime Minister informed the House of Commons that the Silent Column had "passed into innocuous desuetude", and that most of the convictions were quashed on appeal; but on those who traffic in fear the signs that it is present are apt to make a more vivid impression than the signs that it has been brought under control.

Men are easily persuaded to believe what they ardently wish to be true. The British, for instance, started the war with the conviction that Germany was desperately short of raw materials, and many able papers were written to prove that, though she could probably wage a limited campaign for eight to ten weeks (or some similar brief period), she would run out of petrol in less than half that time if she embarked on a major offensive. On 25 May the Chiefs of Staff (who then had no reason to suppose that the BEF could be extricated from the Continent) reviewed the strategical possibilities which would be open to them after France had fallen; they reached the stout-hearted but absurd conclusion that, given American economic assistance on a generous scale, Britain might well produce a critical economic situation in Germany within a year. When both the collection and the assessment of evidence are influenced by wishful thinking, the judgment finally arrived at is seldom of an unwelcome or disturbing character.

The Germans were studying the British Press and radio intensively. Anyone who did this in the hope of finding cracks in the monolith of the national front would not have been disappointed. Apart from such obvious phenomena as the detention of Sir Oswald Mosley and other leading Fascists (including several retired officers and one Member of Parliament), they could not have failed to observe that a number of small, curious and often inexplicable events were occurring almost every day.

On 12 May, for instance, the BBC, after announcing on behalf of the Air Ministry an important order regarding the call-up of RAF reservists, withdrew it in the next bulletin, saying that there had been a mistake. This matter was never satisfactorily cleared up. The order, purporting to come from the Air Ministry, was received at Broadcasting House by telephone but the Air Ministry denied having sent it; at the time it was assumed by the British authorities to have been the work of an enemy agent, but it seems in retrospect more likely to have been the result of a muddle.

Reports of prosecutions for various forms of outwardly treasonable activity were at this period frequently published in the Press and on the wireless. A BBC news bulletin on 7 June announced that, "among actions taken to-day under the Defence Regulations", an employee at an Admiralty chart depot had been sentenced to three months' imprisonment for possessing documents which might be useful to the enemy; a German cap and a list of aerodromes were found in his coat-pocket. The same bulletin revealed that at Bognor Regis "six well-known people associated with the Fascist movement" had been detained by the police. *The Times* reported on 7 June that several officials of the Peace Pledge Union had been charged with "endeavouring to cause disaffection among persons in his Majesty's service"; on 8 June that a violinist had been accused of assisting the enemy by posting up in a telephone kiosk a label giving the NBBS wave-length; and on 11 June that a member of the Irish Republican Army had been sentenced to three months' imprisonment and a fine of £100 for "having in his possession a military map which might be directly or indirectly of use to the enemy." Provincial and local papers carried similar items of intelligence.

The offences were never serious, but the fact that a number of small fry were being caught was capable of suggesting—to anyone anxious to believe it—that activities of this kind were widespread. Apart from citizens who, during the "Silent Column" campaign, were brought before the magistrates on a charge of uttering defeatist statements, a fair number were prosecuted for spreading rumours which they had heard on the NBBS transmissions. For the Germans a gratifying aspect of these cases (which were reported in obscure paragraphs on back pages) was the fact that the accused, many of whom were women, almost always insisted that they had no idea that the enemy had anything to do with the New British Broadcasting Station.

From time to time there were even more encouraging incidents. It would not have been humanly possible for a German intelligence officer to place any save the most auspicious interpretation on this item from *The Times* of 28 May: "Police took possession of a pencilled note signed 'C', and containing the words 'Guess where?', from the door of a storage building in Barnet which caught fire on Saturday evening. The store was completely destroyed." On 23 July a Fascist was given seven years' imprisonment for damaging nine telephone kiosks with the avowed intention of preventing members of the public from ringing up the ARP service.[1] A few days earlier a schoolmaster had been convicted of spreading disaffection among his pupils.

These were all small clues. But they were clues pointing to a solution at which the Germans hoped to arrive. It cannot be proved that they were allowed a disproportionate importance, but it would be surprising if they were not.

It is essential to remember the background against which they presented themselves to the intelligence staffs whose duty it was to evaluate them. The unobtrusive paragraphs recording the disloyal or unpatriotic actions of unimportant individuals were comparable to the artist's signature on a valuable and crowded canvas. In the foreground—in the accounts of Parliamentary debates, the leaders,

[1] *The Times*, 24 July 1940. A similar though less serious form of mischief had worried and perplexed the authorities a few weeks earlier. An official historian records that "bogus [air-raid] warning messages were still enough of a nuisance to justify the Ministry [of Home Security] addressing a circular on this matter to chief officers of Police." (O'Brien.)

the correspondence columns, the reports of fresh exhortations by the Ministry of Information, fresh warnings from the Ministry of Home Security and other quarters—the effigies of treason, sabotage, defeatism, rumour-mongering and all the other phenomena for which the Germans were on the look-out bulked large. Arrests, internments, the cordoning off of restricted areas, the imposition of fines on householders for allowing a light to show during the black-out, the increase of crime in the darkened streets, the grievances of the Home Guard, the protests—roughly equal in volume—against bureaucratic inertia and bureaucratic interference, the intermittent fuss about the rights of conscientious objectors, the glimpses of a degenerate night-life in the capital [1]—this welter of evidence could hardly fail to arouse high hopes that life in Britain bore a serviceable resemblance to its image as projected by NBBS. The little paragraphs were just what was needed to confirm Hitler's diagnosis.

The only clandestine report which the Germans are known to have received on the state of affairs in Britain at this period was brief, but it was also reassuring.

Its sender was Anna Wolkoff,[2] the daughter of a former Admiral in the Imperial Russian Navy, and it was addressed to William Joyce at the *Rundfunkhaus*, Berlin. Anna Wolkoff held extreme anti-Semitic and pro-German views and was under close surveillance by the British security authorities. It was in fact to a young lady in their service that Wolkoff entrusted her letter to Joyce, in the belief that it would be forwarded to Germany in the Rumanian diplomatic bag and thus elude the censorship.

The letter was written in a makeshift code. Part of it was taken up with not unintelligent suggestions ("Stick to plutocracy. Avoid

[1] On 1 August the Home Secretary announced in the Commons that he had made orders "under Defence Regulation 42C directing the closing of six bottle-parties, known respectively as Boogey-Woogey, El Morocco, Hi-de-Hi. Mac's, Paradise and Stork". He went on to say that this measure left seventeen of these establishments—which were in effect nightclubs owing a precarious existence to some loophole in the regulations abolishing them—within the Metropolitan Police District.

[2] See also pp. 187–188.

King") for improving the effectiveness of German propaganda broadcasts from Hamburg and Bremen. But it included also some general observations: "Here *Kriegshetze* [war-fever] only among Blimps. Workers fed up. Wives more so. Troops not keen. Anti-semitism spreading like flame everywhere—all classes. . . . Churchill not popular. . . . Cost of living steeply mounting . . ." and so on.[1] The security authorities, after studying this missive, arranged for it to be forwarded to Joyce in Berlin.

"Acknowledge this," Anna Wolkoff had asked, "by Carlyle reference radio." A few days after her letter should have reached its destination this was done. NBBS, with commendable resource, solved the problem of working a literary reference into their dia-tribes by attacking French culture: "We thank the French for nothing. Where is their Shakespeare? Who is their Carlyle?" Wolkoff was arrested on 18 May.

It would be wrong to attach undue importance to one clandestine communication, but its receipt must have pleased the Germans. It came, not from an agent by a prearranged channel, but spon-taneously from a private individual in the heart of the enemy camp. It gave practical advice about the reception of broadcasts on different wave-lengths; and it drew, in a thumbnail sketch, exactly the sort of picture of England which Hitler saw in his dreams. Neither it, nor any of the other evidence that British unity was a façade behind which the forces of disintegration were potently at work, *created* a delusion; the delusion already existed, a main pillar in the cardboard Stonehenge of the Nazi *Weltanschauung*. But these small clues, pondered by deluded men, helped to strengthen their delusion until an implicit faith in its validity became a mainspring of policy.

It is time now to return to the point from which we began this survey of German psychological warfare in support of *Operation Sea Lion*: to the clumsily but carefully simulated landing of several groups of parachutists on the night of 13/14 August.

NBBS exploited the operation in a manner which leaves no doubt that the ruse and the broadcasts were closely linked. They were, in

[1] The Earl Jowitt: *Some Were Spies*. London, 1954.

a sense, interdependent. The fake parachute drop was intended to give a show of substance to the legend, ceaselessly propagated by NBBS, that Britain swarmed with Fifth Columnists; while the broadcasts, which betrayed an accurate knowledge of the various stage-properties used in the drops, would, it was hoped, lend verisimilitude to the whole thing. The Germans reckoned that it would be impossible for the British authorities to *prove* that nobody had been dropped[1]; and as long as this was so, NBBS's knowing references to the success of the operation, and in particular to the hiding of the parachutists by the Fifth Column, were bound to enhance NBBS's credit and to strengthen the grip which its disturbing allegations had, or should have, established upon the minds of the islanders.

On 14 August, within a few hours of the operation being carried out and *before* any mention of it had been made by the BBC or the Press,[2] NBBS announced that parachutists "in civilian clothes or British uniform" had landed near Birmingham, Manchester and Glasgow. On the 15th this news was repeated and amplified, and on the 16th—by which time an official communiqué had made it clear that the British regarded the whole business as a hoax—NBBS said that this scepticism suited Germany's purposes admirably. The parachutists were in fact being sheltered by Fifth Columnists. They had with them, among other things, clear and detailed photographs of the Manchester Ship Canal, the Birmingham waterworks and other installations. What had the RAF been doing when these photographs were taken?[3]

NBBS continued until 20 August to build up the parachutists, stressing the uncanny accuracy of the maps, plans and lists of names

[1] The Germans had overlooked the possibility of the parachutes landing, as several did, in standing corn, where the absence of tracks made it obvious that nobody had been attached to them.

[2] *The Times* reported it on 15 August; and on the same day the Ministry of Information, in a communiqué describing it as a "propaganda move", said that it had already been mentioned on the German wireless.

[3] The photograph of the Manchester Ship Canal was probably that reproduced in the *Bildheft*, one of the booklets prepared by the Germans for issue to the invading troops. It contained a large number of views of scenery and buildings, most if not all of which had appeared in English illustrated papers before the war. See pp. 191 *et seq.* for fuller details.

which they had brought with them.[1] They even claimed that, in the confusion of the search for the intruders, three policemen had been shot dead; and they called attention to the cipher messages which were now being broadcast on the main German transmissions from Hamburg and elsewhere and which conveyed instructions (of an imprecise and general nature) to the parachutists and their collaborators. In short, an elaborate and well-planned charade was staged[2]; it involved the preparation of a great deal of documentary and other evidence, the diversion of several aircraft at an inconvenient moment, and the co-ordination of plain language broadcasts on the "black" radio with transmissions in cipher on the normal programmes intended for English listeners; and its sole object was to create or strengthen the belief in Britain that (as NBBS put it on 20 August) "our defences are being undermined from within" and disintegration was on the way.

Three days later came the first of the curious broadcasts, referred to earlier in this chapter, which revealed south-east England as the invaders' objective.

No documentary evidence survives to implicate Hitler personally

[1] These, like the photograph of the Manchester Ship Canal, were almost certainly extracted from the Baedeker-like compilations referred to in the preceding footnote.

[2] An interesting sidelight on the importance attached to this ruse is provided by the following facts:

(i) On 14 May, and on various subsequent dates, the BBC had broadcast to Germany warnings that German parachutists who descended on Britain dressed otherwise than in "recognised German uniform" would be shot out of hand. (See Chapter 5).

(ii) The German Government replied, through neutral diplomatic channels, with a vehement protest that their airborne troops never wore anything but German uniform and that any failure to treat them in accordance with the usages of war would be followed by reprisals.

(iii) No satisfactory reply having been received, a second protest was prepared, and this was actually on its way to London (where it was received on 19 August) when NBBS was doing its utmost to convince the British that a large number of German parachutists had landed dressed "in civilian clothes or British uniform".

It will be remembered that the German Foreign Office as well as OKW had liaison officers attached to NBBS. The fact that the latter's broadcasts were at liberty to sabotage the Foreign Office's interests is a further indication that NBBS was at times manipulated from the highest level.

in the conception of the fake parachute landings; but it is beyond question that his approval was necessary for their execution. The testimony of General Schmid suggests that he was pleased with the affair, while that of General von Wedel shows that he did at times take a direct hand in matters pertaining to NBBS. Finally there is the decision to compromise the main *Sea Lion* objective; even if this is interpreted as a far-fetched and unpractical attempt at double bluff, a series of broadcasts indicating that the Germans intended to land, very shortly, in south-east England could not possibly have gone out without the Fuehrer's sanction. Psychological warfare (as it came later to be called) is an ancillary of strategy; and the central enigma of German strategy in the summer of 1940 can be solved only on the assumption that the author of that strategy discerned possibilities in this field which did not exist.

This central problem can be stated as follows: By the third week in July or thereabouts Hitler had reluctantly accepted the fact—already obvious to less astute observers—that the British were not going to do what he wanted them to do, which was to seek an accommodation. He turned, with no great enthusiasm, to the invasion which he had ordered to be mounted. To the Leader of the German people and the Supreme Commander of their Armed Forces two courses were now open: he could have thrown himself into the project and acted as a driving force, or he could have recognised that the difficulties were likely to prove insuperable and taken steps to ensure that, if they did, the minimum damage would be inflicted on German prestige.

Hitler did neither of these things. Although he showed some interest in the launching of the air offensive, he held himself aloof from the amphibious preparations on which everything depended; yet at the same time he told everyone—the British, the neutrals, his Italian allies—that invasion was coming. On 15 July Ciano recorded the receipt by Mussolini of "a long letter" from Hitler: it "announces the attack on England as something definitely decided, but declines in a definite and courteous way the offer to send an Italian expeditionary force". On 17 August the German Press Attaché in Rome told Ciano that a landing was "imminent"; on 7 September Mussolini considered "the landing of the Germans in England as a certainty"; and on 19 September (by which date the invasion fleet was already being dispersed) Ribbentrop was saying, in Rome, that "the landing is ready and possible. English territorial defence is non-existent. A single German division will suffice to bring about a complete collapse." In German domestic propaganda the emphasis on invasion fluctuated slightly from week to week, but its general tone has been sufficiently exemplified in the extracts from NBBS broadcasts.

More significant, however, than what he led his enemies and the outside world to believe was what Hitler told his own people. The Germans were left in no doubt that *Wir fahren gegen Engelland* was the basis of German strategy, hitherto unfailingly successful. The sabre was rattled in their ears less loudly but not much less consistently than in those of the British; as late as 15 September the military correspondent of the *Boersen Zeitung*, General Hasse, was allowed if not encouraged to write: "Invasion will probably follow shortly".

Finally there is Hitler's only public announcement on the subject. It was made on 4 September, little more than a fortnight before *Sea Lion* was due to be launched, and it was uttered, as an eye-witness recorded the same night, with great zest and emphasis.[1] Hitler was speaking at the *Sportpalast*; the fact that he was to speak was kept secret until the last moment, in deference to the RAF. The occasion was the opening of the eighth Winter Relief campaign, but Hitler's main concern was to vow vengeance against the British, whose bombers were now carrying the war into Germany almost every night. After promising overwhelming retaliation in kind, Hitler aroused a tumult of applause with the words: "When people are very curious in Great Britain, and ask '*Yes, but why doesn't he come?*' we reply: '*Calm yourselves! Calm yourselves! He is coming! He is coming!*'" The pledge was unequivocal. Why was it given?

We do not know. Yet there must have been some explanation

[1] "He had to stop because of the hysterical applause of the audience, which consisted mostly of German women nurses and social workers. . . . Here the young nurses and social workers were quite beside themselves and applauded phrenetically. . . . His listeners found it very funny. . . . The man squeezed every ounce of humour and sarcasm out of his voice." (Shirer.)

for the ambiguity of Hitler's attitude to invasion, for the contrast between his proclaimed confidence in the outcome of his plans and his readiness to admit in private that they were a "last resort", full of peril and uncertainty.

It is important to remember that Hitler's objective was not the conquest of England but her "elimination as a base from which the war against Germany can be fought".[1] His attitude to *Sea Lion* makes sense if, and only if, he believed that this objective could be achieved either without an invasion or by an invasion from which most of the risks had been removed. The weather he could not control; but if he could (as NBBS put it) "undermine Britain's defences from within", if he could (as he had so often dreamed of doing) subvert, confuse and demoralise his enemy before launching his assault, *Sea Lion* would become a much more hopeful project.

Three days after he had ranted to an audience of thousands "*He is coming! He is coming!*" Hitler concentrated his air offensive on London. The decision to do so saved Fighter Command from mortal attrition and spatchcocked German strategy; but it held out hopes of demoralising the British administration. For weeks he had striven with considerable ingenuity to subvert and confuse the population; and evidence from Britain itself had given him some reason to suppose that his endeavours were meeting with success. He had ceased, tardily, to hope that the British Government would come forward with proposals for a compromise; but he had entertained the delusion that they would do so for a remarkably long time, and he had entertained it in the teeth of much evidence that he was wrong.

If he was wrong about the Government—a handful of public men of whose records he at least knew something—he was not likely to be right about the people, of whom he knew nothing at all. He had a contempt for the masses—in *Mein Kampf* he had called his own countrymen "the stupid flock of German sheep" before he promoted them to *Herrenvolk*—and through the "black" radio and by more overt means he practised assiduously on the minds of the British. There is no doubt what he wanted them to be. He wanted everyone

[1] Directive No. 16 (16 July).

in the islands (the Scots and the Welsh were allotted additional duties in the cause of separatism) to be a traitor, a pacifist, an anti-Semite or a coward.

To say that Hitler wanted this to be so is an understatement; Hitler *willed* that it should be so. He was fifty-one years old, he had risen from self-doubt in the gutter to be dictator of a State moulded to his own conception of what a State should be, he had conquered most of Europe in a matter of weeks, and he was on his way to conquer the world. It was not only imperative that the British should bow to his will; it was, as he then saw it, inevitable.

Hitler's ego, cushioned on political and military successes of the most dramatic kind, dominated in the summer of 1940 the land-mass of Europe. He had swallowed Austria and Czechoslovakia, Poland, Denmark and Norway, the Low Countries and France in successive gulps. Italy was his jackal, Russia (the next victim) his dupe, Japan a thunderbolt up his sleeve, Spain at the worst a toady. There remained only the small archipelago laved by what he had been brought up to call the German Ocean.

The British should have sued for peace; they had not done so. It should have been possible for him to overwhelm them by direct assault; the prospects of this were doubtful. There remained the formula which he had long held dear—disintegration from within. It was his own private recipe, his secret weapon; "Why should I demoralise the enemy by military means if I can do so better and more cheaply in other ways?"

Not for the first time in his career, but for the first time disastrously, Hitler gambled. It was because he had no experience of losing and could not believe in this contingency that *Sea Lion* came within an ace of being launched. Hitler's commanders-in-chief plan-ned the invasion of a resolute and united island. Hitler let these plans go forward; but all the time he had his secret weapon up his sleeve—the wand which no mere general or admiral could wave—and in his heart of hearts he was convinced that, with a little sub-versive prodding from within and some intensive bludgeoning from above, the British would either give up the struggle or would fight ineffectively.

In these surmises Hitler was proved at fault; but the fact that he
failed in his purpose should not be allowed to obscure the nature of
that purpose. This was to subvert and demoralise the United Kingdom
as a prelude to the occupation (if this proved necessary) of some
parts of it by the armed forces of the German Reich.

CHAPTER NINE

Leadership in a Dark Hour

You are to go to Mill Hill, pick up a Lanchester armoured car and take it to Chequers. The car is for the Prime Minister's use. One of you will ride in front and will show your identity card at any road-block where it is required. The other will ride (on motor-cycle) behind the car in case of breakdown. . . . Do not say the Prime Minister is in the car.

From a written order given to two iunior liaison officers at GHQ Home Forces on 15 September 1940

"THE elimination of Churchill must be an essential feature of any attack on British morale. It would no doubt have an infuriating and therefore temporarily invigorating effect on the population, but that would wear off. And there is no other statesman who could possibly take his place as the focus and fountain-head of British morale."

The quotation is from a paper prepared for the British Chiefs of Staff in January 1942 by a small but able inter-service committee. Its members had been relieved of all ordinary duties, immured in a secluded set of offices, and ordered to write, from the point of view of the German Supreme Command, an appreciation of the problems involved in invading the United Kingdom. Whether their opposite numbers in Germany would have paid a similar tribute to Churchill's indispensability there is no means of telling[1]; but it was deserved, and never more so than during the period with which we are concerned.

When they looked back on the war after it was over, the British, and indeed other nations as well, saw Churchill as a kind of institution, at once the helmsman and the figurehead of a proud, battered, triumphant ship. But when he took over the helm on the evening of 10 May 1940, the ship, ill-found and already badly damaged,

[1] The legend that one or other of the German clandestine organisations tried to arrange the assassination of the British Prime Minister survives in a number of versions. All appear to be baseless.

immediately sustained still graver injuries and began, by all appearances, to sink. Never had the country's need for leadership been
greater; but although Churchill's emergence was acclaimed by
almost all and welcomed, in their hearts if not in their heads, by
even his severest critics, his position as leader was at first gravely
compromised by the far-reaching crisis of confidence which had
brought down Chamberlain.

As the bad news from Norway was followed by worse news
from France, the nation's angry, bewildered disillusionment surged
up and overflowed in all directions. "There was considerable
pressure", Churchill wrote afterwards, "for a purge of the 'guilty
men'." Exaggerated fears of the Fifth Column gave rise to vague
rumours of treason in high places. Just below the surface lay a
suspicion that the entire apparatus of administration and of war
was irrecoverably rotten, that the country had been let down so
badly that no faith could any longer be placed in the utterances of
Ministers, the plans of departments or the decisions of commanders.
Churchill had not only to win for himself the confidence of his
countrymen; he had to restore their confidence in the whole fabric
of direction and command.

Under the bludgeonings of fate which Britain sustained in May
and June the nation held its head high; but its heart was assailed,
not merely by the impact of successive disasters and the approach
of mortal danger, but by a sense (which was quite new to it)
of impotence and inadequacy. The Germans swept on to the
Channel coast. The whole pattern of British land-strategy was
expunged as briskly as impertinent scrawls are wiped off a black-
board by a teacher who is anxious to impart his lesson. And Germany had won all these quick tricks without playing—against the
British Isles—any of her trumps; for it was in this light that her
powerful air forces had been regarded for more than two years.

If there were misgivings in Britain, there was despair in France,
to whose destinies those of the United Kingdom seemed to be so
closely bound that it was at first scarcely possible to contemplate
waging a war from which she had been eliminated. To Churchill's
pressing domestic cares was added the delicate and urgent duty of
sustaining a stricken ally. In the first four weeks of his premiership

he flew five times to France and on 16 June was starting on a sixth journey when news came that it was too late, that the end was at hand.

Of these macabre excursions Churchill has given a full account. His position as an emissary was invidious. The British Expeditionary Force of 12 divisions was but a small contribution to the needs of the hour; the additional fighter squadrons for which the French pleaded had to be withheld against a contingency which Frenchmen, most of whom shared Hitler's belief that the British would not fight on alone, regarded at best as hypothetical; and Britain herself, immune as yet from the ravages of war, had in French eyes the unbecoming status of an *embusquée*. The strain of playing—and each time losing—these unrewarding hands added immeasurably to the burden of the new Prime Minister's dilemmas. "It was a severe experience for me", he admitted afterwards. "Here to all of us was real agony of mind and soul."

An equally important, and more fruitful, outlet for Churchill's statesmanship was the American connection. The long series of messages which the Former Naval Person addressed to President Roosevelt had always a powerful and often a decisive influence on the policies of a still neutral administration and on the climate of opinion in which they were formed. It was, for instance, mainly by the use of this channel of communication that, after nearly four months of negotiation, fifty old but at the time invaluable American destroyers were obtained in return for the lease of British bases in Newfoundland and the Caribbean. Churchill's part in the correspondence, which he began within five days of taking office, is a remarkable study in finesse. It was not merely his own growing prestige which lent cogency to his arguments; it was the tact, the timing and the force of the arguments themselves.

It was in these weeks that Churchill established the position of leadership which—although in 1942 he twice seemed momentarily in danger of losing it—he held throughout the war. The foundations of that position were, like the foundations of ultimate victory, laid in the hectic summer of 1940, and may be here passed briefly in review.

So great was the emergency when he took office, and so impressed were people with the advantages which in war a totalitarian system appeared to have over a democratic one, that in May or June 1940 the British would have been ready to accept a wide measure of autocratic and centralised control. They would not have tolerated it for long; but at the time it seemed to many, if not a panacea, at least a straw worth clutching.

Churchill both relished power and needed as much of it as he could get into his own hands if he and his colleagues were going to save the country. In *Their Finest Hour* he wrote: "Power, for the sake of lording it over fellow creatures or adding to personal pomp, is rightly judged base. But power in a national crisis, when a man believes he knows what orders should be given, is a blessing." During his first few weeks in office he could have helped himself with both hands (and been thanked for doing so) to more power than was good either for him or for the country.

He showed in this matter frugality and discrimination. "The fundamental changes in the machinery of war direction were more real than apparent. . . . In calling myself, with the King's approval, Minister of Defence I had made no legal or constitutional change. I had been careful not to define my rights and duties. I asked for no special powers. . . . It was however understood and accepted that I should assume the general direction of the war, subject to the support of the War Cabinet and of the House of Commons."

The Great Captain dispensed with a commission. He did however as Minister of Defence assume the chairmanship of the Chiefs of Staff Committee, and in the same capacity he brought under his direct control the Joint Planning Committee, an inter-service body by which strategical possibilities were assessed and either rejected or developed.

Thus Churchill gathered the reins of war into his hands. The specious attractions of putting the constitution or the machinery of administration into some sort of martial fancy dress to meet the emergency were rejected; and the Prime Minister remained the servant of the House of Commons. In this role he never scamped his duties, showing always a jealous regard for the rights and the susceptibilities of Parliament; and there can be no doubt that this firm adherence to the established order of things, though on the short view it involved a certain waste of time and (since the Germans could read full reports of all debates not held in secret session) a certain risk to security, was a main foundation of the nation's unity and of the Prime Minister's authority.

These wise arrangements buttressed the position of the helmsman, but they do not explain the figurehead. The nation got its first taste of Churchill's quality as a leader in war when he told the House of Commons, three days after taking office: "I have nothing to offer but blood, toil, tears and sweat." "In all our long history," he wrote afterwards, "no Prime Minister had ever been able to present to Parliament a programme at once so short and so popular."

But those eleven words outlined not only a programme but a personality. Churchill had a gusto for war; it was one of the secrets of his hold over the British in this crisis. As a small boy he had possessed (he tells us in *My Early Life*) fifteen hundred toy soldiers. At Sandhurst he mused: "If only it had been a hundred years earlier what splendid times we should have had! Fancy being nineteen in 1793 with more than twenty years of war against Napoleon in front of one!" Since in the 1890s the Queen lacked enemies for the 4th Hussars to fight, Churchill marched to the sound of the Spanish guns in Cuba. In India pertinacity and string-pulling secured him attachments first to the Malakand Field Force and then to the Tirah Expedition. At the age of twenty-four he charged with the 21st Lancers at Omdurman and in the Boer War saw action at Spion Kop and half a dozen other battles. In 1914 he was First Lord of the Admiralty and when, later, the fiasco in the Dardanelles obliged him to resign, he commanded a battalion of the Royal Scots Fusiliers on the Western Front. War was in his blood; he was a connoisseur of its problems, a student of its techniques, and a good judge of its hazards. Looking back on his five years' sway over the Chiefs of Staff Committee, he wrote: "There was no division, as in the previous war, between politicians and soldiers, between the 'Frocks' and the 'Brass Hats'—odious terms which darkened counsel." The main reason for this was that the interests and outlooks of both professions were fused in the mind of the nation's leader.

Churchill's zest and pugnacity were infectious. He later described "the buoyant and imperturbable temper of Britain, which I had the honour to express" as an important factor in the kingdom's survival. But he was in truth something more than the interpreter of a mood which his own words and deeds did much to evoke, to animate and to steel. The nation's will was a sword-blade; his was the hand on the hilt.

He had an instinctive understanding of the stimuli to which the human spirit responds. He lost no opportunity of imparting to others his own conviction that Britain's predicament was above all a great occasion, a great opportunity, that the grim scene was one in which even the humblest actor was lucky in having a part to play.

We are fighting by ourselves alone [he said on 14 July], but we are not fighting for ourselves alone. Here in this strong City of Refuge which enshrines the title-deeds of human progress and is of deep consequence to Christian civilisation; here, girt about by the seas and oceans where the Navy reigns; shielded from above by the prowess and devotion of our airmen—we await undismayed the impending assault.

The people found this magniloquence heart-warming; it was thunder, but it was also the truth. Not less to the point, though in a different key, was this sentence dictated in a minute a few days earlier: "It is a great mistake to tell the workpeople that they are tired."

To the excellent Mr Somervell, a master at Harrow in the later years of the nineteenth century, the nation became at this period indebted. Mr Somervell, "a most delightful man . . . was charged with teaching the stupidest boys the most disregarded thing— namely, to write mere English. . . . As I remained in the Third Fourth (β) three times as long as anyone else, I had three times as much of it." Decisions are the bones of leadership; words are its flesh. Churchill's, whether written or spoken, were used with an assured artistry; they had at all levels a strong formative influence on the climate of resistance.

Each of his speeches and broadcasts was an event. His language, at once orotund and spare, fascinated his listeners. Echoes of Gibbon (devoured long ago in the cantonments of Bangalore) and of Bunyan, occasional hints of a Shakespearean usage ("contemplating our dangers with a *dis*illusioned eye"), were interspersed with gleeful schoolboy sallies; and idiosyncrasies of utterance, such as a staunch refusal to give foreign words like "Nazi" any save the most insular pronunciation, lent a relish of intimacy to each performance.

Churchill's invective was admirable. It did people's hearts good, after the severe impact of the first great air-attacks on London, to hear Hitler described on 11 September as "this wicked man, the repository and embodiment of many forms of soul-destroying hate, this monstrous product of former wrongs and shame". But in a situation where there was every temptation to rant, to objurgate, to strike an attitude of righteous indignation, he almost always preferred to use the weapons of humour and irony, so much more difficult to wield, so much more deadly.

This gave to his utterances a kind of lilt. It offered the same sort of bonus which men get when, viewing the bulldog jaw of a commander, they note that the firm lips have an upward, humorous curve. Churchill did not, like other politicians, *make* jokes; he shared them. He never played down to his audience. A lesser artist might, for instance, have made Italy's entry into the war the occasion for vehement denunciation or crude derision. Churchill handled it with a feline urbanity; his touch, as so often, was lighter when he ended than when he began, and the effect of a secret smile, of a private joke in which all can share, was unmistakable. "We shall be delighted", he said on 18 June, "to offer Signor Mussolini a free and safeguarded passage through the Straits of Gibraltar in order that he may play the part to which he aspires. There is a general curiosity in the British Fleet to find out whether the Italians are up to the level they were at in the last war or whether they have fallen off at all." If he had ended "or whether they are even worse", he would have scored a hit and pleased the groundlings; by employing a subtler twist of denigration he gave to the passage that characteristic lilt of gaiety and evoked in his hearers the agreeable sensation of being made privy to a personal code of humour.

His lightness of touch never deserted him even when things were at their blackest. It was an attribute which helped more, perhaps, than any of his other gifts as a speaker to communicate to his hearers some of his inner serenity and dauntlessness. Two extracts from a speech made on 8 October, when the bombing of London had reached a peak of fearful severity, will serve to illustrate his therapeutic use of humour.

On that particular Thursday night 180 persons were killed in London as a result of 251 tons of bombs. That is to say, *it took one ton of bombs to kill three-quarters of a person.*

And

Statisticians may amuse themselves by calculating that after making allowance for the law of diminishing returns, through the same house being struck twice or three times over, it would take ten years, at the present rate, for half the houses of London to be demolished. *After that, of course, progress would be much slower.*

The terrible dangers thus blandly mocked did not disappear, but they lost some of their hold on men's minds.

It may be possible for future historians, with access to all the archives, to lay at Churchill's door inconsistencies, follies, perhaps blunders, committed during the summer of 1940; but even if this happens his essential stature in this crisis will remain undiminished. Tireless, resourceful, ebullient and wise, he stood like a rock against the storm. He rallied a shaken nation and reasserted its right to victory. "Hitler", he said after he had been Prime Minister for two months, "has not yet been withstood by a nation with a will-power the equal of his own"; and it occurred to no pedant to point out that Britain had been "withstanding" Hitler since she declared war on Germany nearly a year earlier. Things were different now. Even to his most fervent adherents Chamberlain had never seemed more than a giant-killer. All recognised his successor as a giant. History will never dwarf him.

Behind, and above, the Prime Minister stood the King.

George VI had succeeded to the throne on the abdication of his elder brother in 1936. The distressing and rather unbecoming crisis which surrounded Edward VIII's renunciation of his rights and duties was at first believed in some foreign countries, and notably in Germany, to have done irretrievable damage to the traditions of the monarchy and the status of the Monarch. This was soon seen to be a fallacy; but no British king in modern times had inherited from his predecessor problems of greater delicacy than those which Edward VIII, a dazzling and much-loved figure, bequeathed to his shy, inarticulate brother, who was then forty-one years old.

By the time war broke out in 1939 the new King, with the staunch and imaginative support of his Queen, had won the hearts of his people and the respect of his Ministers; the abdication, which at the time had seemed to mark the end of an era, was almost forgotten, and although the legend on the 1914 recruiting posters—"Your King and Country Need You"—had been replaced by more abstract and impersonal appeals supposedly better suited to the taste of a more sophisticated age, George VI was no less the emblem and focus of his subject's loyalties than his father had been in the Kaiser's War.

But nothing in the Kaiser's War (in which George VI had seen action at the Battle of Jutland) had seemed likely to place the person of the Monarch in peril; and this the threat of invasion in 1940 clearly did. There was no blinking the fact that, if the Germans managed to land in strength, the capture of the King and his family was an undertaking to which for obvious reasons they might well be tempted to divert part of their forces.[1]

Amid the extreme uncertainties and the pardonably exaggerated fears of late May and early June a strong case might have been made out for getting the King and his family away to safety in Canada. The nation's gold was being sent across the Atlantic, and the evacuation of children was being encouraged. The King's constitutional responsibilities extended beyond the United Kingdom to the Commonwealth and Empire; and it might well have been argued

[1] On the eve of the Scandinavian operations, a couple of months earlier, an OKW order dated 2 April 1940 had begun:

"The Fuehrer has directed that the escape of the Kings of Denmark and Norway from their countries at the time of the occupation must be prevented by all means. . . . It will be essential to keep the residences of the sovereigns under close surveillance and, if necessary, to prevent the Kings from leaving their palaces. . . . In the manner in which these measures are carried out due regard will be given to the positions of the sovereigns as far as that is possible. The duration and extent of the measures of surveillance will further be dependent upon the attitude and conduct of the sovereigns."

Documents on German Foreign Policy 1918–1945. Series D, Vol. IX.
London, 1956.

that the Imperial as well as the national interest demanded the Sovereign's removal, at any rate for a time, out of harm's way. For the consequences of his capture would have been as odious and hurtful to the British as they would have been gratifying to the Germans.

This precaution does not seem to have been advocated from any quarter; and it can be said with certainty that if any proposals of this nature had been made to the King they would have been received very ill and rejected out of hand. Even the minor and uncontroversial alternative of sending the small Princesses—then aged fourteen and nine—overseas was never entertained by their father and mother. Within the Cabinet, Churchill recorded afterwards, the question of abandoning the struggle was not broached in even the most academic manner; and within the Royal Family an equally strong and equally instinctive inhibition precluded the consideration, let alone the adoption, of any measures which might have implied a lack of faith in the nation's power to defend herself.

In these matters no decision was taken, no communiqué issued; they were not discussed. The fact that the King and Queen stayed at their posts and never contemplated evacuating their children was not the outcome of heart-searching and a high resolve; it was the by-product of a tradition and an attitude of mind, and by their subjects it was taken for granted. It called, nevertheless, for coolness and firmness of judgment in a testing time and should not go unremarked, for it was of great value to the country's cause.

Soon after Dunkirk King Haakon of Norway and Queen Wilhelmina of the Netherlands were guests at Buckingham Palace, where they arrived with little more than the clothes they stood up in. Both had been harried out of their countries by the Germans; both had had to face and weigh the risks of capture by their enemies. Their experiences underlined the need to provide the Sovereign with a personal bodyguard, for this was in the days when invasion by airborne forces was thought imminent; and for this duty a contingent known as the Coats Mission was formed.

It was commanded by Lieutenant-Colonel J. S. Coats of the Coldstream Guards. It comprised one company of that regiment

The return from Dunkirk.

In the restaurant-car at Compiègne, 21 June 1940.
Hitler (second from the right) dictates his terms to the French.

Members of the British Union of Fascists at the
Tomb of the Unknown Warrior in 1932.

An Englishman's Home. A scene from the 1909
production at Wyndham's Theatre.

"Meanwhile, in Britain, the entire population, faced by the threat
of invasion, has been flung into a state of complete panic." Pont.

In the occupied Channel Islands.
A German officer talking to a police constable in Jersey, July 1940.

Street scene. London, 8 September 1940.

Bombed out.

The King visits a badly bombed area in Lambeth.

The Prime Minister inspects one of the earlier road-blocks.

A barrage balloon off duty, September 1940.

(transported in civilian motor coaches) and four armoured cars, two manned by the 12th Lancers and two by the Northamptonshire Yeomanry. Coats had no written orders, but was told that in an emergency it would be his duty to escort the King and Queen (who were in theory each supposed to keep one suitcase packed against this contingency) to a place of safety. There were, naturally, no means of telling in advance what places would be safe, but four large country houses in remote regions were earmarked as possible refuges. Service in what George VI once called "my private army" was much sought after, and the Coats Mission was not disbanded until the danger of invasion had passed away.

When the bombing started there were those who felt that the King should, for the nation's sake if not for his own, withdraw from the main danger area to Balmoral or Sandringham. George VI would have regarded any such suggestion as ridiculous and in poor taste. He and the Queen continued to carry out their public engagements in the capital, in south-east England and elsewhere, and divided most of their time between Windsor Castle and Buckingham Palace, where at this period the air-raid shelter, in one of the downstairs servants' rooms, combined the maximum of discomfort with the minimum of protection.

Buckingham Palace was hit several times. The most serious "incident" (as the results of bombing attacks were officially known) occurred on 13 September, when the building was straddled by a stick of six bombs dropped by a low-flying aircraft. Two of these burst in the Quadrangle, some eighty yards from the window behind which the King and Queen were discussing the day's arrangements with the King's secretary, Sir Alexander Hardinge. The narrowness of their escape was not realised until Churchill, who had himself been unaware of it at the time, revealed it after the war in *Their Finest Hour*.

The day was rainy and the clouds were low, and in these bad conditions only a handful of German aircraft were dispatched against London. However, the War Office and several other government buildings in Whitehall were hit, in addition to Buckingham Palace. It seems safe to infer that these attacks were carried out by pilots specially selected for their skill and experience, and that the bombing of the Palace, perhaps the most readily identifiable building in that part of London, was deliberate.

If it was, it was a psychological error on the Germans' part. It emphasised the extent to which the King and Queen were sharing the dangers to which Londoners were exposed, and it strengthened both the hatred in which the Germans were held and the country's determination to resist them.

"The war," Churchill wrote to the King rather more than three months later, "has drawn the Throne and the people more closely together than was ever before recorded, and Your Majesties are more beloved by all classes and conditions than any of the princes of the past." This was true, and perhaps the main single reason for it lay in the conduct of the King and Queen during the Blitz. They not only stayed in London when they need not have stayed, but they repeatedly made impromptu visits to the districts which had suffered worst, and which might be bombed again at any moment. On these occasions there could be no barriers of formality, no protocol, no prearranged programme to engender artificiality and constraint. Royalty stumbled over the rubble, picked its way through the broken glass and, when the siren sounded, went down into the shelter like everybody else. To humble people this seemed a wonderful thing, and, although it may have been irrational, they felt a lifting of the heart.

The Times in its obituary of George VI on 7 February 1952 wrote:

In time of war the King, whose public appearances are shrouded under the cloak of security, must suffer some eclipse in the public eye, especially when the Prime Minister is a personality of outstanding colour and vigour. As King George V found when Mr Lloyd George was Prime Minister, some of the fierce light which beats upon the Throne withdraws itself from Buckingham Palace and sheds its beams upon Downing Street. Mr Churchill, fully conscious of this, was determined that the King should not be pushed into the background, and when confidence between them was fully established he showed every consideration to the King and lost no opportunity of publicly praising his steadfastness and his devotion to duty.[1]

[1] In private and informal conversations Churchill habitually referred to his Sovereign as "our noble King".

It was perhaps through this quality of steadfastness that the King made his greatest contribution to his country's cause in the summer of 1940. His was the simple, unquestioning, rather conventional type of courage, and the way in which he bore himself—even though, as has been said, everyone took his bearing very much for granted—set unobtrusively a fine example. It was a time in which ancient virtues and traditional values meant a great deal, and through the anxious weeks after Dunkirk the people found the same sort of comfort in their King as on the battlefields of long ago a hard-pressed regiment found in its colours, held high amid much danger and confusion. "It was a great help to Britain to have so good a King and Queen," wrote Churchill afterwards; and the *New York Herald Tribune* was not found guilty of hyperbole when it described them as Ministers of Morale.

In any trial of strength, whether between teams or tribes or nations, leadership must count, however the odds are reckoned. In June 1940 the odds, except at sea, were heavily against Great Britain. But in the German camp the standard of leadership was at best meretricious. The Fuehrer, unchallenged and widely adored, led the nation; but he led it, in the summer of 1940, nowhere. All the panoply of discipline and solidarity, all the upsurge of national aspirations, all the impetus of unprecedented victories went in this decisive hour for nothing.

The Third Reich had the leaders it deserved; they fumbled their chances. Britain, whether she deserved them or not, threw up good leaders, and they saw her through.

CHAPTER TEN

The Sea Affair

The day of Britain's might at sea is past. Aircraft and the U-boat have turned surface fleets into obsolete playthings of the wealthy democracies.

Adolf Hitler, in 1934

Sea-power, when properly understood, is a wonderful thing.

Winston Churchill: *Their Finest Hour*

All that which concerns the sea is profound and final.

Hilaire Belloc: *The Cruise of the "Nona"*

On 3 September 1940 the Prime Minister began a memorandum on "The Munitions Situation" with the words: "The Navy can lose us the war, but only the Air Force can win it." The first half of this statement expressed an axiom of strategy, if not an eternal truth; the second seemed true at the time. The safety of the islands depended ultimately, as it always had, on the Royal Navy's ability to exert command of the surrounding seas; it was only by successfully challenging this command that the Germans could hope to carry out their invasion.

They never did challenge it. Throughout the three months during which they were making, remaking, and postponing their plans, British sea-power played a role which was none the less important for being largely passive. "Study of contempory documents" writes the official historian[1] "leaves little doubt that the quarrelsome vacillations of the German leaders were chiefly caused by the uneasiness which always seems to be produced among our enemies when it becomes apparent that an invasion is to be launched across seas which they do not adequately control. The lessons of 1940 appear to reinforce our knowledge that, although continental enemies have repeatedly tried to find a way to invade these islands without first defeating our maritime forces, no such short cut exists."

[1] Roskill.

It would however be wrong to portray the Royal Navy, at this crisis of British history, as a grey eminence, radiating an impalpable menace from behind northern mists while her light forces were engaged in such unspectacular duties as patrolling, convoy-protection, and the laying and sweeping of mines. Her contribution to the defence of the islands can be assessed at its true value only by going back to the beginning of the period when the threat of invasion was first apprehended, for only thus can we understand the scale of her achievements and the nature of the new dangers and problems that she faced in the performance of a traditional task.

The winter of 1939–40 was exceptionally severe. At the turn of the year a series of violent storms gave way to a long cold spell of almost Arctic intensity. Ports and estuaries became ice-bound. Guns and other tackle were coated in frozen spray. Fog and snow grounded bombers, fighters and reconnaissance aircraft. Yet the operational demand for ships, particularly as escorts for convoys, mounted steadily; and during the 29 days of February 1940 the average time spent at sea by all ships of the Home Fleet was 23 days, a remarkable total at any time and an astonishing one under the prevailing conditions.

The Home Fleet was therefore far from fresh when in April, after being hastily reinforced from other commands, it was launched upon the ill-starred Norwegian operations. It emerged from them with a revised and disquieting estimate of the relations between sea-power and air-power. For a variety of reasons (some of them reflected, in an exaggerated form, in the uncordial relations existing between the German Navy and the Luftwaffe) naval opinion in Great Britain before the war had tended to underrate the capacity of the air arm when employed against warships. Off Norway, and in the tortuous narrow fiords up which ships often had to sail, the error of this judgment was painfully brought home. From a naval point of view the official historian finds that the first lesson of the Norwegian campaign was that: "It could no longer be doubted that, if effective air cover was lacking, warships could not operate protractedly and the Army could not be maintained overseas." This lesson was to condition all the precautions which the

Navy found herself, immediately afterwards, concerting for the defence of the United Kingdom.

In 1940, when people in Britain discussed the prospects of invasion, they sometimes spoke of the English Channel as a tank-trap.[1] Its true defensive value lay in the fact that it was something more; it was a ship-trap. Over the Channel and the Narrow Seas the Home Fleet in its northern bases was suspended like the blade of a guillotine. Throughout the German preparations for invasion the Army (and von Brauchitsch in particular) remained confident of their ability to discharge the duties laid upon them. The Luftwaffe expected a walk-over. Only the German Navy recognised in *Sea Lion* a desperate venture, beset by appalling difficulties and terrible risks.

Yet it was not as a deterrent, not as an uncommitted reserve, that the Royal Navy is seen in retrospect to have made her most vital contribution to Britain's survival. For the fact is that, as a deterrent, British sea-power did not make a decisive impact on her enemy's will. It ought, no doubt, to have done so, but it did not. The knowledge of British naval superiority strengthened Raeder's objections to *Operation Sea Lion*, but it did not cause those objections to prevail. It influenced Hitler's attitude, but it did not alter his purpose. It was not a reassessment of the naval risks involved, but the failure to establish air supremacy, which made Hitler call off the invasion; all the evidence suggests that, had he won the air battle, his armies would have embarked and sailed according to plan. So although what the Royal Navy *was* had considerable importance (and should, if the Germans had understood about sea-power, have had more), what it *did* was of greater, as well as of more direct, consequence to the defence of the islands.

Legend has been less than generous to the Navy for its part in the evacuation of the British Expeditionary Force from France. Partly perhaps because the British have so strong a relish for everything amateur, this is conceived of in the popular memory as having been carried out in its entirety at Dunkirk, largely by gallant civilians in small or otherwise incongruous craft.

[1] "At any rate I must admit you have a very good anti-tank obstacle," Weygand told Churchill at their last meeting on 11 June.

In fact the withdrawals from the Dunkirk beaches were only part of a continuous series of similar operations, all attended by similar hazards. A high proportion of the ships which took part in them were newly returned from Norway, whence 35,000 British and Allied troops had been brought safely back, often in circumstances of great danger and difficulty. At Dunkirk the small-boat amateurs, mustered and directed by the Royal Navy, showed a selfless courage and great resource; but they were auxiliaries only. The services they rendered are not adequately recognised in the official totals of "troops lifted" (from Dunkirk to English ports) for two reasons. The first is that some of the small boats did their best work ferrying between the beaches and the ships lying off them; the second is that both their numbers and their losses are not, as the official historian admits, fully reflected in the hastily compiled records of the time. These figures, nevertheless, speak for themselves.

In all 338,226 troops were "lifted". Of this total the larger fractions included:

> 5,031 in 203 private motor-boats;
> 4,895 in 27 yachts (some of them manned by the Royal Navy);
> 28,709 in 230 trawlers and drifters;
> 48,472 in 38 minesweepers (large);
> 87,910 in 45 personnel vessels (manned by the Royal Navy and the Merchant Navy);
> 102,843 in 56 destroyers and torpedo boats.

However incomplete the statistics, compiled as they were by a process of improvisation against a background of confusion, they show with a general accuracy the contrasts between the results achieved. The 45 "personnel vessels", or transports, brought back nearly a quarter of the troops evacuated; nine ships were lost and eight damaged. The 56 destroyers and torpedo boats, possessing only a fraction of the transports' troop-carrying capacity, were easier to board, faster, and better able to defend themselves against attack from the air; nine were lost and nineteen damaged, but they brought off more soldiers than the big transports could, and four times their number of trawlers and drifters achieved less than half their lift. The amateurs, coming fresh on the scene, made their inspired and inspiring contribution, but it was the Navy who planned and directed the evacuation of Dunkirk, and of this strange operation the destroyers, tired already, were the tireless heroines.

Many accounts have recaptured already this or that aspect of Dunkirk—a word to which, like Waterloo, the British still have some difficulty in restoring its primary function as a place-name. Here it may suffice to quote, from a document in the archives of the Nore Command, the contemporary report by an officer of the Royal Naval Reserve on his experiences off Dunkirk. The spirit in which they were undergone, if not the experiences themselves, are sufficiently typical to suggest why a doomed army was saved.

H.M. Motor Boat *Triton* (Lt. R. H. Irving, RNR) arrived off the beaches at La Panne soon after dawn on 30 May. These, the most easterly of the evacuation beaches, were brought under persistent but probably not heavy fire from German batteries in the Nieuport area during that day. Throughout the morning *Triton* towed boat-loads of troops out through the shallows to destroyers and trawlers waiting off-shore. Her captain's report runs as follows:

At about 1200 hours, when alongside a destroyer, a voice hailed me saying "Well done, motor boat, wait for me." An officer wearing a lambskin coat came on board. He was wet through. However he said he wanted me to carry on as I was doing and then he would have one or two other jobs for me. So I carried on taking off troops to ships. In the late afternoon the officer above mentioned, whose name I then learned was Commodore Stevens, asked me to run him down to a certain position ... as he was going ashore to look for Lord Gort [Commander-in-Chief of the BEF] and, if he got him, I was to take him straight to England.

Enemy batteries were now on and off dropping heavy shells quite close. Commodore Stevens waded ashore through the surf, up to the neck in water. In an hour's time he returned, waded out again, but did not mention Lord Gort's name.... Commodore Stevens and I then carried on taking troops to ships. At 0100 hours 31 May 1940 I rescued seven soldiers from drowning and continued rescue work until 0200 hours (approx.) when I went aground. I knew the tide was rising so did not worry.... Succeeded in floating her at 0400 and carried on as before. Now I was feeling the strain somewhat, but worse lay ahead. At about 0800 there was a strong north wind and very heavy swell and going alongside ships was very difficult.

Commodore Stevens now asked me to take him out to an MTB which had come in and he asked me to continue the good work alone. He said I had done good work, but could not allow me to rest, too much remained to be done. I might say that the Commodore said I was "a good fellow" and on other occasions said I was "a bloody fool". It is not my place to pass remarks about Senior Officers, but this officer, without cap, soaked through, without food, was a great example to me. He helped me to steer, to pass lines, to haul drowning soldiers on board, and very often would say "Come on, the Army. Where have I seen you before? You are so good looking I'm sure I know you." Other times he cursed the lot as stupid.

On the afternoon of the 31st the shelling became "terrific". All other shipping had left that sector of the beaches: "I was the last naval officer to leave La Panne and the last naval boat. The troops had all disappeared." *Triton* moved westwards in quest of more rescue work and finished up with a rope round her starboard screw, fouling the rudder, "a full load of soldiers on board (six wounded), a full boatload towing and soldiers clinging to the stern." Further hazards, mishaps and tribulations, which awaited the *Triton* before she got back to England, can be passed over; but not her captain's tribute to his shipmates:

The crew sent with me [he wrote] knew nothing of making fast ropes or steering, but under fire, in spite of great exhaustion, exhibited, on and off, great interest in all that was happening. I respectfully submit they are worthy of some recognition.

Triton's activities off Dunkirk had no effect upon the course of history; nor are they recorded in the lapidary style proper to an important naval dispatch. But her commander's report illustrates the manner in which the highest professional traditions of the Royal Navy were at the outbreak of the Second World War upheld by the great muster of reservists, volunteers and recruits on whom a small peacetime Service found itself so largely dependent.

Operation Dynamo, as the evacuation from Dunkirk was called, covered a period of nine days. It had been preceded by a series of forays, some planned in advance but most of them improvised as the situation in the Low Countries rapidly deteriorated, to Dutch, Belgian and French ports. The Dutch Royal Family and most of

Holland's reserves of gold and stocks of diamonds were brought safely away. Blockships were sunk in the entrances to Ijmuiden, Zeebrugge and Antwerp, demolition parties were landed and re-embarked at a number of different places. For eight days the destroyers and minesweepers on whom the main burden of these operations fell worked at high pressure; "there seemed to be no limit to the variety of their tasks—embarking, transporting and disembarking troops, evacuating Allied Royalties, missions and legations, bombarding aerodromes and beaches, towing, screening, escorting, repelling air attacks and attacking submarine contacts."[1] In the course of these operations a great quantity of shipping, most of which would otherwise have fallen into German hands, was prevailed upon to sail for England.

When first Holland and then Belgium fell, the Navy found itself involved in the desperate ventures which had as their objects the defence of Boulogne and Calais. A Guards brigade was carried to reinforce the former port and after two days of bitter fighting all save a few of its survivors were re-embarked under a murderous fire from field artillery, machine-guns, tanks and captured French coastal batteries; the destroyers returned this fire over open sights, and after lifting 900 men in these desperate circumstances went in again, by night, and rescued 1,400 more.

At Calais a brigade of Riflemen and a regiment of tanks were landed under roughly similar conditions. Here the garrison received orders that there would be no withdrawal, for the need to delay the German advance on Dunkirk (this was the period 22–26 May) was imperative. But the destroyers continued with reckless impudence to frequent the port, and the small craft manned by naval personnel who relieved them on the last night were still taking off administrative troops and wounded when virtually the whole town was in German hands.

For all the gallantry of the guardsmen, riflemen, Royal Marines and tank crews who fought in them, these delaying actions at Boulogne and Calais were basically an assertion of sea-power; and the valuable time they gained for the defenders of the Dunkirk

[1] Roskill.

perimeter could never have been gained but for the skill and resolution with which the sailors played their part.

No breathing-space intervened between the evacuation of Dunkirk and its half-forgotten sequel, in which nearly 200,000 British and Allied troops, a number of refugees and a great quantity of military stores and equipment were brought to England from the ports of western and north-western France. Only in one instance was the Royal Navy thwarted. At St Valéry, on which 51 (Highland) Division fell back when the French Army of which it formed a part began to disintegrate, fog prevented the small ships and destroyers which had been assembled from entering the harbour on the night of 10 June. On the next day the French general surrendered. The Highlanders took no notice of this and went on fighting; but the odds were too great and in the end they too had to lay down their arms, 6,000 officers and men being taken prisoner—"the only instance in this campaign [the official historian points out] where a considerable body of British troops fell back to the sea but could not be rescued." Yet even at St Valéry 2,137 British and 1,184 French troops were taken off from the eastern end of the perimeter.

By mid-June the "reconstituted BEF" (52 Division, the remnants of 1 Armoured Division, the leading elements of 1 Canadian Division and various composite forces) had been brought back from Cherbourg, St Malo and Brest, and these ports had fallen into German hands. Large-scale evacuations continued all down the Biscay coast as far as the Spanish frontier, but after the 17th, when the French Government asked for an armistice, few demolitions could be carried out owing to the objections of the local authorities. In the space of roughly one month the Navy landed in British ports a total of 558,032 fighting men,[1] and with them roughly 300 guns, 3,000 vehicles and 2,000 tons of stores.[2] In addition 22,656 civilians

[1] Of these 368,491 were British. Allied troops included some 25,000 Poles and 5,000 Czechs, later to form the nucleus of important national contingents.

[2] In fact a far greater quantity of arms and equipment could, and should, have been removed from the Continent. At many places, and especially at Brest, alarmist intelligence about the proximity of enemy forces caused the evacuation of *matériel* to be abandoned prematurely; but this was not the Navy's fault.

were removed from the Channel Islands, and probably another 10,000 or 15,000 British subjects from various parts of Europe were brought home to safety.

Over the whole period the severe losses suffered by the Royal Navy and the Merchant Navy were, considering the scope of the operations and the risks accepted, remarkably light. Virtually all were caused by air-attack, shore-based artillery, mining or accidents. The German Navy made no serious attempt to dispute its adversary's liberty of action. E-boats—small, fast, highly manoeuvrable craft armed with torpedoes and adept in the use of smoke to cover their withdrawal—sank one destroyer and did other damage off Dunkirk; seven U-boats, detailed to interfere with subsequent evacuations further west, did not sink a ship and do not appear to have carried out any attacks despite the abundance of targets, most of which were inadequately if at all protected.

However daringly executed, a military evacuation is an ignoble proceeding. To its immediate beneficiaries this ultimate truth is seldom apparent. The tired soldiers sleep or sing or vomit on the crowded decks; but in them there is a sense of lightness, a glow of gratitude and hope. It looks as if, after all, they are going to be saved, and for the time being they are relieved of responsibility. They are in luck; they feel privileged. So do their families, so does their nation, when the news of their rescue gets abroad. The fact of an army's defeat is obscured by the fact of the men's survival; and because the enemy has been cheated of his prey the completeness of his victory is, for the time being, overlooked.[1]

But if an evacuated expeditionary force carries home with it a variety of comforting illusions, it leaves behind it bitterness and a

[1] At Narvik at the end of May Allied forces under British command inflicted on the German Army the only defeat it suffered in Europe during the first two and a half years of the war. They were immediately afterwards withdrawn, because the Royal Navy, with more pressing commitments nearer home, could no longer support a sideshow in the Arctic Circle. The end of the difficult affair at Narvik attracted little attention at the time and is to-day scarcely remembered as a victory. If the Germans had won the campaign, had driven the British and Allied contingents into the sea and enforced a compulsory instead of a voluntary evacuation, it can hardly be doubted that Narvik would occupy a place of greater lustre and prominence in the annals of the British than it does or ever will.

squalid havoc. In Dutch, Belgian and French ports much the same sights met the eyes of the inhabitants after the last British destroyer had slipped her moorings. To the injuries done by the enemy's fire the wanton litter created by the discards of an ally in full flight added insult; for even the most orderly evacuation gives off a stench of waste and loss and irresponsibility, and sets a stage upon which the hapless, inevitable straggler is bound, even if sober, to bring further disrenown on the evacuated army.

Despite all this, the effect of the British withdrawals upon the morale of Europe was salutary. Audacious and imperturbable, the Royal Navy stood out in the general ruin as the one force capable of frustrating the conqueror's designs; and although in the heat and bitterness of the moment harsh things were said, as they always are in a time of defeat, about the departing British, the sea-power which made their departure possible was recognised as a symbol of hope, the only portent on a dark horizon capable of good augury. "The psychological impact upon the free people was immense, for it had shown that Hitler's all-conquering armies could be denied the full fruits of their land victories by the skilful and determined application of maritime power."[1]

To Britain's immediate needs the recovery of nearly half a million fighting men[2] made a contribution of supreme importance, all the more so since they included, among the survivors of the BEF, the flower of her Regular Army and her best trained Territorial troops; these withdrawals, Churchill pointed out to the Chiefs of Staff, had "revolutionised the Home Defence position". When it is remembered that *Operation Dynamo*, as originally conceived, had envisaged the evacuation over a period of two days of no more than 45,000 men, it will be seen how vastly the country's chances of survival had been improved by the Navy's resource and devotion. Throughout the rest of the summer British sea-power was to exert, mostly from a distance, a powerful influence upon the German plans to conquer the islands; but even before these plans took shape

[1] Roskill.

[2] From the total of 558,000 must be substracted those French troops who elected to return home after the Armistice and also men whose wounds incapacitated them for further active service.

the Navy had given the nation two priceless assets with which to oppose them—an army, and a high heart.

In framing their plans to deal with a seaborne invasion the Admiralty judged, correctly, that the Germans would choose the shortest route, but expected diversions or subsidiary landings elsewhere. The Naval Staff, using phraseology which disarmingly recalls the prospectus of some Victorian paddle-steamer company, hoped to attack the invaders "before departure": failing that, at "the point of arrival" or—best of all—"on passage". Of these hopes the first and the third could be realised only if reconnaissance was effective and intelligence adequate.

Neither condition had obtained during the Norwegian campaign. Aircraft were not yet equipped with radar; the sighting of ships at sea and the photographing of enemy bases were possible only in favourable weather. Intelligence, which had been unreliable or non-existent in Norway, showed few signs of being any better in western Europe. Considerations of this kind combined with a general exaggeration of German capabilities to produce an element of over-insurance in the British naval dispositions. These were largely made to meet a contingency which did not exist and ought perhaps to have been recognised as a chimaera: namely, the concentration and dispatch of a sizeable (and inevitably slow) invasion fleet against the islands in circumstances which would achieve a large measure of surprise.

The Admiralty's reference to a single "point of arrival", though it was a figure of speech rather than a precise strategical conception, is perhaps a clue to the extent by which they failed to visualise the true nature of the problems confronting the Germans, whose landing-front, even after it had been reluctantly contracted, included three separate beach-heads, with an option on a fourth. And although it was right to make allowance, even in mid-summer, for a period of bad visibility, the Admiralty's pessimistic view of the results to be obtained by air reconnaissance may have been unduly influenced by Coastal Command's failure, while operating at extreme range in the aftermath of a northern winter, to locate in Scandinavian waters single German warships whose probable course was unknown. It seems, in short, that the British had a right to rely on considerably more warning of invasion than they chose to allow themselves, and need not have tied up in a purely defensive role a number of ships which would—until the receipt of the warning—have been better employed on other duties.

The front line was manned by four destroyer flotillas of 36 ships; they were based on the Humber, Harwich, Sheerness and Dover[1] and were allotted (considering the resources available) lavish cruiser support. Some 400 trawlers and drifters of the Auxiliary Patrol and a further 700 patrol vessels of various types formed a screen of mobile vedettes round the coasts of the island from Duncansby Head in the extreme north-east of Scotland southabout to the Solway Firth; at first these craft were very lightly armed, but their fire-power was gradually increased.

What with the losses off Norway and France, the maintenance of a strong striking-force of destroyers as a precaution against a seaborne *coup de main* seriously impaired the Navy's ability to discharge other essential and more normal duties. The official historian writes: "The Home Fleet and the Western Approaches Command were . . . called on to sacrifice flotilla vessels to the southern commands to an extent which greatly restricted the operational capacity of the former and reduced almost to vanishing point the escorts which the latter was able to provide for our Atlantic convoys."[2] The Prime Minister decreed on 1 July that "losses in the Western Approaches must be accepted meanwhile"; but a month later he noted that these losses were "most grievous. . . . No doubt this is largely due to the shortage of destroyers through invasion precautions. . . . Anyhow, we cannot go on like this."[3]

The following table of sinkings shows how gravely the Navy's control of the seas had been weakened by the diversion of so many of its light forces to anti-invasion duties:

British Shipping Losses from all Causes (Summer 1940)

March	107,009 tons
April	158,218 „
May	288,461 „

---

[1] The flotilla at Dover was withdrawn to Portsmouth after some of the earlier German air-attacks.

[2] Roskill.   [3] *Their Finest Hour.*

June	585,496 tons (Dunkirk, etc.)
July	386,913 „
August	397,229 „
September	448,621 „

The number of U-boats operating during these months was small, yet the average number of kills per U-boat was probably higher than at any other time during the war. These sinkings represent the one positive contribution made by *Operation Sea Lion* to the German cause.

It is easier to understand than to applaud the decision to maintain, throughout the summer, a pattern of naval defence which had so crippling an effect on the exercise of sea-power in the wider sense. In June the destroyer flotillas in the Nore and neighbouring Commands were the one sure answer to a mortal threat. As the summer wore on the Army became more and more competent to fulfil its traditional role when invasion threatens, which is—as someone once put it—to act as goalkeeper for the Navy. But with so much at stake, and so little known of the enemy's capabilities, to remove the Navy from the goal-mouth was a measure not lightly to be undertaken; and the destroyers were kept in stations where their operational value was, and was bound to be, very small until the invaders took the initiative and set sail.

In retrospect it seems strange that the premises on which these dispositions were originally made in June, and which were repeatedly challenged by the Commander-in-Chief, Home Fleet (Admiral Forbes), were never seriously called in question at the highest level. Not only did the Army become steadily better qualified to carry out what Forbes called "its immemorial role of holding up the first flight of an invading force", but experience showed that no major secrets could, during the summer, be hidden for more than a very short time from aerial reconnaissance of the European coastline.

Moreover the British saw as clearly as the Germans did that—as the Chiefs of Staff put it on 26 May—"the crux of the matter is air superiority"; and nobody supposed that air superiority could be achieved by a lightning onslaught of one or two days' duration. The destroyers were not tethered to south and east-coast ports because these were the only bases, or even the most convenient bases, from which they could strike against invasion; they were kept there solely as a precaution against surprise, lest the enemy should make suddenly, with little or no warning, a massive descent upon the shores of Britain.

But how could he arrive without warning if, as everyone agreed, he must fight and win a major air-battle before he sailed? As a strategical concept, the zareba of destroyers round the south and east coasts seems in retrospect to have made less and less sense with every day that passed; and every day the need for the deployment of these ships elsewhere became more apparent, and more urgent. Kennelled for week after week in the southern English harbours, where the assets of their speed, their agility and their fire-power brought the Royal Navy only negligible returns, these powerful flotillas were compelled to abjure the first principle of sea-power, which is flexibility. The light of after-knowledge is not necessary to show that they could have intervened against an invading fleet at short notice from distant stations; early on 10 May, for instance, the destroyer-leader *Codrington* raised steam in Scapa Flow and arrived in Dover 23 hours later after a voyage of 530 miles. Even allowing for the difficulties and delays of refuelling, perhaps under heavy air-attack, no undue risk would have been accepted if part at least of the zareba had been dismantled and some of the destroyers made conditionally available for duty in the Western Approaches and elsewhere. But if those who were affected by them criticise decisions taken in a matter of life and death, it at least indicates that the critics are not dead.

At the time the chief critic was the Commander-in-Chief, Home Fleet. His views did not prevail; but they still deserve a hearing, and their general tenor is well conveyed in some pungent observations on the Auxiliary Patrol. In September the Admiralty wanted to convert some of the trawlers serving with this far-flung force into minesweepers, while the Ministry of Agriculture and Fisheries, supported by the Ministry of Food, were urging that both trawlers and drifters should resume their normal activity of fishing.

After the shore-commands had made known their views Admiral Forbes wrote:

I regret to find that my brother Commanders-in-Chief are in disagreement with me. . . . The main cause of this difference of opinion seems to arise from an idea . . . that the Army of the present day is to take no hand, or only a very slight one, in preventing an invading force from actually landing on our shores, but that the Army's chief role is to have a battle with the invaders after they have landed. A subsidiary reason appears to be [the belief] that it is quite an easy matter for the enemy to land large masses of tanks, mechanical transport, ammunition, etc., on an open beach or in a small harbour. In the past it has never been considered that a superior Navy could prevent a raid by sea, but that if it had "control of the sea" it should be capable of preventing invasion. . . .

Apart from the principles mentioned above, it appears necessary to investigate whether we are using our forces in the most economical way. . . . I understand that [the Auxiliary Patrol] have the dual role of reporting and then fighting the enemy. As regards reporting, compared with the past we have the overwhelming advantage of air reconnaissance. As regards fighting, is the employment of seven drifters and one yacht capable of moving at ten knots the most economical method of bringing a comparatively small number of Lewis guns into action against an invading force . . . or can this be better and more economically done by the Army with the same number of Lewis guns in motor vehicles moving at 20 to 30 miles an hour?

As we look back on this old controversy (for the principles involved were basically the same for trawlers and destroyers) it is difficult not to feel that the zareba conception of naval defence owed something to the influence on minds in the Admiralty and elsewhere of a story-book view of invasion. Undue importance was placed on the repulse of the first wave of the assault. The motto "*Ils ne débarqueront pas*" was subconsciously adopted, and insufficient account was taken of the extreme vulnerability to naval action not only of the invader's sea-lanes but of the forces ashore which depended on them. "Let us be masters of the Straits for six hours and we shall be masters of the world", Napoleon wrote to Latouche in 1804; in the following year, after reviewing the Grande Armée at Boulogne, he doubled his estimate ("If we have the power of crossing but for twelve hours, England is no more!"). But Hitler, as we shall see, needed to have "the power of crossing" for more than twenty times twelve hours before the landing of his first wave would have been completed. It was not one single, elusive fleet any more than it was a single "point of arrival" with which the Royal

Navy had to reckon; and it is clear now that the destroyers and their supporting cruisers would, as Forbes argued then, have been better employed in a less static role.

After its exacting rescue-work finished at the end of June, the Royal Navy in home waters exchanged the role of a Scarlet Pimpernel for the less dramatic duties of a watchdog. Its heavy forces were a Fairy Godmother whose aid never had to be invoked but whose wand, wielded from Scapa and Rosyth, laid upon the German Navy a spell which cast a blight over, though it did not stop, their preparations to invade. Its light forces were, like Cinderella, allotted humdrum and sometimes unworthy tasks.

It is often said that a democracy is at a disadvantage in war; and in peacetime the British sometimes inveigh against the traditional hierarchies and channels of command which exist within the armed services. Since in the senior of these services these hierarchies and channels were in the critical summer of 1940 almost inextricably confused, it may here be convenient to examine the whole system of command by which the defence of the islands was directed; for throughout this narrative criticisms abound of the German arrangements, which were on paper more monolithic but which did not work well, and it would be unfair not to show the other side of the picture.

At the summit the British, like the Germans, allotted to their leader a double role. Churchill was Prime Minister and Minister of Defence; Hitler was Chancellor of Germany and Commander-in-Chief of her Armed Forces. Each had arrogated to himself his military responsibilities; and although the benefits derived by their respective nations from their decisions to do so were in practice far from equal, each was in theory wise to take his decision.

In Whitehall the Minister of Defence presided over the Chiefs of Staff Committee and answered to the War Cabinet. Below this level the structure of command was complex. From the Admiralty the Naval Staff exercised a broad control over the North Atlantic Station (headquarters at Gibraltar), the South Atlantic Station (Freetown, Sierra Leone), the America and West Indies Station (Bermuda), the East Indies Station (Ceylon), and the China Station

(Singapore and Hong Kong); it also controlled the fleet in home waters. This comprised the Home Fleet (normally based on Scapa Flow) and five main shore-commands—Portsmouth, the Nore (Chatham), the Western Approaches (Plymouth), Rosyth and Dover. Of these the commander-in-chiefs were co-equal[1]; but their responsibilities and their outlook varied widely and, since the necessity constantly arose for ships to be transferred from one command to another (and since the Admiralty, whence these transfers were ordered, is automatically unpopular with all commanders-in-chief), a fertile field existed for friction and disagreement.

In the Army, command was more centralised. But the Commander-in-Chief, Home Forces, on whom lay the main responsibility for defeating the German Army if it landed, had to concert his arrangements with a bewildering galaxy of opposite numbers. Apart from the four naval commanders-in-chief and the Flag Officer, Dover, there were Bomber Command, Fighter Command and Coastal Command (which in 1941 was placed under the Admiralty's operational control), to say nothing of Anti-Aircraft Command, over whom the Air Ministry had a partial jurisdiction. There was also the Ministry of Home Security, under whose aegis the Regional Commissioners exercised duties which would assume great importance in time of invasion.

Weaknesses in this system (if such it can be called) of command revealed themselves during exercises, and it can scarcely be doubted that, if *Sea Lion* had been launched, stresses severer than it was designed to bear would have been placed upon its cumbrous and intricate machinery. But to supersede it by, or rather to superimpose upon it, the improvised and untried apparatus of a Supreme Command would, in the short time and with the meagre resources available, have added still further to the confusion, and no major reorganisation was attempted. Few doubted that, if the crisis came, the defence of the islands would in practice be largely directed by a former cavalry officer, smoking a cigar.

---

[1] With the exception of Dover. Normally a sub-command of the Nore, it had been given an independent status but was commanded by a flag officer, not a commander-in-chief.

CHAPTER ELEVEN

Margins of Error (1)
British Intelligence about the Germans

Sherlock Holmes clapped his hands softly together and chuckled. " 'Pon my word, Watson, you are coming along wonderfully. You have really done very well indeed. It is true that you have missed everything of importance, but you have hit upon the method."

Conan Doyle: *A Case of Identity*

"THE difficulty of obtaining information is increased by the fact that there is little actual contact with the enemy land forces."[1] Seldom, and in the history of modern warfare never, had two military machines, about—as both believed—to be locked in a decisive struggle, been so curiously insulated from each other. On a clear day it was possible, with the help of binoculars, to tell the time by the clock-tower in Calais from the battlements of Dover Castle; but between the two armies the Channel interposed an unnatural void in which their curiosities about each other remained suspended. They were like insects deprived of their antennae. However fallible and incomplete, the normal apparatus of patrols and listening-posts, prisoners, captured equipment, pay-books taken from corpses, and statements by bewildered civilians, serves to create between two forces poised for battle a sense of mutual familiarity which all ranks find vaguely comforting.

Denied all clues of this kind (save, to the British, the meagre harvest of a few gallant but ill-found Commando raids), the Intelligence Staffs on both sides of the Channel fell back on more

[1] From *Notes on German Preparations for Invasion of the United Kingdom*, prepared by the General Staff (M.I.14). The first edition of this secret document was not printed until April 1941, but its appreciation of the basic factors in the situation, though worked out in greater detail, is essentially the same as that made in the previous summer.

impersonal methods—on photographic reconnaissance, on various forms of wireless intelligence, on studying each other's newspapers and broadcasts and on reports from neutral sources. Both also employed secret agents. Neither, at this stage of the war, achieved results which can fairly be called impressive.

In the field of intelligence there was a fundamental difference between the requirements of the two adversaries. To the Germans, holding the initiative, accurate information was no more than a valuable asset; to the British it was a vital necessity.

It soon came to be realised in London that the timing of the enemy's seaborne attack was virtually dictated by the need to land his first wave at or just before dawn and at or about high tide. High water occurs at different times on different sectors of the English coast; but the enemy's need for fighter-cover over his main beach-heads limited the extent of the coastal area threatened and thus narrowed down—to roughly a week in every lunar month—the period in which first the south and then the east coast became ripe for assault. Although, however, conditions for a landing in Norfolk became suitable five days later than they became suitable for a landing in Sussex, this still left a wide margin for potentially fatal miscalculations about the enemy's objectives; and there was more-over the supposedly ubiquitous threat of airborne attack (of whose scale, as we have seen, an exaggerated estimate was formed) as well as the probability of diversionary raids and feints. It was impossible to be strong everywhere; the 28 under-strength divisions of which GHQ Home Forces disposed were—apart from more obvious deficiencies in training and equipment—seriously lacking in mobility,[1] and there were small prospects of rectifying by flexibility and resource any major miscalculations regarding German strategy. It was thus of cardinal importance for the British to discover, or to deduce correctly, the areas selected by the enemy for his main landings; and the Royal Navy—envisaging, as the Admiralty put it in May, "the happy possibility that our reconnaissance might enable us to inter-

---

[1] "It is of paramount importance", GHQ Home Forces were plaintively insisting in June, "that all mobile columns should be really mobile"; and although a motley assortment of troop-carrying vehicles was acquired by requisitioning from civilian sources, the C.-in-C., Home Forces (Brooke), was still pressing, at a conference on 6 August, for a "higher standard of mobility".

cept the expedition on passage"—was vitally concerned to know from which bases the seaborne invaders would sail.

To these all-important questions the British began by returning the wrong answer; and when, late in the day, the right answer presented itself to them they accepted its validity with an ill grace. It might be the truth, they argued, but it could hardly be the whole truth; and in some quarters it was held not to be the truth at all, but a piece of Hitlerian chicanery. Throughout the period their intelligence staffs were not well informed; nor, in evaluating such data as they had to work on, did they show any marked flair for arriving at the truth.

The only important matter of fact on which the intelligence available to the British was at fault throughout the summer of 1940 was the operational strength of the German Navy. This was exaggerated. The Admiralty were unaware that the two modern battle-cruisers, *Scharnhorst* and *Gneisenau*, had been damaged by torpedoes and were out of action; and the Germans were credited with having, in addition, six light or heavy cruisers in effective service, whereas in fact they only had two.[1] These misapprehensions, however, did not seriously distort the British view of their enemy's capabilities; for they still left him with barely adequate naval support for any considerable expedition across the sea.

For three and a half months—from mid-May until the beginning of September—the British strove hard to divine the Germans' intentions. They failed almost completely to do so. They were correct in assuming that the enemy's main attack or attacks (as distinct from diversionary operations) would not be launched outside the radius of his fighter-cover; they were also right in thinking that he would go for London if he got ashore. The German Navy, even on their unduly pessimistic estimate of its strength, was not considered capable of producing two separate armadas simultaneously; and the question which the British had to answer boiled down to this: Would Hitler attack the east coast south of the Wash, or the south coast east of Weymouth?

The importance of finding the right answer was great, and appeared to be greater than it was, since the Navy—taking, as we

[1] Roskill.

saw in the preceding chapter, an ungenerous view of the RAF's capabilities—held that no more than 24 hours' notice of invasion could be guaranteed. This assumption that the Germans could achieve what would in effect be strategical surprise enhanced the already obvious importance of disposing to the greatest advantage the forces in GHQ Reserve; for Brooke, who had succeeded Ironside as Commander-in-Chief, Home Forces, on 20 July, was quick to realise that the Thames Estuary and the great labyrinth of London were an obstacle across which—particularly if road and rail communications were being interrupted by bombing—the passage of major reinforcements from Southern Command to Eastern Command or vice versa would be a slow and difficult enterprise.

East coast or south coast? Heads or tails? It seemed essential to guess right. The British guessed wrong.

The idea that the Germans would attack the east coast was held with tenacity and abandoned with reluctance. On 10 July the Prime Minister received from the First Sea Lord, Admiral Pound, a closely reasoned paper prepared by the Naval Staff, whose conclusions were that, while "it appears probable that a total of some 100,000 men might reach these shores without being intercepted by naval forces," their subsequent maintenance would be virtually impossible. The 100,000 men were conjecturally subdivided among the following objectives:

South coast from Bay of Biscay ports	20,000
„ „ „ Channel ports	5,000
East coast from Dutch and Belgian ports	12,000
„ „ „ German ports	50,000
Shetland, Iceland and coast of Scotland from Norwegian ports	10,000
	97,000

It will be seen that only a quarter of this hypothetical force was directed on the south coast, and that less than a fifth of it was envisaged as embarking at the ports of northern France, Holland and Belgium in which the Germans had begun, a week earlier, to make preparations for the dispatch to England of an army several times its size.

On the same day Churchill—who throughout took a sceptical view of the possibilities open to an invader—scouted, in particular, the concept of a cross-Channel operation. "It will be very difficult," he wrote, "for the enemy to place large well-equipped bodies of troops on the east coast of England. . . . Even more unlikely is it that the south coast would be attacked."

This view continued not only to prevail, but to serve as a basis for strategy. "We may seem at present", the Chiefs of Staff ruminated on 13 August, "to be slightly over-insured along the south coast." They were in fact heavily under-insured. Only five divisions, with three available from GHQ Reserve, held the coast from Dover to north Cornwall; a total of 15½ divisions, with two more in reserve, were allotted to the sectors Cromarty–Wash and Wash–Dover. It was not until early September that the unmistakable evidence of the barge concentrations in the Channel ports made it clear that (in Churchill's words) "the front to be attacked was altogether different from *or additional to* the east coast, on which the Chiefs of Staff, the Admiralty and I, in full agreement, still laid the major emphasis".[1] A regrouping of Home Forces was quickly put in hand, and by mid-September the number of divisions available for the defence of southern England had been increased from a maximum of eight to a maximum of sixteen.

For three months, then, both the Minister of Defence and his principal Service advisers were mistaken in their forecast of the enemy's strategy, which—though it only took shape midway through this period—never contemplated any alternative to a cross-Channel operation. Their error was not induced by the cunning of the Germans, whose intermittent attempts to deceive their intended victim were puerile. The fact of the matter was that, until the beginning of September, the British lacked, and were in the circumstances almost bound to lack, any evidence as to where the blow would fall.

What made them so confident that it would fall on the east coast

[1] *Their Finest Hour.*

and not on the south? Conditions for an amphibious assault were better on the open, gently shelving east coast than on the south, whose beaches are mostly flanked or dominated by cliffs or overlooked by escarpments of downland; and the East Anglian plain offered greater opportunities for mechanised warfare than the intricate, quilted terrain of Kent and Sussex. The fact that the Germans chose the south coast, Churchill stoutly maintained afterwards, "does not mean that . . . they were thinking rightly and we wrongly".

Negative information was, until late in August, a powerful factor in favour of the east coast. As the alarums and frenzied speculations of June died away and the danger was brought into some sort of focus, the British ceased to believe in an assault which could be delivered without warning (although, as we have seen, this conception continued throughout the summer to influence their naval dispositions). Their arrangements for photographic reconnaissance, though still inadequate, gave them regular coverage of the Continental coast between Statlandet, in the Shetland Narrows, and Brest. Longer sorties enlarged their field of vision, but the adequacy of this coverage naturally decreased as the distance to be flown increased. Thus the Intelligence Staffs had to take into account two different brands of negative information about potential invasion bases. The Baltic ports—threatening the east coast if they threatened anything—were a permanently unknown quantity as far as photographic reconnaissance went; while from the ports nearer home (of which the nearest, threatening the south coast, were the most easily and therefore the most fully covered) the cameras in the Hudsons and the unarmed, high-flying Spitfires continued to bring back, not a menacing question-mark, but an unequivocal No. In them, for week after week, no shipping was being accumulated, no dumps formed.

Short of a cryptographic windfall which the Intelligence Staffs had no reason to expect, aerial reconnaissance was the only reliable source from which a clue to German strategy might be forthcoming. The combination of its *non possumus* in the Baltic and its *non est* in the Narrow Seas implied a threat to the east coast and immunity for the south coast; and force was lent to this interpretation by a popular, and pardonable, fallacy. The British had been energetically preparing to repel an attack on their country since the middle of May; they understandably assumed that Hitler's arrangements to launch an invasion had at the very least kept pace with their own arrangements to defeat it. This, as we have seen, was not the case.

"German plans for the invasion of this country will have been worked out in great detail and secrecy." The sentence, taken from *Notes on German Parachutists* issued by GHQ Home Forces on 18 June, is but one of many clear indications that the British, once they had tumbled to the idea that they were going to be invaded, expected the thing to be done in style.[1] After the first shock of alarm had passed, there were many who thought that Hitler might lose his nerve; none suspected that he had not made up his mind. Prudently, but mistakenly, they credited him with deep-laid plans, concerted long in advance of his opportunity; and when, as July went and August came, they saw in the ports nearest to their shores no signs of those plans being implemented, it was natural to assume that they were maturing in bases beyond the effective scope of the RAF's reconnaissance. All this strengthened their forebodings about the east coast.

The daily proceedings of the Invasion Warning Sub-Committee (it is convenient, and seems permissible, to retain the designation under which the Combined Intelligence Committee held its first meeting in the Admiralty on 31 May) offer an interesting study. This inter-service body, under a naval chairman, was only one of several intelligence agencies, and its conclusions were not necessarily accepted as authoritative by the Chiefs of Staff (to whom, however, unlike any comparable offshoot of the Service Ministries, it reported directly every day). The committee did nevertheless scrutinise all the evidence available in London which might seem to have a bearing on the enemy's intentions, and it is thus possible to obtain from its minutes some idea of what this evidence was and how it was assessed.

A German descent on Ireland was much on the committee's minds during the first week of June. Among other disturbing reports was one that "German soldiers in civilian clothes are embarking at

[1] See also the second footnote on p. 85.

Naples for Spain, whence they will be sent from Cadiz for an attack on Ireland." It is typical of the hectic, nightmarish atmosphere of the Dunkirk period—this was on 3 June—that this far-fetched contingency was carefully pondered. "It is known", commented the committee, "that young German male tourists have been arriving in Galicia. Some of them have uniforms with them and this is known to the police, who do not interfere. It is considered unlikely that an expedition will be organised in this manner but the situation will be watched." A few days later the committee dismissed as "unlikely" a report of German plans "for the mounting of long-range guns in the Calais-Boulogne area which may be used to cover a landing in the Dover area".

On 21 June (the day after Raeder for the second time discussed invasion with Hitler) the committee considered the report of a conversation in which the German Military Attaché in Ankara had outlined to a senior Turkish staff officer the German plan; he gave —prophetically, it must be presumed—an accurate forecast of the form which *Operation Sea Lion* finally took. "Presents no new features" was all the committee found to say about this curious scoop; but it was probably among the scraps of evidence indicating that "the enemy's plans might include the Channel" which caused Churchill—basically sceptical but tirelessly vigilant—to decide, on 27 June, that "it would be well if the Chiefs of Staff gave their attention to this rumour".

On the following day an almost identical preview of German intentions reached London from His Majesty's Ambassador in Bucharest. It laid, correctly, emphasis on the use of long-range artillery and minefields to cover the crossing of the Channel in its narrowest part. The committee, giving ground slightly, recommended that a sharp look-out should be kept for these fabled guns.[1]

[1] The two reports quoted above—and in particular the second, whose provenance suggests a "plant"—might be held to support the theory, which gained some currency in Germany after the war, that Admiral Canaris (then head of the *Abwehr* but executed in 1945 on a charge of treason) was actively trying to assist the British by forewarning them of Hitler's plans for invasion. On the dates in question no plans had been formulated, let alone made final. It cannot be proved that Canaris—who was Puckish, intuitive and unpredictable—had no hand in the transmission of this intelligence; but no evidence survives to implicate him in what may well have been a case of intelligent anticipation.

Despite, however, reliable information, received at the end of July, that the Luftwaffe had been forbidden to attack harbour installations in Channel ports, no menace to the south coast was discerned. As late as 23 August the committee, reviewing the general situation, concluded: "No serious threat of invasion yet exists from the Netherlands, French or south-west Norwegian ports. This is evidenced by the lack of shipping concentrations on these coasts."

On 29 August, however, photographs of Kiel and Emden showed that there were 40–50 merchant ships at Kiel, and 350 large motor launches at Emden, which had not been there a fortnight earlier; the launches were of a type not previously seen at Emden. The Invasion Warning Sub-Committee agreed that this was a "new and unusual feature" but remained unimpressed. Both concentrations, they felt, might have some sort of significance; but the merchant ships at Kiel were quite possibly held up there by "suspected mining or other temporary restrictions", while for the presence of 350 possible invasion-craft at Emden "some simple explanation in connection with canal or other water traffic may be the reason".

On 3 September photographs showed sudden and startling increases in the number of barges at Ostend (50 since 31 August), Terneuzen (140 since 16 August) and the south end of the Beveland Canal (90 since 1 September). The committee refused to be stampeded. "Ghent", they pointed out, "is important for (*a*) iron and steel; (*b*) textiles; (*c*) oil fuel storage. Probably barges are going south . . . to fetch these valuable products. . . . But movements preliminary to invasion are not impossible." The increase of barges at Ostend "is abnormal, but might be accounted for by the removal of obstructions in the canal system".

On 5 September the committee received with composure the news that leave throughout the German Army was being cancelled on the 8th. "Army leave", they pointed out, "is stopped from time to time without special incident." Photographs showing further increases of ships, barges, launches and even (at Cuxhaven) "three of the special *Stickenhorn* rafts" elicited only, on 6 September, the comment: "There is little evidence other than the movement of small craft towards the Channel ports to show that preparations for invasion of the U.K. are more advanced than they have been for some time. . . . If there is an intention to invade the expedition is [probably] being held in readiness in the Baltic or Hamburg."

At 2007 hours on the following day the code-word *Cromwell*, generally, though mistakenly,[1] taken to mean that invasion was either imminent or in progress, was issued to Home Forces. This false alarm seems to have shaken the *sangfroid* of the Invasion Warning Sub-Committee. They continued to expect the "main" expedition to come from Hamburg or the Baltic,[2] and they evolved a rather precious theory that the barge concentrations, so blatantly assembled, were really a decoy designed to divert our bombers from German targets and our attention from some more recondite operation. But they ceased to disbelieve automatically the evidence of their own eyes.

The Invasion Warning Sub-Committee was not (it must be repeated) the only agency drawing deductions from evidence which, neither plentiful nor illuminating until the end of August, became thereafter almost impossible to misinterpret. The committee's scepticism was viewed with alarm at the War Office, in one of whose remoter basements M.I.14 (the section of the Military Intelligence Directorate dealing with Germany) led a troglodytic and increasingly anxious existence. To them the lessons of the reconnaissance photographs (which now no longer arrived in a large envelope accompanied by a slip bearing the legend "With the Managing Director's compliments", for the civilian firm responsible for the production of the most important photographs had been absorbed into the Air Ministry a few weeks earlier) seemed unmistakable; and officers of this section, when they emerged into the sunlit, sociable streets found it difficult, in the light of their own knowledge of cross-Channel developments, to stomach the carefree

---

[1] See p. 281.

[2] As late as 11 September the GHQ Home Forces Intelligence Summary, while admitting that south-east England was immediately threatened, held that "the main effort is still likely from North German ports but there is no indication of its direction". On the 12th Home Forces toyed with the idea of either an attack on the east coast south of the Tyne or an airborne descent on London (where on that day all the main railway termini were reported closed by bombing). The cross-Channel threat had, the Summary implied, become almost too conspicuous to be true.

demeanour of their friends. M.I.14 did not know everything, or make all the right deductions from what they did know; but they were on the right track. There was some justification for the comment recorded on 13 September in the war diary of the Operations Branch of OKW. It referred to the Prime Minister's broadcast of 11 September, in which he had given in general terms an outline of the German preparations. "Churchill", the diarist (Greiner) wrote, "seems to be remarkably well-informed about *Operation Sea Lion*."

When conventional methods of obtaining intelligence draw a blank, as they did for the British throughout much of the summer, there is often a tendency to resort to esoteric expedients.

A minor example of this occurred in 1943, when the Japanese, after capturing Hong Kong, Malaya and finally Burma in the previous year, inflicted a local but crushing defeat on Indian Army forces in the Arakan. One of the main tactical problems in jungle warfare had proved to be the extreme difficulty of accurately locating the enemy's automatic weapons in dense cover, even when they came into action—as they often did—at little more than point-blank range. A temporary officer in the RAF, who in happier times had been an enthusiastic water-diviner, claimed to be able to solve this problem. The gift of dowsing, he asserted, was more widely distributed among the human race than most people realised, and it was particularly common among Indians, who formed at that time the bulk of the forces under British command confronting the Japanese. His own experiments had proved that it was just as easy to divine metal as it was to divine water; and he asked only for his powers, which he believed to be shared by at least one man in every section of infantry, to be tested against British weapons concealed in a training area.

They were tested. A form of martial hunt-the-thimble was organised, but the machine-gun-diviner failed in every instance to locate his quarry. He was returned to duty.

Research has failed to disclose what eventually happened to another water-diviner—then serving in the Royal Engineers—whose claims to be able to assess the imminence of invasion were for a time taken seriously in some quarters. This officer maintained that his gifts enabled him not only to locate but to estimate the size and rate of growth of the supply-dumps which the Germans were accumulating at the invasion ports. Accurate data of this kind were clearly a valuable guide to the enemy's state of readiness, and the ordnance-diviner was installed in comfortable quarters on the east coast and supplied with aerial photographs and other material calculated to stimulate his extra-sensory powers. Although he achieved nothing to the purpose, this was probably his finest hour.

Equally few traces have been left in the country's annals by the Hungarian astrologer whose aid was also enlisted in this crisis of her fortunes. The fact that Hitler was known to place considerable reliance on this branch of superstition provided some reason for the employment of a soothsayer in (so to speak) a counter-battery role; and M.I.14 were ordered to supply him with the dates of birth of all German officers above the rank of colonel whose particulars were recorded in their files. Apart from causing this small diversion of effort (which led to the useful discovery that more than half the War Office dossiers referred to officers who were either dead or in retirement) the soothsayer does not appear to have made any important contribution to the defence of the United Kingdom.[1]

Trivial though these details are, they may help to recapture some of the story-book atmosphere of those exciting months. Almost anything might happen, almost anything was worth trying. Carrier pigeons in cages were, for instance, dropped in fairly large numbers over Occupied Europe; written instructions told the finders what sort of military information was needed and how to send it back. The birds who returned in the summer of 1940 carried, at best, only simple, pathetic messages expressing faith in victory or hatred of the Boches; later in the war there were occasions when the pigeons brought accurate and valuable reports, and at least one man was shot by the Germans for sending them.

It is not quite true to say that in the field of intelligence the British,

[1] He did, however, record—apparently in the late autumn of 1940—his conviction that, astrologically speaking, "the first really good opportunity for the invasion of an island came only in the last ten days of May 1941". It was in these ten days that the Germans captured Crete. (Louis de Wohl: *The Stars in War and Peace*. London, 1952.)

once more, lost every battle but the last; but certainly it was late in the day before they arrived at a correct forecast of German strategy. There were several reasons for this. They overestimated the operational strength of the German Navy; they assumed, prudently but as it happened wrongly, that German plans for invasion were more advanced and more workmanlike than in fact they were; and above all they found it impossible to believe that Hitler, who for all their derision still remained a formidable and hypnotic figure, would come at them, as Julius Caesar and the Duke of Normandy had, by the shortest and most obvious way. As long as counter-invasion intelligence remained largely a matter of guesswork, the British tended to guess wrong; but from the moment, in the last days of August, when a body of relevant evidence began to come their way, they interpreted it sensibly and got the answer more or less right.

It would however be going too far to say that contemporary records bear out the conclusion, reached at this period by their enemies, that intelligence is "a field in which the British, by virtue of their tradition, their experience, and certain facets of their national character—unscrupulousness, self-control, cool deliberateness and ruthless action—have achieved an unquestionable degree of mastery".[1]

[1] *Informationsheft GB*. An analysis of certain British institutions printed in Germany in August 1940 for issue to the invading forces and described in the following chapter.

CHAPTER TWELVE

Margins of Error (2)
German Intelligence about the British

Geld
1 crown (kraun) = 1 krone = 2½ shillings
2 pennies   = twopence (tap'penß)
2 shilling 6 pence = 2 sh. 6d. oder 2′ 6″.

| Können Sie mir den | Can you show me | kan juh schoh mi |
| Weg nach Y zeigen? | the way to Y? | dhe ueh tu Y? |

From *Militärgeographische Angaben über England*,
a handbook printed for the use of the invading troops in August 1940

"You don't know much," said the Duchess, "and that's a fact."
Lewis Carroll: *Alice in Wonderland*

"WE are divided from England by a ditch 37 kilometres wide and we are not even able to get to know what is happening there!"[1] It was not until October 1941 that Hitler uttered these words, but they would have been equally apropos in the previous summer. "The intelligence available on the military preparedness of the island and on the coastal defences is meagre and not very reliable", Keitel complained to Ciano on 7 July; and although it came afterwards to be widely believed in Germany that the High Command knew all they needed to know for the purposes of an invasion, the evidence which has survived shows that this was hardly the case.

There was no single question to which the Germans needed an answer as badly as the British needed to know which sector of their coast was going to be attacked. It was however of great importance, as far as the Army was concerned, that the Germans should be adequately informed about the British order of battle—about, that is to say, the identities, the composition and the whereabouts

[1] *Adolf Hitler: Libres Propos sur la Guerre et la Paix.* Flammarion, Paris, 1952.

of the field formations who were waiting to repel them. It is doubtful whether more than a minority of senior officers held the view, put forward by Jodl at an OKW conference on 31 July, that "the German forces need to reckon only with a poor British army, which has not had time to apply the lessons learnt in this war"[1]; a more usual opinion was (as Hitler put it to his commanders-in-chief on 21 July) that "a defensively prepared and utterly determined enemy faces us". In any case all confident pre-conceptions became dangerously obsolete when it began to appear that the invading forces, so far from comprising 40 divisions, would have to be reduced to less than a third of that number.

As the weeks went by, and more and more difficulties appeared, and more and more operational handicaps were perforce accepted, the attackers knew, or had to assume, that the defenders' strength was increasing, until in the end reasonably accurate intelligence about the British dispositions in south-east England and the reserves available for that sector was a vital requirement for the commanders of 9 and 16 Armies.

No one in the German camp seems to have worried unduly on this score. The intelligence which the *Abwehr* supplied to OKW was jejune and erratic, and is not unfairly typified by the statement, made on 13 August in a report on British morale, that "even the Dunkirk combatants are not inclined to peace". The *Abwehr* made the following estimates of British strength: their minor but rather improbable fluctuations passed without comment.

23 August   34½ divisions (22 completely operational)
2 September   35½ divisions (16 allotted to coastal defence, 19½ in reserve)
17 September 34½ divisions (20 allotted to coastal defence, including 14 fully operational: 14½ in reserve, including 4 fully operational)

The actual strength of Home Forces at this time was 29 divisions; there were also eight independent brigades, of which six were armoured. All these formations were, in varying degrees, well below their establishment in personnel, weapons and equipment.

A more detailed, and more misleading, view of British dispositions

[1] See also p. 249 for a remarkable expression of OKH's optimism at this period.

survives in a map of the United Kingdom, overprinted under OKH auspices for use by 9 and 16 Armies, on what was to have been the eve of the invasion. This shows a total of 37 British divisions, and appears to be based largely on wireless intelligence. These formations can be subdivided as follows:

Divisions identified in their correct locations	5
Divisions identified within 30 miles of their correct locations	10
Divisions identified but placed in a completely wrong area	9
Divisions identified but marked "whereabouts unknown"	5
Divisions identified but not in existence	8
	37

Since all the divisions under the command of Home Forces had been identified, if not correctly located, and since the overestimate, by eight divisions, of the total British strength was for practical purposes largely offset by the Germans' failure to identify the eight independent brigades, the overall picture provided by the map would have given reasonably sound guidance to planners at a high level. But the German commanders in the bridgeheads, for whose benefit the map had been prepared, would have been in for some disconcerting shocks when (for instance) they encountered in Kent a division which they believed to be in Wales. XII Corps, the formation holding the south-eastern tip of England, was wrongly identified as XI Corps,[1] which lay in East Anglia, and the only one of its component divisions to be correctly identified was located in the wrong place. These may sound trivial technicalities, but in an awkward battle a commander's confidence is not increased if he discovers that most of what he thought he knew about the enemy is seriously wide of the mark.

Potentially more damaging than any of the curious errors which

[1] This mistake may well have originated in the fact that HQ XII Corps, an operational command, was superimposed shortly after Dunkirk on No. 11 District Headquarters, a purely administrative organisation. Specialists in such matters will find it odd that an *erratum* of this nature should have remained uncorrected for three months.

they made in piecing together the British order of battle was OKH's underestimate of the speed with which, once a bridgehead had been established, the defenders might be expected to counter-attack it. They believed, and based their planning on the belief, that it would take the British four days and nights to bring their reserves into action. This appreciation may have been influenced by the Luftwaffe's grandiloquent claims about its capacity to cut road and rail communications leading to the coast; but even so it seems strangely complacent and unrealistic. The whole British strategy was based on the swift deployment of that "mass of manoeuvre" which (as Churchill had cause to remember) had been fatally lacking in France; there would have been no breathing-space for the bridgeheads.[1]

In the OKH order-of-battle map a small but interesting sidelight is thrown on the limitations of the German Intelligence Service. Of the two British divisions stationed at that time in Northern Ireland, one is located by the Germans in London and the other is in the "whereabouts unknown" category; the garrison of Northern Ireland is tentatively estimated as comprising one unidentified division and "garrison troops and foreign formations of unknown strength". With a German Legation and a small German business community in Dublin, and with plenty of Irishmen on both sides of the Ulster border harbouring grievances against the British, this gap in the Germans' knowledge is unexpected; and it reflects small credit on the talents of the only spy known to have been in unsupervised wireless communication with the *Abwehr* from the British Isles during this period.

Dr Herman Goertz, a lieutenant on the reserve of the Luftwaffe, was dropped by parachute in County Meath on the night of 5/6 May 1940. He was fifty years old and in 1936 had been sentenced to four years' imprisonment for spying, conscientiously but not very

[1] Cf. the minute on "Defence Against Invasion" sent by Churchill to the Chiefs of Staff Committee on 5 August: "The defence of any part of the coast must be measured, not by the forces on the coast, but by the number of *hours* within which strong counter-attacks by mobile troops can be brought to bear upon the landing places. Such attacks should be hurled with the utmost speed and fury upon the enemy at his weakest moment."

usefully, on RAF airfields. In Maidstone gaol, where he served his sentence, he met several members of the Irish Republican Army. His mission in 1940, which seems to have been loosely if at all defined, had some connection with an unpractical plan, code-named *Kathleen*, for a German invasion of Ireland; this had been submitted to the *Abwehr* in Hamburg by an emissary of the IRA.

Goertz was dropped—in the wrong place—wearing German uniform and carrying military identity papers made out in a false name. He failed to recover the parachute and container with his wireless set and other equipment in it, and set off to walk to a rendezvous in County Wicklow, 70 miles away. He swam the River Boyne "with", as he afterwards wrote, "great difficulty since the weight of my fur combination exhausted me. This swim also cost me the loss of my invisible ink." Soon, exhausted by hunger and strain, he was in worse case, and discarded his uniform; "I was now in high boots, breeches and jumper, with a little black beret on my head. . . . I kept my military cap as a vessel for drinks and my war medals for sentimental reasons. . . . I had no Irish money and did not realise that I could use English money quite freely." [1]

Although with Irish help he established wireless contact with Germany and was not arrested by the Irish police until November 1941, Goertz—out of depth in the intricate cross-currents of IRA politics—achieved nothing. In 1947, when told that he was to be repatriated to Germany, he took poison; the reasons for his suicide are not known. He earns a place in this narrative on two counts. The lonely, brave, baffled figure trudging across the empty Irish landscape in jackboots, with a little black beret on his head and a pocket full of 1914–18 medals, is a reminder of how far the German intelligence effort fell short of those standards of subtlety and dissimulation which were expected of it, and against which the precautions taken in the United Kingdom inflicted upon the life of the whole nation a kind of mild, pervasive cramp.

The other interesting thing about Goertz is that early in 1941 (he did not specify the month) the *Abwehr* transmitted to him on several nights in succession the order: "Report immediately about Irish defence forces. Order from the highest authority." These

[1] *Irish Times*, 25 August to 10 September 1947.

instructions were almost certainly an echo of the curious epilogue to *Sea Lion*, when, in the winter of 1940–41, Hitler, after ordering the attack on Russia to be mounted, toyed with the idea of an occupation of Ireland as a means of eliminating Britain from the war before it became a war on two fronts.[1]

The *Abwehr* sponsored one other, and on paper more promising, Irish adventure. Two prominent IRA leaders, Sean Russell and Frank Ryan, had made their way to Germany and volunteered for clandestine operations against Britain. On 8 August 1940 they set off for Ireland in a U-boat, taking with them a few adherents whom they recruited from among the Irishmen in prisoner-of-war camps; they had a wireless transmitter and an assortment of sabotage equipment. Russell was given no specific task but told that his operations were to be co-ordinated with the forthcoming invasion of England; he would be notified of its timing at the last moment "by a signal still to be agreed upon (for instance a bunch of red flowers in front of a particular window in the German Legation in Dublin)".[2]

These primitive methods of communication chime incongruously with the role allotted in the minds of the British security authorities to the German Legation, which was assumed to be a potent and resourceful centre of espionage and subversion.[3] In fact they were never used, for Ryan died of a heart attack while the submarine was on passage and—though it is not clear why this casualty should have been deemed fatal to the expedition's prospects—the party returned to Germany and was disbanded.

As the plans for *Sea Lion* took shape, the extent to which they were hampered by lack of accurate intelligence came to be appreciated by the German Supreme Command, and the *Abwehr*, whose reputation at the time was high, endeavoured to remedy this state of affairs by

[1] See also pp. 296–297.
[2] De Jong.
[3] "The security authorities in London had to reckon with the possibility that the German and Italian Embassies in Dublin might become the focus of a widespread espionage movement throughout the British Isles." J. W. Blake: *Northern Ireland at War*. London, 1956. The two diplomatic missions referred to by the official historian had the status of Legations, not of Embassies, in 1940.

Farewell parade of parachute spies before starting for the Scottish Highlands.
Punch, 3 January 1940

large-scale improvisation. In September a shower of spies descended
on the United Kingdom; all were taken into custody by the British
authorities. They were for the most part low-grade agents who
had not completed their training. The *Abwehr* seems to have
realised that their chances of doing useful work or even of escaping
detection were not high; but they were only expected to remain in
the field for a few weeks, and it was hoped that any who got into
trouble would be got out of it when the German troops arrived.
At any rate a number of inferior spies were more likely to produce
results than no spies at all, and early in September this clandestine
traffic began in earnest. Let us follow the fortunes of two parties
sent across; they give an adequate idea of the *Abwehr*'s methods at
this time.

On 2 September 1940 four German agents embarked at Le
Touquet in a fishing boat which was escorted across the Channel
by two minesweepers. According to one of the men the fishing boat's crew consisted, improbably, of three Russians and a
Latvian; another said it was manned by two Norwegians and one
Russian. All had confused memories of the voyage, and it seems
possible that they were drunk.

The spies were to hunt in couples. One pair, after transhipping to a dinghy, landed near Hythe in the early hours of 3 September. They had a wireless set and an elementary form of cipher, and their orders were to send back information of military importance; they had been given to understand that an invasion of the Kentish coast was imminent. By 5.30 a.m. on the same morning both men, although they separated on landing, had been challenged and made prisoner by sentries of a battalion of the Somersetshire Light Infantry.

This was hardly surprising. The two men were of Dutch nationality. They were completely untrained for their difficult task; their sole qualification for it seems to have lain in the fact that each, having committed some misdemeanour which was known to the Germans, could be blackmailed into undertaking the enterprise. Neither had more than a smattering of English, and one suffered, by virtue of having had a Japanese mother, from the additional hazard of a markedly Oriental appearance; he it was who, when first sighted by an incredulous private of the Somersets in the early dawn, had binoculars and a spare pair of shoes slung round his neck.

The other pair of spies consisted of a German, who spoke excellent French but no English at all, and a man of abstruse origins who claimed to be a Dutchman and who, alone of the four, had a fluent command of English. They landed at Dungeness under cover of darkness on 3 September, and soon after daybreak were suffering acutely from thirst, a fact which lends colour to the theory that on the previous night the whole party had relied on Dutch courage to an unwise extent. The English-speaker, pardonably ignorant of British licensing laws, tried to buy cider at breakfast-time in a public house at Lydd. The landlady pointed out that this transaction could not legally take place until ten o'clock and suggested that meanwhile he should go and look at the church. When he returned (for she was a sensible woman) he was arrested.

His companion, the only German in the party, was not caught until the following day. He had rigged up an aerial in a tree and had begun to send messages (in French) to his controllers. Copies of three of these messages survived and were used in evidence against him at his trial. They were short and from an operational point of view worthless; the news (for instance) that "*this is exact position*

*yesterday evening six o'clock three messerschmitt fired machine guns in my
direction three hundred metres south of water reservoir painted red*" was in
no way calculated to facilitate the establishment of a German bridgehead in Kent.

All four spies were tried, under the Treason Act, 1940, in November. One of the blackmailed Dutchmen was acquitted; the other
three men were hanged in Pentonville Prison in the following month.
Their trials were conducted *in camera*, but short, factual obituary
announcements were published after the executions.

Two men and a woman, who on the night of 30 September 1940
were landed by a rubber dinghy on the coast of Banffshire after
being flown thither from Norway in a seaplane, had—and, except
by virtue of their courage, deserved—no more luck than the agents
deposited in Kent. They were arrested within a few hours of their
arrival. During those hours their conduct had been such as to attract
the maximum of suspicion. This—since both men spoke English with
a strong foreign accent and the documents of all three were clumsily
forged—they were in no position to dispel; and the first of them to
be searched by the police was found to have in his possession, *inter
alia*: a wireless set; a loaded Mauser automatic; an electric torch
marked "made in Bohemia"; a list of bomber and fighter stations
in East Anglia; £327 in English notes; and a segment of German
sausage. Both men—one a German, the other a Swiss—were in due
course hanged. Although *Sea Lion* had for practical purposes been
cancelled before they left Norway, one of them had been given, like
the men in Kent, a purely tactical role connected with the invasion.

The one serious leakage of secret information known to have
occurred during the period was not contrived by the German
intelligence. The principal persons concerned in this strange episode
were a young American born in China, the then Member of Parliament for Peebles and Midlothian, and the daughter of a former
admiral in the Russian Navy. The American, Tyler Kent, was a
thirty-year-old cipher-clerk employed in the United States Embassy.
Five years earlier, while holding a similar position in Moscow, he had
formed the habit of keeping copies of the more important messages
which passed through his hands, and he resumed this practice when

transferred to London in October 1939. According to his own story, his motives, though muddled, were pure. He disapproved of the manner in which American foreign policy was conducted, felt that the loyalty he owed to his country as a whole was at least equal to the loyalty he owed to whichever of her representatives he happened to be serving, and accumulated his hoard of documents against a day when he might feel it his duty to reveal their unsatisfactory contents to influential Congressmen. It seems quite possible that this explanation was more or less true.

In London Kent made the acquaintance of Anna Wolkoff,[1] a lady some ten years older than himself, and was drawn into the orbit of the "Right Club", a small, seedy clique of anti-semites, whose dedicated members went round in the blackout sticking up hand-bills which proclaimed "This is a Jews' War". Prominent among these unbalanced cranks (but unlike some of them a staunch anti-Nazi) was Captain A. H. M. Ramsay, an Old Etonian, a Member of Parliament and an officer with a good record in the First World War; Anna Wolkoff called herself his ADC.

By January 1940 Kent's collection of documents had begun to include copies of the messages exchanged between Churchill (then First Sea Lord) and President Roosevelt; these were des-patched through the United States Embassy. Of those which came into Kent's possession, none was of the first importance but all would have been of value to the enemy. In February he applied for, but was refused, a transfer to Berlin. When at his trial Counsel for the Prosecution asked Kent whether, if his application had been granted, he meant to take the documents with him and make them over to the Germans, Kent replied that the question was hypothetical.

He had however begun to show these documents indiscriminately to his comrades in the fight against the Jews and the Freemasons, Captain Ramsay and Anna Wolkoff. The latter had a close associa-tion with an Assistant Military Attaché of the Italian Embassy. It was not proved that she transmitted to him any of the interesting information to which she now had access; but on 23 May the German Ambassador in Rome (Mackensen) telegraphed to Berlin

[1] See pp. 126-127.

an accurate summary of Roosevelt's reply to Churchill's first message in the "Former Naval Person" series to be sent after he became Prime Minister.[1] Churchill's message was transmitted on 15 May and included a request for 40 or 50 of "your older destroyers". The reply—a sympathetic one—was sent from Washington on the 16th but was not received by the Prime Minister until the 18th. Earlier messages in the same series had passed through Wolkoff's hands and had been photographed; and it seems probable that Kent had thus been indirectly instrumental in furnishing the Italians with copies of these important communications. Certainly the formula employed by Mackensen in prefacing his report ("I am reliably informed from an unimpeachable source . . .") suggests that his excellent intelligence was derived from access to a verbatim version of the President's message; and this impression is strengthened by internal evidence in his telegram. This was a dangerous leakage. The secrets to which Kent (who for more than five years, without incurring suspicion, had been systematically betraying the trust reposed in him by the State Department) now had access really mattered. A grave threat to British security had come fortuitously into existence.

But it had come into existence under the microscope automatically focused by the authorities on such blatantly dubious organisations as the "Right Club". Kent and Wolkoff were arrested on 18 May (the American Ambassador having waived the former's title to diplomatic immunity as a member of the Embassy staff) and tried *in camera* at the Old Bailey. Kent was sentenced to seven years' imprisonment, Anna Wolkoff to ten. Captain Ramsay, who could not be shown to have broken any law by his fervent but tangential activities, was interned under Section 18(B) of the Defence Regulations on 23 May. He continued at intervals, as was his right, to assert in written communications to the Speaker of the House of Commons the thesis that his detention constituted a breach of Parliamentary privilege. The House debated this matter in December 1940 and decided that no breach of its privileges was involved. Ramsay was not released until after the war; he died in 1955.

[1] *Documents on German Foreign Policy 1918–1945.* Series D, Vol. IX. 1956.

In 1940 the schisms, caused mainly by the internecine war between the *Abwehr* under Canaris and the *Sicherheitsdienst* under Himmler, which later reft and stultified German Intelligence, had not begun to provide an explanation for its inefficiency. Its standards, even so, were not high. Some idea of its limitations may be gained from a report dated 5 September 1940 and headed "England: Fortifications on the South Coast", for which a place was found in the files of the Supreme Command of the German Navy. It read as follows:

A secret agent reported on September 2:

The area Tunbridge Wells to Beachy Head, especially the small town of Rye (where there are large sand-hills) and also St Leonards, is distinguished by a special labyrinth of defences. These defences, however, are so well camouflaged that a superficial observer on the sand-hills, bathing spots and fields, would not discover anything extraordinary. This area is extremely well guarded, so that it is almost impossible to reach there without a special pass.

In Hastings, on the other hand, most of the defences can be recognized quite plainly. In the town there are troops of every kind. The presence of numerous small and heavy tanks is most striking.

Numerous armoured cars were also seen in St Leonards and in a small locality where there is a famous golf-course, probably St Joseph.

Comment by the Abwehr:

The agent was not able to give a clearer account of the number of armoured cars in the different localities, or of the regiments he saw there.

From the position of Beachy Head (west of Hastings) and Rye (east of Hastings), it can be deduced that the place in question near St Leonards was the western villa-suburb of Hastings. Tunbridge, which lies on the railway line from Hastings to London, must, according to the sense of the report, also lie on the coast, but, as in the case of St Joseph, this cannot be confirmed from the charts in our possession.

Both Tunbridge Wells and Tonbridge are some thirty miles inland from Beachy Head. It is just possible that the spy's geography was bedevilled by an odd coincidence. In 1940 the post office at Camber-on-Sea (a small village about ten miles east of Hastings) was kept by a Mr Tunbridge, and after the obliteration of all place-names in May the sign over his premises read:

TUNBRIDGE
POST OFFICE AND STORES

But the agent's report is worthless by any standards, and the serious attempts made by the *Abwehr* to evaluate it suggest two things: first, that the receipt of any report from an agent in England was a rare and notable event,[1] and secondly that the *Abwehr*, which was prepared to doubt the reliability of the Ordnance Survey before calling in question the accuracy of an obviously inept spy, did not know its job.

There was, however, one field in which German Intelligence scored an important success. The Royal Navy's official historian writes:

It must be admitted that, during the early months of the war, the procurement by the enemy of intelligence regarding our warship dispositions and movements was superior to our own. It is now plain that the enemy's advantage in this respect was achieved, firstly, through regular air reconnaissance of our bases and, secondly, through the study he had made of our wireless traffic, which could and did reveal to him a great deal.

The Germans had in fact broken and were reading the British naval ciphers, and this was not realised in London until the late summer. Then, in August, the ciphers were changed. A post-war German account[2] reveals how important to their Naval Staff this source of intelligence had been:

A great setback for German naval strategy at this time [was caused] by the change by the Admiralty of naval codes and ciphers. The insight into British operations, which had lasted so long, thus came to an end. Knowledge of British movements had spared German vessels many a surprise encounter with superior forces and this had become an element of operational planning.

1 "It seems incredible," Ciano lamented on 11 September, "but we [the Italians] do not have a single informant in Great Britain. On the other hand, the Germans have many. In London itself there is a German agent who makes radio transmissions up to 29 times a day. *At least it is so stated by Admiral Canaris.*" (*Ciano's Diary.*) The italics, which are not Ciano's, seem to be all the comment needed. Goebbels is said to have seen one agent's report from London in September; this disclosed that the state of emergency in the capital was such that titled ladies had to relieve themselves in Hyde Park. (Wilfred von Oven: *Mit Goebbels bis zum Ende.* Buenos Aires, 1950. Quoted by de Jong.)

2 Quoted by Roskill.

One enduring monument to the work of the German Intelligence in preparing for the invasion of England survives. The German forces were to have been provided with handbooks of an encyclopaedic character, together with a set of seven maps. Each map covered the whole of the United Kingdom and each dealt with a different aspect of its topography—geology, waterways, density of population and so on. There were also street-plans—reproduced from those published by the Automobile Association—of every town and city. Hundreds of thousands of these bulky vade-mecums were captured by the British towards the end of the war; they filled several warehouses.[1]

One of the handbooks was that already referred to in connection with the fake parachute-drops in mid-August. It contained 174 photographs, the majority taken from the air, of views, scenery and buildings in England and Wales. Forty-seven of these photographs had appeared in *The Times* during the previous ten years, and the rest seem to have been methodically collated from the pages of such periodicals as *Country Life* and the *Illustrated London News*; one, for instance, shows the official opening of the Mersey Tunnel for road traffic in 1934. They comprise a number of views of ports and harbours (including the "harbour" of the tiny Cornish village of Mousehole), but many are merely pictures of beauty-spots or famous buildings. From a cultural point of view there may have been something to be said for issuing the German infantry with photographs of Tintern Abbey or Blackpool Tower, but operationally they would have had negligible value.

Another handbook, entitled *Military-Geographical Data about England*, contained a well-ordered mass of information ranging from the bed-capacity of individual hospitals to the suitability of different regions for mechanised warfare. The gasworks at Wigston Magna,

[1] Schellenberg, in 1940 a rising star in the *Sicherheitsdienst*, claims in Chapter X of his *Memoirs* (London, 1956) to have been responsible for the production of these handbooks; "this task [he wrote] occupied a great deal of my time." But Chapter XI makes it clear that he spent most of the relevant weeks in Lisbon, trying to kidnap the Duke of Windsor. There may be a few grains of truth in each of these stories; there are none in Schellenberg's statement that the entire edition of 20,000 handbooks was destroyed in his office during an air-raid in 1943.

the length of the pier at Aberdovey, the museum at Saffron Walden —all were scrupulously set down; and the details extracted from guide-books and works of reference were here and there supplemented by the fruits of elementary peacetime espionage, such as information about the location of airfields, coastal batteries and other permanent military installations.

This solid and creditable piece of work ends with a few hints on the English language, and even provides a short glossary of Welsh and Gaelic words. Its compilers had curious preconceptions about the vocabulary most likely to prove useful during the invasion. "Sewage works", "submarine contours", "War Office" and "lunatic asylum" all occur several times under different headings, and it is not easy to reconstruct circumstances in which a German soldier would have wanted to talk to the British about "the bottom of the sea (bot'tim ov dhe ßie)". Nor has "Where is the next tank?" the hallmark of a phrase that was bound to come in useful sooner or later.

But the most curious of the German handbooks, and the only one marked "Secret", was the *Informationsheft GB*, which appears to have been the work of the Gestapo. It was intended to guide the security and intelligence services both in their quest for loot and in their efforts to eliminate for ever the traditional sources of anti-German feeling in Great Britain.

The first of the latter were the public schools, "which deserve special attention. . . . Vital anti-German propaganda material and documents of political and historical importance are to be found there". After noting that "Eton is booked up to the year 1949" and commenting on the recent increase in former public schoolboys among the leaders of the Labour Party, the authors concluded: "The whole system is calculated to rear men of inflexible will and ruthless energy who regard intellectual problems as a waste of time but know human nature and how to dominate other men in the most unscrupulous fashion."

Scarcely less pernicious than the public schools was the Boy Scout movement. Although its world-wide ramifications "may outwardly concern themselves with the pre-military training of youth in the countries concerned, for England the Boy Scout movement

The Home Guard (steel helmets) training with the Army (packs and Bren-gun carrier): a typical Sunday morning scene in the autumn of 1940.

A flame barrage in action: one of the few successful experiments.

On 27 September 1940 the House of Commons
sustained damaged for the first, but not last time.

A Heinkel III over the Thames during the first
great attack on London, 7 September 1940.

The arm-band and shot-gun stage:
members of the Mid-Devon Hunt patrolling Dartmoor.

The old soldier.

London Docks burning on Sunday, 8 September 1940.

A bomber's-eye view of the barges.

"Must you say 'Well, we're still here' *every* morning?" Pont.

Children being evacuated from London.

Above: A bomb-disposal squad at work on a 12,000-lb. bomb in the grounds of a hospital. The officer is Lt. R. Davies, who was awarded the first George Cross for gallantry in the St Paul's incident. *Below*: A 14-inch gun of the Royal Marines shelling the German heavy batteries on Cap Gris Nez.

represents a camouflaged but powerful instrument of British cultural propaganda and an excellent source of information for the British Intelligence Service. . . . The liquidation of the Austrian Scout movement produced proof, among other things, of the link between the Scout movement and the [British] Secret Service."

A general survey, couched in what can only be described as chop-licking terms, of British museums and art galleries follows. Their contents—in many of which "the German Reich is bound to have a special interest"—have been "stolen from all over the world"; there are a number of portraits of Jews in the National Gallery; and "attention must also be drawn to the treasures of various churches".

Religion is the next item dealt with. It was not viewed favourably. The Church of England is "nothing but a tool of Empire power politics". Roman Catholicism is no better, but in "Britain it is to a large extent maintained by people of Irish extraction. This offers certain limited possibilities for employing Catholicism against people belonging to the Church of England." Most dangerous and objectionable of all was the Religious Division of the Ministry of Information; "the records of this department should be secured without fail".[1] A confused account of the Buchmanite Oxford Group Movement credits Halifax (then Foreign Secretary) with its leadership; his principal lieutenants—all save one of them noble —include the Earl of Athlone and the Marquess of Salisbury.

An ill-informed survey of Communist, left-wing and *émigré* organisations follows, and after that a rambling account of the sinister part played in British national life by Jews and Freemasons. The only reference—a vague and tentative one—to people who might be expected to collaborate with the Germans concerns a group of Ukrainian *émigrés*; there is no mention of the British Union of Fascists, several of whose better-known members appear in the "Special Search List" (*Sonderfahndungsliste GB*), a curious document dealt with later in this chapter. A long but incomplete list of Trades

[1] For a satirical pastiche—from which the above sentence might well have been taken—purporting to describe the religious activities of the Ministry of Information in 1940, see *Put Out More Flags*, by Evelyn Waugh (London, 1942). This novel is an excellent guide to the atmosphere of the period.

Unions and similiar organisations, with the addresses of their head-quarters, includes the Amalgamated Society of Journeyman Felt Hatters and the Rossendale Union of Boot, Shoe and Slipper Operatives; this list seems to have been compiled for the sake of compiling a list.

The organisation of the police—an easier target for analysis than anything attempted in the first 80 pages of the *Informationsheft*—is described with some degree of accuracy. A photostat replica of the Metropolitan Police List for February 1937—a document measuring some 28 inches by 20 inches—is included; and locations are given for the central fingerprint branch (on the third floor in New Scotland Yard), the forensic laboratories at Hendon, the Special Branch card indexes, and the files of the Aliens Records Office at 28 Bow Street.[1]

In the last section of the booklet an attempt is made to analyse the organisation and characteristics of the British Intelligence Service, which "has contributed in no small measure to the creation and preservation of the British Empire". Apart from some scraps of factual information obtained from the interrogation of two captured British officers, this section is marred by inaccuracy and pedantry. The writer's approach to his subject is novelettish; he sees the British Intelligence Service as a mechanism of diabolical potency, wishes that Germany could build up something half as effective,[2] and takes comfort from an article in a Toulon newspaper which notes a falling-off from the Secret Service's pristine omnipotence since "the Irish and colonial elements which once predominated among its personnel" began to be replaced by less *rusés* operators.[3]

[1] The Germans had a special interest in aliens. The exodus of Jewish and other refugees from Germany, Austria and Czechoslovakia, and later from territories occupied during the war, had harmed the German cause. Many of these fugitives had said or written, and in a few cases done, things which rendered them liable to the barbaric reprisals which under the Nazis passed for justice.

[2] "What we need", Hitler had once declared, "is something like the British Secret Service—an Order, doing its work with passion." (Rauschning.)

[3] For an even sillier thesis on this subject, see *Der Englische Geheimdienst* by Dr Alfred Seid, a booklet published in Hamburg in 1940 and later circulated as an official document. The author traces the origins of the Secret Service back to the Plantaganets, identifies Christopher Marlowe and Ben Jonson with its nefarious activities, and includes among its achievements the sinking of the cruiser *Hampshire*, with Kitchener on board, in 1916.

At the end of the *Informationsheft* there are four pages of passport-type photographs—thirty in all—of men and women, mostly with German or Central European names. It appears from the "Special Search List" that these individuals were to be arrested on sight. The main body of this list consists of some 2,300 names and addresses of British citizens or aliens resident in Britain; against each appears the number of the Gestapo section in whose files particulars of the individual are to be found.

Most of the Britons on the list were persons of some prominence—peers, members of parliament, writers, publishers, editors, trade unionists, diplomats and so on. Men and women of every political persuasion are included, and there is little to suggest that the list was a "Black List" or that any action was necessarily intended against the individuals whose names—freely misprinted [1]—appeared on it.

The list almost certainly represents a collation of all the names of British citizens or residents recorded, for whatever reason, on the files of the German security authorities. Some people appeared on it because they were known, from their speeches or writings, to be anti-German; others seem to have been there for such arbitrary or coincidental reasons as the fact that they had business connections with Germany, had held a diplomatic or consular post in Europe, or had written about world affairs. The impression that the list was made up by lumping indiscriminately together all the British names to be found in the dossiers of the security authorities is strengthened by an appendix to it; this records the registration numbers of some twenty British-owned cars "which have been in Germany in suspicious circumstances". [2]

It is easy to smile at the errors and naïvetés of these painstaking

[1] The misprints may have been due to hasty proof-reading, but there are in addition many easily avoidable inaccuracies. For example, Colonel Strong, who in 1940 was head of M.I.14 and had served as Assistant Military Attaché in Germany immediately before the war, is shown as a naval officer.

[2] It is often said that the Germans compiled a "White List", containing the names of Britons on whose collaboration they believed they could rely. Those who vouch for its existence have, in my experience, never actually seen it themselves, and it seems improbable that any such list was in fact made, or, if made, had any pretensions to accuracy.

documents. In fact they represented a considerable achievement. Compiled and printed in a matter of weeks—they were ready for issue to the staffs concerned by the end of August—they would not greatly have aided the fighting troops in the mêlée of an invasion; but to the invaders' administrative services, and later to an army of occupation, they would have been of real value. When, earlier in the year, von Falkenhorst had received his orders to lead the invasion of Norway, his first action had been to go out and buy a Baedeker. This time the German General Staff had eliminated the need for any such makeshifts.

The complete set of documents—the maps, photographs, street-plans, topographical data, tables translating yards into metres and shillings into marks, summaries of British constitutional history and all the rest of it—was large enough to fill a small haversack. Those who ordered this work to be done and those who, in a very short time, did it can hardly be dismissed as dilettantes, or accused of not taking *Operation Sea Lion* seriously.

CHAPTER THIRTEEN

Expedients and Improvisations

Mr Loftus: Is the honourable gentleman aware that the Mayor of Lowestoft has twice camouflaged his car?

Hansard, 19 September 1940

AT the time of Dunkirk the British Army was quite incapable of preventing the Germans, if they eluded the Royal Navy, from landing on the coast; and its ability to outfight an invading force of any size once it had got ashore was, to say the least, open to doubt.

If the half-trained soldiers, with five or ten rounds apiece, were not prepared to admit this, their leaders were. The Chiefs of Staff, in an otherwise sturdily optimistic appreciation of the situation at the end of May, felt obliged to record their view that: "Should the Germans succeed in establishing a force with its vehicles in this country, our Army forces have not got the offensive power to drive it out."

Almost all the fully-trained men, and almost all the available arms and ammunition, had been sent overseas. It was not only the BEF in France that had drained the depots and the arsenals. The Middle East, where Wavell faced superior Italian forces on four or five widely separated fronts, had to be supplied. So had the fortresses—Gibraltar and Malta, Hong Kong and Singapore. India, Burma and West Africa had their needs; and at the end of the queue isolated garrisons plaintively made known their small but cumulative wartime wants from Belize, Sarawak, the Seychelles and other outposts.

The last formations to join the BEF had been seriously deficient in training and equipment:

It was with this travesty of an armoured division [wrote one of their commanders afterwards]—a formation with less than half its proper armoured strength, without any field guns or a proper complement of anti-tank and anti-aircraft guns, without infantry, without air support, without the bulk of its ancillary services, and with part of its head-quarters in a three-ply wooden "armoured" command vehicle—that I was ordered to force a crossing over a defended, unfordable river, and afterwards to advance some sixty miles, through four *real* armoured divisions, to the help of the British Expeditionary Force.[1]

The fact that such a scratch force was thought fit to take the field augured badly for the state of the reserves left behind.

A document survives which gives a general but accurate picture of the strength of Home Forces on 8 June. It was prepared for the Assistant Chief of the Naval Staff on the basis of information supplied by the War Office, and was studied in the Admiralty with despondency.

After pointing out that three weeks were expected to elapse before the BEF was reformed, the War Office disclosed that meanwhile fifteen infantry divisions (including one in Northern Ireland) and one armoured division were in being.[2] The average strength of the infantry divisions was just under 11,000 all ranks, or rather more than half their establishment. Of the sixteen divisions, two had done no divisional training, five had done very little, and nine had reached a standard described as "fair".

After listing various holding battalions, training centres, and home defence battalions composed of old soldiers armed only with rifles, and noting that most of these were already committed to the static defence of vulnerable points, the report dealt with *Equipment at present available*. The most important items were the following:

2 pounder anti-tank guns[3]	54
Bren guns[4]	about 2,300

---

[1] Joan Bright: *The 9th Queen's Royal Lancers, 1936–1945*. Aldershot, 1951.

[2] 51 (Highland) Division was still fighting in France, whence only a few survivors returned. So were the remnants of 1 Armoured Division. On 13 June 1 Canadian Division, 52 Division and certain other forces were placed under orders to cross to France; but the "reconstituted BEF", as it was officially called, had to be withdrawn through Brest and Cherbourg soon after it had landed. (Col. C. P. Stacey: *Official History of the Canadian Army in the Second World War*, Vol. 1. Ottawa, 1955.)

[3] In France these guns had proved useless against all save the lightest German tanks.

[4] 2,300 Bren guns would have barely sufficed to bring five divisions up to the scale of equipment authorised in those days.

2 in. and 3 in. mortars	very few and little ammunition
Armoured cars	37 (in England)
	15 (in N. Ireland)
Light tanks	395
Infantry tanks	72
Cruiser tanks	33
Field guns	420 (with 200 rounds per gun)
Medium and heavy guns[1]	163 (with 150 rounds per gun)

These slender totals did not represent the reserves of equipment standing in Ordnance Depots; they were *all* the weapons with which inexperienced troops would have had to oppose the invader had he got ashore early in June. With the cupboard as bare as this, it was inevitable that the British should turn to improvisation.

An account has been given in Chapter 5 of the events which led to the mustering of the Local Defence Volunteers—announced in a broadcast by Eden on 14 May—as a measure to meet the emergency created by the successful German offensive in France and the Low Countries. The response was immediate. Within six days more than a quarter of a million men had been enrolled, and by August the Home Guard (as the volunteers had been redesignated) had a strength of more than a million.

The problems attending the overnight creation of a citizen army, for which no arms, no uniforms and no organisation existed when it was urgently called to the colours, were diverse and formidable. Police stations, besieged by applicants, ran out of enrolment forms. At first nobody knew what to do with these forms when they had been completed; the police had been forbidden to hand them over to anyone other than "a properly appointed commander", but no properly appointed commanders existed, nor was there any machinery for appointing them. At this juncture the Lords Lieutenant of counties were brought in to play, in consultation with the senior military commander in their area, much the same parts as they had played in the days of the Armada and of Napoleon. They selected retired officers as Area, Zone or Group Organisers, and these chose commanders for the different localities (some of which had however

[1] There were also 47 coastal-defence batteries of two guns each. These had very little ammunition, and the guns were very old.

already elected or acclaimed their own). At that time it was envisaged that no unit larger than a company would be formed and that rank would be dispensed with; later officers of the Home Guard were granted the King's Commission, and in populous areas the companies were expanded to battalions, which were controlled by a Zone Headquarters. On 30 May GHQ Home Forces, which expected at any moment to have a decisive battle on its hands, passed on the complex and growing burden of Home Guard administration to the War Office, where in due course a Director-General with a small staff was appointed to look after this huge part-time army. On 3 August 1940 Home Guard units were formally affiliated to their county regiments and permitted to wear their badges.[1]

"How does one fly to arms?" The question is asked by a lukewarm patriot in the Edwardian melodrama about invasion, *An Englishman's Home.* In 1909 the playwright could evade it; in 1940 the British Government and people could not. To have raised a quarter of a million men in six days was on paper a creditable achievement; in practice it would make little difference to the prospects of the airborne invaders—then expected to arrive at any moment—until the men had been given arms and ammunition, and the novices (the majority were old soldiers) trained in their use.

The total available stock of rifles in the country was believed to be 70,000; these were supplemented by a miscellaneous collection of 20,000 firearms handed in to police stations as the result of an appeal (they included several from the gunroom at Sandringham). To this meagre armoury a number of picturesque additions were made. In Manchester several rifles used in the Indian Mutiny were obtained from the Zoological Gardens. Four dozen rusty Lee Enfields, relics of some forgotten tableau or drama, were discovered among the stage properties at Drury Lane. The Norwich Museum yielded not only ancient muskets but a sentry box of the same period. In Essex an unexpected windfall made possible the formation of a Cutlass Platoon, twenty-four strong, under the command of a former naval rating. Rook-rifles, kukris, assegais, ancestral sabres, golf clubs, axes and many improvised variants of the bludgeon and the spear were carried on patrol in the early days; "these" (it was

[1] Graves.

suggested in the orders of one unit) "could be usefully supplemented by a packet of pepper to interfere with the vision of any persistent unwelcome visitor".[1] Some men, no doubt, took up these weapons as a gesture or for a joke; but mostly they were borne for the simple and sufficient reason that, although they were not good weapons, they were better than none at all.

The first recorded Home Guard patrols were sent out by what later became the Worthing Battalion of the Sussex Home Guard twenty-four hours after Eden's broadcast appeal on 14 May; and on 17 May an order from Eastern Command for patrols to be carried out by 1,500 Home Guards in Kent and Sussex seems to have been complied with. At this stage the volunteers were called by the news-papers "Parashots"; and a War Office statement ("the need is greatest in small towns, villages and less densely populated areas") underlined the overriding importance attached to the danger of airborne invasion.

The reactions of German propaganda to the Home Guard were vehement, and many a worthy citizen, armed only with a brassard and an ash-plant, felt obscurely flattered at being reviled as an unscrupulous *franc tireur*, a member of a "murder-band" whose mere existence constituted a breach of international law. Ponderous attempts to ridicule the "Broomstick Army"[2] were made from time to time; but a more normal tone was one of acrimonious indigna-tion, and threats of reprisals ("British people, you will do well to heed our warning") were frequent. Anyone who found time to study the spate of verbiage transmitted from Hamburg and Bremen could only deduce from it that the Germans did in fact contemplate an airborne invasion and thought the Home Guard capable of jeopardising its success. This deduction was, as we have seen, wide of the mark.

The legend that at the time of Dunkirk the Home Guard was extensively armed with pikes is, like many other legends of the period, not in accordance with the facts; but it is less baseless than

[1] Quoted by Graves.

[2] In fact at this period recruits in at least one regimental depot of the Army proper were learning their arms drill with broomsticks for lack of more con-ventional weapons. (Lt.-Col. The Lord Birdwood: *The Worcestershire Regiment: 1922–50*. Aldershot, 1952.)

some. Pikes, or to be accurate lengths of iron tubing with a bayonet-like blade at the end, were issued in bulk to many Home Guard units; they were officially recommended as "balanced instruments particularly useful for street fighting". But this did not happen until September 1941, and it seriously annoyed the Home Guard, who by that time were well armed with sub-machine guns as well as rifles, grenades and even a primitive form of anti-tank gun. They took a pride in the equipment and the skill at arms which they had acquired in sixteen arduous months, felt slighted by being saddled with a medieval weapon, and failed in any case to see how one man could be expected to carry a pike as well as a rifle or tommy-gun. The well-meant ironmongery, though destined to occupy a small, romantic niche in the folklore of the Second World War, was consigned with contumely to their unit stores. In some localities its arrival was held responsible for mild outbreaks of absenteeism among Home Guard personnel.

Gradually the offensive spirit of the stout-hearted citizens began to be matched by their equipment. "I do not want you to misjudge the shotgun," the Commander-in-Chief, Home Forces, told senior Home Guard commanders on 5 June. "I have now coming out over a million rounds of solid ammunition, which is something that will kill a leopard at two hundred yards"; but Ironside felt obliged to qualify this heartening statement with the warning that there would be "perhaps only three or four cartridges in the men's pockets to begin with".

Soon the first rifles began to arrive from America, and eager hands divested them of the coating of grease in which they had been embalmed since the end of the First World War.[1] Concrete obstacles were replacing the farm-waggons with which the first road-blocks had been improvised[2]; trenches had been dug, and new pill-boxes were being built. Pronunciation-tests for suspects were issued—

[1] In addition to the government-purchased rifles, the generosity of private American citizens made available, through the "American Committee for the Defence of British Homes", a number of sporting rifles, shotguns, pistols and binoculars. The Committee was formed in New York in September, and by the end of the year had shipped 160 cases of arms to Britain.

[2] At Margate it had been hoped to block the advance of German tanks through the town by means of bathing machines filled with sand. (Graves.)

Soothe, Wrong, Wretch, Rats, Those. Denim battledress[1] slowly replaced the brassards, although it was some time before everyone had a uniform; a section-commander near Dover, reporting an incident in which he had waded out to capture the crew of a German bomber that had crashed near the foreshore, concluded: "I should like to add that I have ruined my suit, not having been issued with a uniform. Can I have some compensation for same, please?"

The answer was No. The Home Guard received no pay, and at first virtually no public funds were made available to meet out-of-pocket expenses incurred by the volunteers. Commercial firms were generous with their help, municipal authorities less so (in their eyes, perhaps, the Home Guard tended to be classed as a poor relation of the Civil Defence organisation, over which they had some statutory control). The units, who trained in the summer evenings after work and at the week-ends, and stood guard or patrolled at night, needed blankets, stoves, lanterns, store-rooms, typewriters, stationery and many other things. Much telephoning was necessary (there are records of the telephones in their *ad hoc* headquarters being disconnected by the Post Office owing to the non-payment of accounts), and men had to travel between their posts and their homes. In those anxious but ebullient days nobody grudged the small sacrifices thus involved, but later the inequity of the situation was recognised, a system of allowances was introduced, and the volunteers found themselves filling up almost as many forms as professional soldiers.

As the Home Guard settled into its harness several knotty and unforeseen problems came up for solution. It was decided that women—despite protests from many of them—could not be enrolled; an "Amazons' Defence Corps", formed by some ladies in Surrey, had a brisk run for its money in the illustrated papers but

---

[1] In Northern Ireland the uniforms were made of black denim. For administrative reasons the volunteers had been enrolled as special constables in the Royal Ulster Constabulary. It was soon realised that members of a police force who took part in military operations forfeited their rights under the Hague Convention. After two years of disputation a formula was found to resolve this delicate problem; but the formula involved the "re-attestation" of volunteers, and the attendant controversies long survived the crisis to which they owed their origin. (Blake.)

failed to achieve embodiment in the forces of the Crown.[1] Clergy could be enrolled but not armed; the Bishop of Truro was cheered when he let fall, during a debate in the House of Lords, the fact that he was a regular member of a night-patrol.[2] It was decreed—with what effect cannot be established—that sentries posted on church-towers were not to carry weapons. "Private armies", mostly raised and equipped by commercial or industrial firms, were a common target for criticism, and so were retired generals who insisted on wearing the uniform and insignia of their old rank while serving as privates.[3] Indignation was expressed in Parliament when it was discovered that a First World War holder of the Victoria Cross had been discharged from the Home Guard in Manchester because, his Russian parents never having been naturalized, he was ineligible under the regulations. These seem not to have been invoked in the case of a sixty-three-year-old Zulu whose father had led one of Cetewayo's *impis* against the British and who had been at one time a lion-tamer; he was among the first volunteers in a coastal district of Glamorgan-shire, where it was hoped that, if the invaders landed, his appearance on the foreshore might suggest to them that a serious error in navi-gation had been made. In 1940 the oldest member of the Home Guard was probably an ex-regimental sergeant-major of the Black Watch, who was still serving on his eightieth birthday two years later.

Although a majority of the Home Guard were old soldiers or sailors, whose combined experience covered a vast diversity of

[1] The ladies inevitably got their way in the end. The War Office was induced to grant a limited number of them the status of "nominated women". To make up for this un-Amazonian designation, they were given a badge and a certificate which said that "Mrs/Miss . . . . . . is authorised to follow the Armed Forces of the Crown." It was hoped that this document would safeguard their interests if they were taken prisoner, though this was by that time a remote contingency. They were employed on administrative rather than on combatant duties.

[2] Another prelate—the Bishop of Chelmsford—had anticipated the mustering of the Local Defence Volunteers by independently raising a band of a hundred armed vigilantes in the Romford area several months before Dunkirk (*The Times*, 16 May 1940). A similar degree of prescience was shown by a titled lady in Herefordshire, who as early as March had organised the tenants and employees on her estate (to the number of eighty) into a force known as "the Much Marcle Watchers". (Graves.)

[3] "In one company in East Sussex", a Member complained in the House of Commons on 2 July, "there are six different generals all dressed up as generals."

campaigning and went as far back as the relief of Khartoum in 1885, it was to the Spanish Civil War of 1936–39 that they looked, at first, for tactical doctrine. In Spain a citizen army had faced regular troops with superior equipment, and the few Britons who had taken part in the fighting were not behindhand in urging the value of the lessons to be learnt, preferably under their direction, from the ingenious tactics of the Republican forces. Several newspapers and periodicals strongly supported the view, always popular and seldom implausible, that Blimps in the War Office were wantonly neglecting the only military methods worthy of study, and of the various Home Guard training centres the most fashionable was the one at Osterley Park, where amid thunderous explosions three anarchists from Catalonia ambushed dummy tanks before an idolatrous week-end audience. "Even a nodding acquaintance with the Spanish instructors", wrote the historian of the Home Guard, "carried more prestige among the LDV than a close friendship with a Hollywood film star would have done in peace time."

As the summer wore on the Home Guard acquired a growing miscellany of weapons, ample stocks of ammunition, and a creditable proficiency in their use. Its strength at the end of the summer was well over a million, but it was a largely static force and it would therefore be misleading to assess its operational influence on the invasion—had it been launched—in terms of its total strength; for the attack on south-east England would initially have had to overcome opposition only from those Home Guard units whose homes lay in its path. The battalions in Belfast, Glasgow, Cardiff, Bristol, Liverpool, Manchester and other places remote from the decisive battlefield about the capital might have seen action; but by the time German troops came within range of their rifles the issue would have been decided and in the conqueror's communiqués the fighting, however fierce, would probably have been described as "mopping-up operations". To say that 9 and 16 Armies had to reckon with a million men at arms over and above the formations of the British Army is to speak loosely.

It is impossible to generalise about the Home Guard. Soldiers are nomads by virtue of their occupation, and the true quality of armies, like that of actors, is revealed by their performance of different roles on different stages. Each unit of the Home Guard rehearsed on its own stage for its own role. They manned motor-launches on Lake Windermere and the Norfolk Broads, rode hunters over the Devonshire moors and ponies over the Welsh hills. Railwaymen drove armoured trains; the London taxis were formed into some sort of motorised unit; patrolmen of the Automobile Association were put into uniform and affiliated; in rural areas gamekeepers and hunt servants found themselves credited with a Red Indian's natural aptitude for war. At a later stage these citizen-soldiers provided gun-crews for the anti-aircraft batteries.

Some Home Guards defended a pinpoint on the map—a bridge, or their own factory, or a country house requisitioned for the use of an organisation engaged on clandestine operations or research. Others, who nightly trudged the downs or the fields or the remoter cliff-tops, had wider territorial responsibilities. The Home Guard did duty in Caithness and Kensington, in Herefordshire and Harrow, in the Mendips and Fleet Street and the Forest of Dean. Everywhere its operational role and its domestic problems varied. The last-ditch defenders of Whitehall, for instance, were spared the chagrin with which the commander of the 9th Battalion of the Cumberland Home Guard felt compelled to modify his pride in having established a carrier-pigeon service, "the first, I believe, of its kind in the Home Guard". "It is a precarious service," he wrote, "owing to the depredations of the numerous peregrine falcons in this area. At times only one out of five pigeons returns safely to its loft." But perhaps enough has been said to indicate the influence of environment on the component units of this remarkable force.

Although the Home Guard were never tested in action, their value to the defence of Great Britain was unquestionable. Apart from weapons and equipment, the Army's greatest need throughout the summer of 1940 was for training; and training was impossible while formations were spreadeagled and fragmented by the requirements of static defence. There were—not counting Northern Ireland —5,000 miles of coast to watch; the official list of "VP's"—vulnerable points—ran into thousands; the defence of aerodromes (a vexed and controversial inter-service issue at that period) threatened to absorb a huge slice of the armed manpower; there were factories and government offices to guard, road-blocks to man, and bridges to protect against the theoretical menace of the saboteur. After the German air offensive began, a steadily increasing number of guards had to be found for the wreckage of aircraft shot down in the fighting; escorts or stretcher-bearers were often needed for their crews.

For all these duties the Home Guard was available. Had it not been, an almost intolerable strain would have been placed upon Home Forces and also, incidentally, on the police; training would have suffered severely and might well have been brought to a standstill. Moreover, as the Home Guard got into its stride, it rendered valuable service by giving its seventeen-year-old recruits a basic training which stood them in good stead when they were called to the colours a year later.

Although it never won a battle-honour, the Home Guard had the distinction of making prisoner the Deputy-Fuehrer of the Third Reich, Rudolf Hess, when on the night of 10/11 May 1941 he baled out from a Messerschmitt 110 over Eaglesham Moor in Renfrewshire. During the Battle of Britain at least one platoon was credited (by the Press, at any rate) with bringing down a German aircraft by rifle-fire. In some districts relations between the Home Guard and the Civil Defence Services had originally been less than cordial; the unpaid volunteers, patrolling the lonely countryside at night, could not but contrast their lot with that of the ARP wardens, who kept a much more comfortable vigil in accommodation provided by the authorities and who were moreover the envied owners—this was always a sore point in the early days—of steel helmets. But when the bombing started, the Civil Defence Services, the police and indeed the stricken population as a whole owed countless debts of gratitude to the Home Guard, whose part in rescue work and kindred activities cost them many casualties and earned them a number of decorations for gallantry.[1]

This is not the place in which to follow the fortunes of the Home Guard after the cancellation of *Operation Sea Lion*. The volunteers,

[1] During the war 1,206 members of the Home Guard lost their lives as a result of wounds, injuries or illness due to their service.

their ranks eventually diluted by a proportion of "directed" personnel, soldiered on until victory was won.[1] At one time the strength of the Home Guard almost touched the two-million mark, and by the end of the war it was a well-armed, highly trained force knit together by a tradition which, if on the martial side it derived from Henry V, had on the social side vaguely Falstaffian affinities. In the well-accoutred warriors who in 1945 marched with the rest of His Majesty's forces in the Victory Parade it would have been difficult to recognise the civilians in brassards, scanning the June skies in 1940 with shotguns in their hands; but it is perhaps the latter whose effigy has the stronger claim on the Home Guard's niche in British history.

Among the expedients with which, after Dunkirk, the British sought to eke out the resources of their hopelessly inadequate armoury was the large-scale use of flame. The Petroleum Warfare Department, an organisation which acknowledged the War Office as its sire and the Ministry of Fuel and Power as its dam, was officially constituted on 9 July 1940, and much thought and experiment were devoted to ringing the coasts of the island with a wall of fire.

This high ideal proved incapable of realisation, and the Department's most practical contribution to the country's defences was probably the Flame Fougasse. This was normally a forty-gallon drum containing a mixture of tar, lime and petrol; steel filings, propelled into the drum by a small explosive charge, ignited the contents and drove them out in a great gerbe of molten liquid, whose adhesive properties caused it to stick, still burning, to a tank or to anything else with which it came into contact. Several thousand of these simple devices were installed, initially by Chemical Warfare Companies of the Royal Engineers and later by the Home Guard, in defiles and other bottlenecks along the south coasts, the barrels being dug into banks at the side of the road and camouflaged. The Fougasse, unlike a minefield, was perfectly safe until the charge was armed and placed in position; they were usually emplaced in "batteries" of four. A more elaborate variant of the same principal

[1] The Home Guard was reactivated in 1952 as a precaution against Russian aggression. It was disbanded again (save for a small organisational cadre) in 1956.

was embodied in the Static Flame Trap, whence petrol in bulk flowed down pipes into a gorge or sunken road—the best example was at Dumpton Gap in Kent—where it was ignited by means of a Molotov cocktail.[1]

It is unlikely that these weapons, sited sparsely and in no great depth, would have caused the invaders many casualties; but even if only two or three of the fire-ambushes had been successfully sprung, the fame of the resultant holocausts might well have imposed caution and delay on the German advance; and the Fougasses—which were later used in Greece and Russia, as well as being incorporated by the Germans in the fortifications of the West Wall—were a cheap and serviceable contribution to the island's defences.

Less cheap, less serviceable, but much more ambitious were the Petroleum Warfare Department's endeavours to "set the sea on fire". One of the few wholly successful experiments, which took place on 24 August on the northern shores of the Solent, is thus described by the then head of the Department:

Ten pipes were rigged from the top of a thirty-foot cliff down into the water well below high water mark and ten Scammel tanker wagons connected to them delivered oil at the rate of about twelve tons an hour. Admiralty flares and a system of sodium and petrol pellets were used for ignition and within a few seconds of the pumps being started a wall of flame of such intensity raged up from the sea surface that it was impossible to remain on the edge of the cliff and the sea itself began to boil.[2]

The high hopes aroused by this marine inferno were never realised. The 24th of August had been a day of dead calm, and although there was one more successful experiment (in March 1941 at Studland Bay, when air-raid wardens in Bournemouth, ten miles away, claimed to be able to read a newspaper by the light of the flames), the opposition of wind and weather was never

---

[1] These home-made incendiaries, consisting merely of a bottle filled with petrol and equipped with an improvised fuse or wick, had first been used by the Finns against the Russians in 1939. They were a staple weapon of the Home Guard in its hand-to-mouth formative stages. The Russian statesman's name was also borrowed, later in the summer, to provide a sobriquet for the clumsy canisters in which the Luftwaffe dropped most of its first incendiary bombs; these were known, for no discoverable reason, as "Molotov Breadbaskets".

[2] Sir Donald Banks: *Flame over Britain*. London, 1948.

effectively overcome. The installation of a Flame Barrage (as it was called) of even the narrowest compass was immensely costly in steel, in labour, and eventually in petroleum products; and although in 1941 the Chiefs of Staff approved the allotment of material for fifty miles of barrage, half to be erected in South-Eastern Command, the only completed sections were short ones at Deal, St Margaret's Bay, the Shakespeare Cliff, Rye, and Studland Bay. These were not begun until long after *Sea Lion* had been cancelled, and not even one platoon of the invading armies would have faced the hazards of a flaming sea.

But here again, as so often in the period, we find the flinty soil of fact bearing a crop of legend. Not only was it believed in Britain that the countless German corpses washed up on the south coast had suffered burning in the sea, but on the other side of the Channel rumours of deaths or injuries to German troops from this cause were current. An American correspondent in Germany saw a hospital train all of whose occupants were said to be suffering from burns, and a story circulated in various forms that the Germans had been testing flame-proof asbestos suits with disastrous results. It is inconceivable that tests of untried equipment of this type would have been carried out on a large scale or caused a noticeable number of casualties, and the origins of this particular legend remain inscrutable. In 1954 a film based on the career of Admiral Canaris gave rise in Germany to a popular belief that in 1940 the whole British coast had in fact been protected by a wall of flame; for in the film agents of the *Abwehr* purloin from the heart of Whitehall a roll of film—it appears to be a film of the actual experiments taken at the time by a British official photographer—showing the more spectacular efforts of the Petroleum Warfare Department, and Canaris has only to exhibit this to the German General Staff to secure the cancellation of *Sea Lion*.

Another and still more far-fetched use of flame was suggested by a well-known industrialist for the defence of airfields. This was an extension of the principle of the fire-ship. Its object was to deter the German pilots involved in an air-landing operation, and the method proposed was to start up twenty old cars stationed round the perimeter of the airfield, with their steering gear locked and just enough petrol to carry them out into the middle, where they would burst into flames. The decision not to proceed with this project was taken after one field-trial.

But the fact that so ludicrous an expedient should have been thought worth testing by a government agency illustrates the pathetic eagerness with which the British cast about them for some means of doing their enemy a mischief if he came among them. All over the country strange engines of war were devised by members of the armed services and by civilian inventors. Some of these survived the tests to which they were subjected and were put into production; the Northover Projector, the Blacker Bombard (later known as the Spigot Mortar), the Smith Gun and the Sticky Bomb all became more or less regular items of Home Guard equipment.[1] Lorries were made approximately bullet-proof by building partitions round the sides and filling the intervening space with pebbles. The public were heartened by photographs showing "the latest type of armoured car" drawn up in serried ranks. These diminutive vehicles were believed to be the fruit of Lord Beaverbrook's inspiration and were known as "Beaverettes"; they were, one of their users recalled, "ordinary civilian-type Standard 14's, with a sheet of armour plate in front and at the sides, and open on top".[2]

An enormous catapult, capable of hurling a four-gallon petrol tin for a short distance, was constructed by the London Midland and Scottish Railway; and the Bank of England produced, from the works where its notes were printed, a modern version of the Roman ballista. At the height of its powers this apparatus was able to throw a Molotov cocktail a hundred yards; it was called "Larwood", after the Nottinghamshire fast bowler.[3]

There is much to smile at in the flimsy or obsolete makeshifts which in the early days played so large a part in the defences of the island, but basically the picture was the same on both sides of the

[1] A Northover Projector, emplaced in the Speaker's dining-room in the House of Commons, was one of the weapons sited to oppose a German advance across Westminster Bridge. The Home Guard unit which provided its crew was composed of Members of both Houses of Parliament and of the staff of the Palace of Westminster.

[2] Major J. D. P. Stirling: *The First and the Last. A History of the 4/7 Royal Dragoon Guards.* London, 1950.

[3] Banks.

Channel. For the Germans victory, and for the British defeat, had suddenly been revealed as dependent on a contingency which neither had foreseen, for which neither had made any preparations, and of which neither had any relevant experience. Both, hastily concerting the measures they thought appropriate, committed follies, blunders and extravagances; but both had only a matter of weeks to work in, and when all is said the state of readiness and efficiency achieved by the British defences at the end of the summer is no less remarkable than the completeness of the German arrangements to launch an invasion.

CHAPTER FOURTEEN

In the Air : The Lull

Women of Britain, give us your aluminium. We want it and we want it now.... We will turn your pots and pans into Spitfires and Hurricanes, Blenheims and Wellingtons. I ask therefore that everyone who has pots and pans, kettles, vacuum-cleaners, hat-pegs, coat-hangers, shoe-trees, bathroom fittings and household ornaments, cigarette boxes or any other articles made wholly or in part of aluminium, should hand them in at once to the local headquarters of the Women's Voluntary Services.

From an appeal made by the Minister of Aircraft Production (Lord Beaverbrook) on 5 July 1940

GERMAN strategy in the air from Dunkirk to the end of the summer reflects more clearly than any other aspect of the period the flaws in Hitler's judgment. His dreams of a British capitulation imposed on the Army, and to a less extent on the Navy, delays which seriously hampered their preparations; and his obsession with those dreams deprived both Services of the drive and inspiration which they had a right to expect from their Supreme Commander, and which Hitler was well qualified to supply. It is however doubtful whether the British gained thereby any positive advantages of importance, for they were bound to be given a respite, and the respite could not in practice have been much shorter than it was. Granted the fact that the Germans had made no preparations for a conquest of Britain before they attacked France, no adequately mounted invasion could have been launched at a much earlier date than that on which an inadequately mounted one was, in the event, ready to sail. It was not to Hitler, but to the Channel, to what Conrad called "the stern and impartial sea", that the islanders owed a breathing-space during which they were able to prepare themselves for the shock of arms.

In the air the circumstances were different. That a defeated enemy must, whenever possible, be pursued is one of the oldest principles of war, and after the evacuation of Dunkirk the Luftwaffe was available for this duty.[1] It is true that its main effort was, for another fortnight or so, concentrated with good effect against the French. But part of its strength could have been—and indeed on the first two nights after the evacuation ended was—diverted against England; and after the Fall of France, despite the exigencies of redeployment, a considerable and increasing weight of attack could have been delivered against the RAF and the industries on which it depended. Nothing of the sort was done.

By abandoning the principle of the pursuit, the Germans gave the RAF "two whole and entirely precious months"[2] in which to build up its depleted strength in men and machines, to extend the radar chain and the network of observer-posts until almost the whole country was covered, and to organise without interference the beginnings of a bomber offensive.

The following figures give some idea of the concrete advantages which Hitler's strategy conferred on the RAF:

On 4 June (the last day of the Dunkirk evacuation) Fighter Command disposed of 446 serviceable aircraft, of which 331 were Hurricanes and Spitfires. Only 36 fighters of these types were immediately available for issue from the Aircraft Storage Units to the squadrons as replacements for casualties.

On 11 August (the eve of "Eagle-day", when the Luftwaffe was to launch its offensive) the number of serviceable aircraft in Fighter Command had increased to 704, including 620 Hurricanes and Spitfires. Instead of 36, 289 were ready for delivery to the squadrons.

During June, July and August, moreover, the production of all types of aircraft exceeded the totals called for (in Air Ministry plans originally laid down in January 1940) by a monthly average of roughly 250 machines.

It is almost beyond question that Hitler was unwise to hold his hand for so long, but one of his reasons for doing so was not in itself unsound. When he struck, he wanted to strike with the full force of which he was capable, and this he could not do until the

---

[1] It is not here intended to imply that the Luftwaffe, after Dunkirk, had beaten the RAF; but the German forces, of which the Luftwaffe was a part, had beaten and driven from the field the British forces, of which the RAF was a part. It is in this sense that the principle of the pursuit is invoked.

[2] Denis Richards: *The Royal Air Force, 1939–45*. Vol. I. London, 1953.

redeployment of the three Air Fleets concerned had been completed (when it had, bad weather at the beginning of August imposed a further week's delay). But these considerations were not the key to his strategy. It was, once more, the mirage of a settlement with Britain which caused Hitler to call off the pursuit and to surrender, for two crucial months, his initiative in the air.

During those two months—the period, to be precise, was from 17 June, when France asked for an armistice, until 12 August, when the Luftwaffe launched its daylight offensive—Hitler made, or allowed Goering to make, a lesser but not unimportant error in the related fields of tactics and psychology. To quote Richards on this phase of the conflict:

> German aircraft ranged over England almost every night. The force employed was never more than sixty or seventy bombers; its losses rarely amounted to more than one or two aircraft. Apart from their reconnaissance and training value, the operations were thus a cheap means of maintaining pressure until the full weight of the German air arm descended on us.

But if these pin-pricks—for they amounted to no more [1]—were a cheap means of maintaining pressure, they were also a profligate method of squandering one of the Luftwaffe's greatest assets, which was the sway it held—from a distance—over the fears and fancies of a community which it had not yet attacked.

If one gun, or one battery of guns, fires every night for several weeks into a position which is to be assaulted with powerful artillery support, the attacking force will diminish its prospects of success. It would have been better if the guns had been silent. In war pin-pricks, inflicted by the weaker adversary upon the stronger, are often the only form of offensive action within the former's scope and may well bring disproportionate rewards (as did, at the end of this period, the RAF's puny but defiant raids on Berlin). But harassing action by the stronger adversary against the weaker is almost always worse than a waste of effort. For the defence learns, before the main assault,

[1] Raeder pointed this out on 11 July, when he submitted to the Fuehrer that "the present attacks on a number of objectives of lesser importance are only pin-pricks, making no impression on the public, and of more inconvenience to ourselves than to them."

many minor lessons which it would have had no time to learn, or anyhow to assimilate and act upon, after the main assault had been launched; and the rewards gained by the assailant are scarcely worth gaining when measured against the elements of surprise and confusion for which they were sacrificed.

A lull in the air would have seemed ominous. The long-vaunted horrors would still have been unimaginable; and the defence would have learnt none of the minor but important lessons of experience which two months of mild marauding by the Luftwaffe taught it. "At first", writes Richards, these tactics "caused great inconvenience and some loss of production—not from the actual damage inflicted, but from the perpetual and protracted air-raid alarms; on 24/25 June, for instance, the whole of the country south of a line from Hull to Liverpool was under the 'red' warning, though only Bristol was threatened by more than one or two aircraft." Not only the RAF, but Anti-Aircraft Command, the Civil Defence services, the railways, the Post Office, factories, hospitals and schools—in short any form of organisation, large or small, was given the opportunity of carrying out a thorough dress-rehearsal before the ordeal of the first night. But perhaps the most important beneficiary from what was in effect a kind of inoculation was the ordinary citizen, whose baptism of fire, however vicarious, equipped him with a valuable measure of self-confidence. The grim ululations of the sirens, the wardens' whistles, the drone of engines in the dark, the crump of gunfire—even if no bombs fell within twenty miles of him, these were unnerving phenomena at first; but after two months they had forfeited their bloodcurdling propensities, and familiarity had bred a measure of contempt.

Before taking part in a cat-and-mouse game, it is as well to make quite sure that you are the cat. The Luftwaffe was certainly no mouse; but in these indecisive and almost playful night-attacks it blunted its claws in one important respect.

The small scale and the inconsequent pattern of the German raids suggested to the British that they had some sort of experimental purpose; and it was not long before this purpose was discovered, and the navigational device known as *Knickebein* compromised. *Knickebein* (which means what on a golf-course would be called "dog-leg") was a system of directional radio-beams, transmitted from German stations, which intersected over the bomber's target and enabled its load to be delivered by remote and almost infallible control. Once the nature and purpose of this device were known, the initiative passed from the cat to the mouse; and before the end of June a special organisation, known as No. 80 Wing of the RAF, had been set up to "bend" the German beams, thus gravely impairing the Luftwaffe's chances of hitting the targets against which it was sent by night. *Knickebein*, a secret weapon of which the British knew nothing until it was used against them, would clearly have needed operational tests before it was brought fully into play; but it was surely a mistake to start those tests so early in the battle that, long before a decision was in view, the weapon had become not only obsolete but double-edged.

On the German as on the British side the main gains from these night operations were of an imponderable nature, the experience acquired in night-flying—a technique to which the Luftwaffe had up till then devoted little study—outweighing the damage done by sporadic and inaccurate bombardment. A more directly profitable form of activity were the attacks by dive-bombers, lavishly protected by fighters, on coastal convoys in the Channel. British shipping losses were not particularly heavy—some 40,000 tons were sunk by these operations in the month preceding the Battle of Britain—but considerable strain was placed on Fighter Command, who could hope only for very short warning of an attack and, lacking the time to concentrate adequate strength against it, were generally in action against heavy odds. Nevertheless, between 10 July and 10 August the British destroyed 227 German aircraft for the loss of 96.

Three Air Fleets, with a total strength of some 3,500 aircraft, were committed to the operations against the United Kingdom: *Luftflotte* 2, under Kesselring, in the Low Countries and north-east France; *Luftflotte* 3, under Sperrle, in north and north-west France; and *Luftflotte* 5, under Stumpf, in Norway and Denmark. Their redeployment on new bases which had to be stocked, and in many cases repaired or improved, before they were fully operational, was a formidable task; and it was not until 24 July that the trial of strength between the two air forces began with a prelude of skirmishing.

The British were unaware that it had begun, and for them the date failed to survive as a minor landmark of the period. The inference that something must have been amiss with the German plans is correct. Goering at this stage attempted to use a tactical weapon—the fighter—as an instrument of strategy, and it is hardly surprising that he failed. His object was to destroy Fighter Command and thus clear the way for his bombers. "Free chase over south-east England" was the standard briefing for the squadrons of *Luftflotten* 2 and 3.[1] They made two or three sorties a day, normally crossing the coast at over 20,000 feet, a considerable height for those days.

The Germans hoped, somewhat callowly, that these provocative tactics would bring to battle not only the squadrons already stationed in the area but, as these were destroyed or crippled, the whole of the rest of Fighter Command. The Messerschmitt 109, with a tactical endurance of roughly eighty minutes, could spend only about twenty of those minutes over English soil, and, as Galland, himself commanding a Fighter Group at the time, wrote afterwards: "The German fighters found themselves in a similar predicament to a dog on a chain which wants to attack the foe, but cannot harm him because of his limited orbit."

The RAF knew about the chain and saw no reason to oblige the dog. Some fighting took place, especially when the Germans began to despatch small numbers of bombers or dive-bombers with the fighters (to whose pilots these aircraft were known as "decoy ducks"); but this coat-trailing did not lead to the hoped-for series of decisive battles, nor were the results of such actions as did take place favourable to the Luftwaffe. It was only in the attacks on shipping and coastal targets in the Channel (in which, for instance, on 8 August the RAF lost 20 aircraft against the Luftwaffe's 28)

[1] Adolf Galland: *The First and the Last*. London, 1955. It seems possible that the writer's memories of operations carried out by his own *Gruppe* in July have been diluted with memories of fighter sweeps carried out by the Luftwaffe in greater strength during October; but he was in a position to know the purpose of the summer sorties, and his evidence on this point cannot be disregarded.

that the Germans achieved a small measure of the lethal attrition they had aimed at.

Nobody in the German camp, or for that matter in the British, ever deviated from the sound principle that air supremacy over south-east England and the Channel was an essential prerequisite to invasion. It was needed not merely for the assault, but for several essential preliminaries to the assault. The German Navy, in particular, had not only to lay some millions of mines in two vast cordons stretching from the coast of France to the coast of England; they had also to sweep the existing British minefields in the path of the invasion flotillas. For both these vital tasks air supremacy was essential.

On 31 July Raeder reported to Hitler that: "Minesweeping has begun with exploratory sweeps but can be carried out according to plan *only if we have air superiority*. It will take three weeks if the weather is favourable. . . . Mine-laying will begin at the end of August *if we have air superiority*, and will last about two weeks." When, rather more than a month later, a vast invasion fleet began to assemble in the Channel ports, mastery of the air became more than ever important for the invaders, working as they were within the narrowest margin of time. Although "it must be confirmed that the activity of the British forces [bombing and mine-laying by the RAF] has undoubtedly been successful", the Naval Staff were on 10 September still prepared to "provisionally guarantee" a state of readiness by D-day (21 September); but they pointed out in measured terms that "clear air superiority", which they had always insisted on as "the most important prerequisite for the operation", had not so far been achieved.

The Germans, from Hitler downwards, seriously overestimated the Luftwaffe's capacities as an agent of terror and destruction. In the Polish and Norwegian campaigns it had been virtually unopposed; in *Operation Yellow* it had enjoyed not only an immense numerical superiority over its adversaries but also the advantages of working (as it had been specifically designed to work) in direct support of a powerful army whose swift advance dislodged the French and British squadrons from their forward bases and thus started a kind of organisational rot which could only be partially stopped by improvisation. After the Fall of France the Germans had some excuse for regarding their air force as irresistible.

"It will take between a fortnight and a month to smash the enemy air force", its Chief of Staff told Halder on 11 July; although it sounds like a casual boast, this prophecy may well have been an echo of Goering's orders to *Luftflotte* 5, issued on the same day. From these it is clear that he expected to destroy the fighter defence of southern England in four days, the rest of the RAF in four weeks.

This over-confidence, coupled as it was with an underestimate of the British population's steadiness under fire, may partly explain the slapdash and erratic character of German strategy in the air. We have seen how, on the first two nights after Dunkirk, conventional small-scale attacks were carried out against airfields in East Anglia: how these were followed, first, by a complete moratorium lasting ten days and thereafter by five weeks of inoculatory pin-pricks[1]; and how at the end of July the Germans attempted to bring Fighter Command to battle without giving it anything worth fighting for.

It may here be well to remind the reader that there existed among the principal persons in Germany at that time, whether they were political leaders or military commanders, no loyalty in the sense in which this concept was understood in the opposing camp. The members of what Bullock has well called "the gutter-élite" sur-rounding Hitler were united by the ties which normally unite revolutionaries, gangsters and place-seekers whose conjoint or con-verging efforts have been crowned with success, and these ties, like ropes which have been tarred, were rendered more durable by a rich, Teutonic integument of perverted idealism and a profound faith—half-treacly, half-shrewd—in the genius of Adolf Hitler.

This faith was shared in full measure at a lower level. To the biddings of their Fuehrer and his dubious oligarchy the obedience of

[1] The value of this phase of the Luftwaffe's operations—"this warming up process", as the official historian calls it—to civil defence organisations in the United Kingdom is made clear in *Civil Defence*, by O'Brien.

90 million Germans was, in the summer heyday of 1940, for practical purposes complete and unquestioning. At the summit, among his chosen chiefs, Hitler, like all dictators, compelled a lickspittle allegiance and, like all tricksters, promoted mutual distrust. But below the summit no slur can be cast on the loyalty with which the German nation followed their leader in 1940 towards the bright uplands of victory and, later, through deepening shadows into the abyss of self-destruction. It was only at the highest level that small, tortuous cracks in the synthetic monolith of National Socialism affected the destinies of *Operation Sea Lion*.

The German Navy, well accustomed to the peripheral role of a poor relation, not so much misunderstood as un-understood by whatever central government ruled a race of landsmen, viewed the Hitlerian caucus with detached but fatalistic disapproval. The Army, traditionally nearer the centre of German politics, took more activist views but never translated them into action. After the Fall of France the various half-baked plots to kidnap or assassinate Hitler (of which before *Operation Yellow* was launched there had been a small, untidy burgeoning) were forgotten in the heady atmosphere of triumph and promotions, and OKH transferred their disapproval of Hitler to the military lackeys of OKW, who from the ivory tower of the Supreme Command issued the orders of a still suspect oracle for an extremely awkward operation.

Goering alone, as Commander-in-Chief of the Luftwaffe, straddled both worlds and might perhaps, had he been so minded, have pulled the whole operation together. His was the responsibility for leading the attack, for making the invasion possible; he had Hitler's ear and could perhaps have recalled him from his dreams. He made nothing of these duties and these chances. He played a lone hand, he played it badly, and he sometimes played it in fancy dress; Galland, summoned from the Channel coast to Karinhall in late September, found his Commander-in-Chief "wearing a green suède hunting jacket over a silk blouse with long, puffed sleeves, high hunting boots, and in his belt a hunting knife in the shape of an old Germanic sword". Goering was, Galland adds, "in the best of humour". He had small cause to be, for by that time the Luftwaffe had been beaten, the ships and the barges were being furtively dispersed and the "military blow against England" had been indefinitely post-poned.

Raeder, at every stage, put the difficulties before Hitler but lacked the nerve, or the standing, or both, to point out that they added up to impossibilities. Goering squabbled—*de haut en bas*—with Raeder and virtually ignored the Army, in direct support of whom the Luftwaffe's operations were theoretically being carried out. A natural braggart, he was incapable of calling attention to the limitations of his own service even when he was made tardily aware of them; and as the day approached for the full fury of the Luftwaffe to be unleashed on England he did not feel it his duty to sound a note of caution about the results to be expected from its operations. He was a deeply conceited man, as well as a vain one; it does not seem to have crossed his mind that the blow he was about to deliver could be anything but a *coup de grâce*.

CHAPTER FIFTEEN

In the Air : The Storm

Many are the Examples, of the great oddes between Number and Courage.

Bacon

ON 30 July Hitler ordered Goering, in terms which seem to echo an impatient or impulsive mood, to prepare, "immediately and with the greatest haste", to start "the great battle of the German Air Force against England". Goering's final directive for *Operation Eagle* was issued on 2 August, and on the following day Hitler travelled from the Berghof to Berlin to be present at the launching of the attack.

The weather was unkind.[1] *Adlertag* was postponed and Hitler went back to the Berghof. It was not until 12 August that the Luftwaffe was able to strike in force; but the Germans—possibly because Hitler did not return to Berlin until the 13th—do not regard *Operation Eagle* as having been formally inaugurated until that day.

No attempt will be made here to retell in tactical terms the whole story of the Battle of Britain. To do so would overweight the narrative with material which is available elsewhere and to which compression would do an injustice. The general account which follows will concern itself mainly with those aspects of a decisive struggle which bear most directly on the invasion-project.

At the outset the German attacks were mainly concentrated on airfields in south and south-east England. On the first day (12 August) they also attacked, and damaged, five radar stations, of which one in the Isle of Wight was out of action for eleven days. These stations, whose tall spinneys of 350-foot masts offered unmistakable

---

[1] The German meteorological service was always at a disadvantage compared with its opposite number in Britain. Most of Europe's weather reaches the continent by way of the Atlantic, and the Germans were often flying uncomfortably blind as far as conditions over the target were concerned. "The British could nearly always forecast the weather early enough to make provision for it. We were always surprised by it." (Galland.)

targets, were (excepting perhaps the person of the Prime Minister) the most important objectives for German bombs which the island contained.

At this stage of the war both sides possessed radar. The British were experimenting with the airborne sets which in 1941 turned the night-fighter from a blind hunter into a killer; but in the summer of 1940 radar was a purely defensive device. It provided a screen within which the intruder automatically forfeited surprise and was always at a tactical disadvantage which could be offset only by sheer weight of numbers.

Some idea of the benefits—all the more valuable since the British pilots were always fighting against odds—which it conferred on the defence may be gathered from the evidence of one of the men who led the attack:

> In battle we [Germans] had to rely on our own human eyes. The British fighter pilots could depend on the radar eye, which was far more reliable and had a longer range. When we made contact with the enemy our briefings were already three hours old[1], the British only as many seconds old—the time it took to assess the latest position by means of radar to the transmission of attacking orders from Fighter Control to the already airborne force.[2]

In fact, although at this stage the British radar gave extremely accurate bearings, it was a much less reliable guide to the height and numbers of the attacking force. But it was indispensable to the country's survival.

To knock out one of the five radar stations attacked on the first day was an achievement of real value—or would have been, had the Germans maintained their objective. But, with the inconsequence which was a feature of their strategy throughout this crucial period, the Luftwaffe forthwith abandoned these targets; and on 15 August Goering, presiding over a conference of his three Air Fleet commanders at Karinhall, concluded that "it is doubtful whether there is any point in continuing the attacks on radar sites, in view of the fact that not one of those attacked has so far been put out of opera-

---

[1] It is difficult to see why the time-lag should have been as long as three hours; it must nevertheless always have been substantial.

[2] Galland.

tion". His dubiety seems to have been accepted as a firm definition of policy, and only two more attacks on radar stations took place.

Here, early in the battle, we get a glimpse of fuddled thinking at the highest level in the German camp. The radar stations were an Achilles heel, or something very like one. The fact must have been recognised up to a point, or they would not have been singled out on the first day. By the fourth day it was believed, erroneously, that the attacks had been wholly ineffective; yet no effort had been made to improve on the first day's results. Finally (most singular of all) the commander-in-chief of an air force confidently committed to depriving the British Isles, in six weeks, of both the will and the means to resist was prepared to accept as indestructible a number of flimsy and conspicuous installations sited on the most readily accessible parts of enemy territory. The mental processes which combined to formulate this aspect of German air strategy are not easy to fathom.

When an army passes to the offensive two criteria are applied in retrospect to its operations: Were the things that it tried to do the right things or the wrong things? And how far did it succeed in doing them? A commander of land forces, though he seldom can (and almost never should) try to answer the first question until the whole campaign is over, can usually answer the second. Either he has stormed the hill, broken the line, forced the river-crossing; or he has failed to do so.

In the air both questions are—or were in 1940—apt to remain imponderable; but some light was in those days thrown on a commander's capacity by his answers to a third. What did he think, at the time, that he had done? Goering emerges with small credit from this test.

In fairness to the Germans it must be remembered that they were pioneers. Their bomb-loads were small,[1] their bomb-sights primitive,

[1] In the summer of 1940 the average bomb-load carried by the average German bomber over the average distance which had to be traversed from a base in Western Europe to a target in England was less than 2,000 lb. These bombers were two-engined. The average bomb-load dropped by a four-engined Allied aircraft on Germany in 1944-5 was many times as great and was delivered, thanks to scientific

and their crews (who normally saw the results of an attack, whether successful or unsuccessful, in terms of an impressive pyro-technical display) pardonably inclined to exaggerate the destruction they had wrought. Moreover the planning and execution of a sustained attack against an air force, none of whose bases was in any danger of being overrun until the attack had succeeded, was an entirely novel problem, and one to which any tendency to rest on laurels won in earlier campaigns provided the worst possible approach.

But when all this had been said, the margin by which the Luftwaffe exaggerated or misinterpreted the effect of its daylight attacks on ground targets remains very wide indeed. Both sides—the British certainly, the Germans possibly, in good faith—overestimated from day to day the number of aircraft shot down in combat by their pilots; in the conditions of those times this was inevitable, especially after a day of heavy and confused fighting. But the Luftwaffe totted up these swollen claims against the background of a wholly un-realistic estimate of the RAF's total strength, and thus were always much nearer to final victory on paper than they were in fact. Their intelligence was bad (on 16 August, for instance, only three of the eight airfields attacked were in use by Fighter Command) and their claims of damage done were over-sanguine if not deliberately dishonest; on 13 August, when Halder was told that eight "major bases" had been "virtually destroyed", the facts were that of ten RAF stations attacked seven had received minor damage while no bombs at all had fallen on the other three. By 16 August German intelligence estimated that British fighter strength had been reduced to 430, of which only 300 were operational.

These errors, possibly flavoured at times with self-deception, were an unsound basis for strategy, especially for the sort of opportunist strategy, with frequent changes of method and objective, on which Goering relied in the fighting which was meant to pave the

developments and operational experience, with greater precision and effect. (The heaviest recorded bomb-load carried—in a Lancaster Mark X—by the RAF is believed to have been 22,000 lb, or nearly 10 tons. The United States Air Force achieved a still heavier weight of attack.) Sustained onslaughts with such missiles failed to break the spirit of the hard-pressed German people or completely to paralyse the life of the nation.

way for invasion. It is small wonder that in OKW's ivory tower a note of near-perplexity was sometimes sounded. "British fighter defence severely crippled", Greiner wrote in the war diary on 3 September; yet an entry on 28 September records the fact that "lately the British fighters have again been opposing the German formations above the Channel". Admittedly OKW was at all times somewhat remote from reality; but it is difficult not to feel that the Supreme Command of the German Armed Forces ought to have been better informed about the progress of a decisive battle than it was.

An important feature of the German plan was the night-attacks on aircraft plants which went hand-in-hand with their daylight operations against Fighter Command and its bases. In execution these attacks were marred by a low level of accuracy, so that although much miscellaneous damage was done the targets themselves were seldom hit. In conception it is at least arguable that the attacks should have started earlier. There is a limit to the number of tasks (which, however closely they may be related at a theoretical level, involve completely different types of operation) that even the most powerful air force can carry out simultaneously in the course of six weeks; there is a certain *folie de grandeur* about the belief that it would be possible for the Luftwaffe to destroy both the RAF and the industries on which it depended in one short offensive, while at the same time discharging a number of other duties connected with preparations for the invasion and intensification of the blockade. The Germans were right to attack aircraft factories, but wrong to defer these attacks to the last moment.

On 15 August all three Air Fleets combined, for the first and—as it turned out—the last time, to deliver a crushing blow against the island and its defences. It is true that less than a third of the 1790 aircraft committed to the day's operations were bombers; but this was in 1940 an unprecedented scale of attack. It should have marked the beginning of the end.

And so it did, though in a contrary sense to that hoped for by the Germans. Five grand assaults were delivered during the day. Some formations were routed, all were heavily punished and only one—

"Eglantine Cottage? Go down the lane past the Messerschmitt, bear left and keep on past the two Dorniers, then turn sharp right and it's just past the first Junkers." *Punch*, 4 September 1940.

composed of fighter-bombers and directed on factories in the Croydon area—did any serious damage. *Luftflotte* 5, operating from Scandinavia, suffered a reverse so decisive that it was never again committed to daylight operations against England. Its bombers, escorted by ME 110's (which had a longer range but less manoeuvrability than the ME 109's), crossed the north-east coast, the first wave near Blyth, the second near Scarborough. They were intercepted well out to sea. Their escorts, short of petrol and in any case no match for Hurricanes and Spitfires, were unable to accompany them inland. Few of the raiders attacked, and only one of them hit, the airfields and factories which they had come to destroy.

Judging by the foreseeable inadequacy of their arrangements for fighter escort, it is probable that *Luftflotte* 5 expected to find the north of England sparsely if at all defended; but though the fiasco in which they were involved on 15 August may have been due to the Luftwaffe's tendency to under-value the strength and capabilities of the RAF, their Commander-in-Chief was already beginning to revise his preconceptions. On this day Goering ordered that no more than one officer should be included in any air-crew detailed for operations over England.

The German losses were 76 aircraft, the British 34. But in London that evening the official communiqué gave the day's total as 182 enemy planes certainly destroyed, with a further 53 probably destroyed; and the whole nation rejoiced. When the true figures became known after the war, this wide margin of error (where no error at all had been suspected at the time) caused perplexity, coupled with a sense of disillusion. Richards, after rehearsing the many practical reasons why all such "stop press" claims were bound to be inflated after a great and confused air-battle ("though whenever the fighting was less intense the pilots' claims were extremely accurate"), makes the following comment on the utility of unwitting braggadocio:

It must . . . be admitted that the figure of 182, like that of 185 for 15 September [when the true total was 56], though subsequently shown to be wrong, had an important psychological effect during the battle. For it undoubtedly inspired not only the fighter pilots but the whole nation to still greater miracles of effort.

After the war the publication by the British Government—following the scrutiny of German documents to which, of course, at least one of their allies also had access—of the true figures caused a small shock of disillusion. This shock would have been less disconcerting, and its effects more ephemeral, if the figures had been provisionally revised at some stage between the desperate days and nights of 1940 and the relaxed aftermath of victory in 1945. It was within the knowledge of the Air Ministry (though not at the time when the communiqués were issued) that the number of German aircraft brought down on British soil after twenty-four hours' fighting never exceeded fifty; a few more were known, from a study of signals intelligence, to have met disaster over the sea or on the mainland of Europe; and a few could be assumed to have come down without trace in the Channel or the North Sea. But the total German losses, known or fairly estimated when the results of each day's actions had been fully assessed, never ran into three figures; and it might have been well if the great discrepancies between the honest but inevitably exaggerated "stop press" claims and the post-mortem verdicts of the intelligence staff, had been made public before, years later, the exhumed facts demanded an autopsy in their own right.

But this is a counsel of perfection; for at no stage in the war could the British Government have afforded to take a step calculated to dishearten their own people, to weaken their credit among their allies, and to provide the propaganda services of their enemies with a golden opportunity.

It seems worth pointing out that, had the statistics of German aircraft destroyed in the Battle of Britain been deliberately falsified, they would quickly have become suspect. Had it even been believed, within the squadrons of Fighter Command and the staffs who dealt with their operational reports, that pilots' claims were being evaluated by lax or over-indulgent standards, the belief would soon have gained currency throughout the country. For on the British, though not on the German, side the battle was fought by men who slept in their own country. They were young, intelligent and gifted with that hard-bitten quizzicality which insulates the mind against the stresses imposed on it by recurrent danger and unremitting strain. They argued in their messes, boasted or were silent in bars, shared victories and doubts with the women they loved. They were jealous of their prowess and hotly resentful of any attempt to clothe it in false values. Had the fighter pilots believed that their claims were being doctored, exaggerated or even scrutinised without proper care, the whole nation would have come—in a matter, almost, of hours—to share that belief.

There is some evidence that the morale of the Luftwaffe was adversely affected by the grandiose claims made on their behalf by the German Propaganda Ministry,[1] or at least by the overweening tone in which these claims were presented to the German public; and it is true that the margin of error in the German statistics of air-

---

[1] Some idea of the readiness with which official credence was given to completely bogus claims by German fighter-pilots can be gained from *The One That Got Away*, by Kendal Burt and James Leasor. (London, 1956.)

craft destroyed was out of all proportion to the British margin of error. Between 10 July and 31 October 1940 the British claimed 2698 aircraft, shot down 1733: the Germans claimed 3058, shot down 915.[1] Thus the British overstated their case by 55 per cent, the Germans by 234 per cent.

Although this huge discrepancy was partly due to deliberate falsification by the German Propaganda Ministry, it was also partly the product of natural causes. For the Luftwaffe was losing the battle, and in war it is normal for the losing side to make, in self-vindication, claims which history is unlikely to substantiate. The pilots themselves, though sceptical of the official figures, had no means of judging their true fraudulence. The attacking squadrons were dispersed in a wide arc over five occupied countries, and the men—unlike their opponents, who when off duty converged on one form or another of the parish pump—had scant opportunity for comparing notes and piecing together a general picture of how things were going outside their own unit.

Besides eliminating—except by night—the threat to Britain from Germany's dearly won bases in Scandinavia, the RAF's victory on 15 August had the effect of accentuating the defensive element already noticeable in German tactics. On that day less than a third of the attacking aircraft had been bombers; on the 16th the proportion was reduced to less than a quarter. There was moreover an increasing tendency for the large fighter escorts to be misemployed. Instead of being used in their natural role of skirmishing flank-guards with full liberty of manoeuvre, their orders—in deference to the wishes of the bomber crews, who felt happier if they could see the fighters close alongside or overhead—often confined them to a role which worried and handicapped the pilots.

On 17 August there was something of a lull. On the following day heavy attacks did a good deal of damage but cost the Luftwaffe 71 aircraft against the RAF's loss of 27. It was on this day that the *Stukas* were withdrawn from operations against inland objectives. These dive-bombers (Junkers 87's)—cheaply manufactured, easy to fly and highly effective in precision attacks against ground targets—

[1] Richards.

had given excellent service in Poland, Norway and France. A special attachment caused them, as they plunged almost vertically downwards, to emit a shrill, deafening scream and this, superimposed on the roar of their engines and the rattle of their guns, heightened the demoralising effect of their attacks. But to machine-gunners or even to riflemen who kept their heads they offered a fair target; they were troubled by the barrage-balloons; and their lack of speed made them easy meat for the British fighters. An engine of war which had left the scars of terror over half Europe was unable to face the hazards of the English sky. "Their pinpoint accuracy", wrote Galland, who watched the process, "lost its effect because of the interference on the part of the defence. . . . The renunciation of such a weapon of attack, from which it had expected so much, was certainly no easy decision for the German command."[1]

But the withdrawal of the dive-bomber squadrons (which had originally mustered some 250 fully operational aircraft) still left the Luftwaffe with a great numerical superiority, and by the last week in August the strain on Fighter Command was beginning to tell. From the 19th to the 23rd cloud reduced the scale of the German attacks, but on the 24th they were over again in force; and for the next thirteen days—until 6 September—a daily average of nearly a thousand aircraft assailed England.

This was not what came to be remembered as "The Blitz"—the vengeful, semi-indiscriminate pounding of London by night. For the first time, and for roughly a fortnight, Goering's tactics marched with Hitler's strategy; for the first time Fighter Command came close to defeat. "Once the enemy air force has been annihilated," Goering told the commanders of his Air Fleets on 19 August, "our attacks will be directed as ordered against other vital targets." He meant targets connected with the invasion.

Only four days earlier, before the disastrous issue of the all-out operations on 15 August was known at Karinhall, Goering had said

[1] It was however a sensible decision. The dive-bombers were designed for the close support of ground troops and had made their name in this role. Withdrawn from the air-battle, they remained available as a substitute for artillery in the assault phase of *Operation Sea Lion;* and in early September the concentration of *Stuka* squadrons in the Pas de Calais area was one of the many indications received by the British that invasion was imminent.

the same thing in the same place to the same men: "We must concentrate our attacks on the destruction of the enemy air forces". Little, at high cost, had been achieved since then. But now, in the last week of August, the Luftwaffe for the first time had recourse to a potentially lethal pattern of attack.

Up to now the German offensive in the air had essayed, more or less simultaneously, three different tasks. It had tried to overwhelm the outposts of the British defence, and in the process to draw into the fight and liquidate the supposedly meagre British reserves; it had probed the left, or north-easterly, flank, which should in theory have been ill defended; and it had done its best to hamstring Fighter Command by destroying its main sources of supply, the aircraft factories. In all three tasks the Germans had failed; and in the first two, which were immediate to their purpose, they knew that they had failed. They turned now to a narrower and more rewarding field.

It was from a study of signals intelligence that the Germans came to realise the cardinal importance of the Sector Stations. At Fighter Command Headquarters, Dowding was in the normal position of a commander-in-chief; he planned the battle but he did not fight it himself; once it had been joined, he could influence its outcome only by the judicious use of his reserves. The actual fighting was controlled from Group Headquarters; and the Sector Stations were the agencies through which control was exercised. As Richards puts it, "[Fighter] Command and Group were the brain of our defensive system; the Sectors were the nerve-centres". Group ordered the squadrons up; thereafter the Sector Stations (each of which normally handled three squadrons) passed on to the pilots, by radio-telephone, the latest combat-intelligence and thus guided them into battle on advantageous terms.

These continual, urgent colloquies between ground and air were audible to the German monitors, and it needed only a moderate talent for jigsaw puzzles to understand how vital a role the Sector Stations were playing, and how disastrous to the squadrons they controlled it would be if they ceased, even temporarily, to play it. On 24 August the Luftwaffe began a series of heavy attacks on the inner zone of airfields on which No. 11 Group's seven Sector

Stations were deployed and on which the defence of south-east England and the capital depended.[1]

The outlook for Fighter Command was already bleak enough when these hard shrewd blows were delivered. The sheer weight of numbers was beginning to tell, and casualties in men and machines exceeded replacements by an ominous and increasing margin.

From 8–18 August the RAF lost 154 pilots killed, missing or badly wounded; during the same period only 63 joined the squadrons from the training units, and these, being as yet raw, were less serviceable than the men whose places they took. There was, too, a more imponderable form of wastage, for upon the pilots who survived (and for whom, as Richards says, "two or three sorties a day was normal, six or seven not uncommon") the strain was slowly becoming unendurable. There was a rush of volunteers from establishments where bomber and reconnaissance pilots were trained, and arrangements were made to assimilate these after a short period of re-training; but stopgaps could not remedy a situation which would very soon be desperate.

The figures of aircraft losses told the same story. Over the same ten days—8–18 August—the RAF shot down 367 German aircraft (and believed, of course, that they had shot down many more). They lost 213 fighters, of which 30 were destroyed on the ground; but less than 150 Hurricanes and Spitfires were produced during the period, and the squadrons could be brought up to strength in machines only by drawing on reserves.

For the handful of men in England who knew the facts the truth must, by 19 August, have been plain to see; since the strength of the Luftwaffe, and the capacity of the industries behind it, were not then known with certainty, the exaggerated British estimate of German casualties in the fighting cannot have seriously distorted their vision of that truth. All the evidence pointed to the inescapable conclusion that in this great slogging match the Luftwaffe would, within a few weeks, reduce Fighter Command to a guerrilla force, powerless to thwart the main aims of German strategy. This fact was recognised; yet in the mood of the hour, shot through by

[1] They were Tangmere, Debden, Kenley, Biggin Hill, Hornchurch, North Weald and Northolt.

a blind, happy-go-lucky faith in victory, the grim verdict of the statistics seemed an academic thing, with small power to dismay. And in a sense it was academic. It was not within the power of the British to close the gap between casualties and replacements or even —save negligibly—to prevent it widening; only (as it seemed) some vagary of the climate could retard this process by reducing the scale of the operations. The nation's leaders faced no torturing alternatives. There was nothing to do but to fight on, and hope for the best.

In this situation the Luftwaffe's attacks on No. 11 Group's Sector Stations, which began in earnest on 24 August, were the worst possible omen. Hitherto it had been by a process of attrition that the Germans had laid the foundations of a British defeat in the air. In every day's fighting the Luftwaffe had been worsted; but in every day's fighting the victors had suffered losses whose cumulative effect was bound in the end to prove mortal. And these losses had been sustained in repelling attacks on objectives which were not *immediately* vital to German strategy.

What German strategy needed was supremacy—not superiority— in the air over south-east England, the Channel and the Continental ports from which invasion was to come. This requirement had implications, such as the neutralisation of Bomber Command and Coastal Command, which were never fully taken into account by the Germans; but their first task, both in reality and in their own estimation, was to eliminate Fighter Command. Skirmishing and coat-trailing before "Eagle-day" furthered this purpose. Thereafter —from 12 to 24 August—they had concentrated their attacks either on forward airfields (like Manston and West Malling in Kent) which were expendable, or on factories whose total destruction, had it been achieved, would still not have crippled the British defences within the requisite period of less than forty days.

What the situation demanded was a knock-out blow. Hitler had decreed it, Goering had promised it, Raeder kept on complaining that it had not been delivered, the sanguine von Brauchitsch took it for granted. But until 24 August the Luftwaffe's tactics had not been shaped for a knock-out, let alone a swift one. Now, for the first time since Goering had called off the attacks on radar stations, the Germans struck at their adversary's vitals.

They achieved very fair results. Of all the erratic changes in German tactics the decision to concentrate on the Sector Stations covering London was alone completely sound. True, it gave Fighter Command—since these targets lay further inland—an opportunity to intercept in strength instead of scrambling squadrons into the air piecemeal, which had been the only answer to the tip-and-run raids on peripheral objectives. But in fact the pace was so hot, the squadrons so fully committed, and the battered Sector Stations so hard put to it to continue functioning at all, that this theoretical advantage did not mean a great deal to the RAF.

No Sector Station was completely knocked out. But severe and cumulative damage, especially at Biggin Hill and Kenley, was beginning to atrophy these nerve-centres, where courage of the highest order was displayed by the girls of the Women's Auxiliary Air Force manning the communications systems.[1] The fortnight during which the Luftwaffe persisted in these attacks, and which ended on 6 September, cost the Luftwaffe 378 aircraft; but the RAF lost 277. This proportion of 5–7 was the best the Germans achieved; and at the same time they were inflicting much miscellaneous damage on ground targets. "The scales", Churchill wrote afterwards, "had tilted against Fighter Command. . . . There was much anxiety."

Then suddenly on 7 September there came a change. Late in the afternoon the Luftwaffe began its first concentrated attack on London. All through the evening, all through that night until just before dawn on the 8th, relays of aircraft showered high explosive and incendiary bombs on the sprawling capital. Similar operations were thereafter carried out by an average of 200 bombers for fifty-seven consecutive nights. The cratered, rubble-strewn Sector Stations were reprieved.

[1] One of the exigencies of service in the WAAF is recalled by this passage from *Survivor's Story*, by Air Marshal Sir Gerald Gibbs (London, 1956):

"In the beginning we tried to get the girls to leave those rooms in which R/T [radio-telephonic communications] was broadcast from the aircraft during air fighting—for the language was terrible. But it wasn't idle blasphemy or obscenity, it was the voice of men in the midst of fighting for their lives—and dying. The girls refused to leave their jobs and said they didn't mind the language as much as we thought. They added that it was nice of us to think of their being like that, all the same."

To those who endured it, as to those who launched it, the onslaught on London seemed to represent a strategic climax, to be the culmination of a master-plan. In fact it was not a climax but a quirk of German strategy. The Blitz was a confession of inadequacy, a gamble on terror undertaken because other weapons had failed to produce the swift decision that was required and expected of them; and strangely enough it was begun (as will be told in Chapter 19) because of a comparatively trivial blunder unwittingly committed by a few German aircraft a fortnight earlier.

From the moment when he directed Goering's air-fleets on London, Hitler destroyed such prospects as remained to him of invading England in 1940; and by his intervention as a strategist at this juncture he rendered services to Fighter Command comparable to those he had rendered to the British Expeditionary Force when he sanctioned a delay in the advance of German armour on Dunkirk at the end of May.

But it is time now to cross to the other camp and review the preparations there being made for *Operation Sea Lion*.

CHAPTER SIXTEEN

The Legend of German Dilettantism

Poins. What says Monsieur Remorse?
Shakespeare: *Henry IV, Part I*

IN Germany after the war it became customary to speak of *Operation Sea Lion* as an almost whimsical project which nobody took seriously at the time. Ex-generals claimed that the Army's preparations went forward in the relaxed and academic atmosphere of a *Kriegspiel*. Kesselring, at the time commanding *Luftflotte* 2, remembered being "convinced that the operation would never be started". "It is only possible", he wrote, "to understand the antecedents of *Sea Lion* . . . on the assumption that the High Command continually flirted with the idea of an invasion as a conscience-salve for its failure to make up its mind by reason of a number of political and military misgivings." Others have advanced kindred variations of the theme that the invasion-project was only a kind of strategical doodling.

They are not supported by the facts. Of these the most important is that Hitler—then a demi-god bathed in a shining aura of success—ordered that invasion should be carried out. His orders may, for reasons analysed in earlier chapters, have lacked alacrity but they did not lack compulsion. They were issued before he fully realised the difficulties of the operation; but when he did realise the difficulties he did not cancel the orders. Nor did he, even provisionally, commit the great military machine which he had driven headlong to the Channel coast to any alternative strategy. Had there existed, for instance, a plan for the systematic reduction of England by bombing it would be possible to argue that the three Air Fleets, poised in a great arc to pave the way for *Sea Lion*, had all the time an ulterior role, that they stood in much the same relation to invasion as invasion itself had stood to Hitler's hopes of a British surrender. But no such plan existed.[1] The air offensive against London and other cities was not planned as an insurance against invasion proving impossible. In fact it was not planned in advance at all. " *In this operation,*" Directive No. 16 had decreed, " *elements of the Air Force will do the work of the artillery.*" This was exactly what the Luftwaffe were doing when *Sea Lion* was cancelled; and one of the reasons why they went on doing it afterwards was that they had been given nothing else to do.

It is true that in the summer of 1940 Hitler's mind dwelt increasingly on Russia. In a memorandum on 9 October 1939, and again in an harangue to his commanders-in-chief on 23 November, he had implied that his ultimate purposes included an attack on Russia. But on the second occasion he had said: "We can oppose Russia only when we are at peace in the West." To this sound principle he meant to adhere; for he abhorred the prospect of a war on two fronts, to the dangers of which his political testament, *Mein Kampf,* had made repeated and emphatic reference. (More than seven million copies of this long, turbid book had been sold in Germany, and although it had perhaps found more purchasers than readers its main themes were widely known.) In June 1940, before France had fallen, he told Jodl that he would move against Russia "the moment our military position makes it at all possible"; in July he told Keitel that he wanted to do so in the autumn of 1940.[2]

But when he made this last statement he still expected a prompt British capitulation as a matter of course; and during the weeks when *Sea Lion* was being mounted he confined his actions in the East to such purely defensive or precautionary measures as the fortification of the north Norwegian fiords and the dispatch of a military mission to prepare bases in Rumania "in case a war with

---

[1] Directive No. 17 (issued on 1 August), which called for an intensification of air and sea warfare against England, did indeed lay down a bombing policy in general terms; but it was a short-term policy, aimed at creating conditions which would make invasion either unnecessary or—failing that—practicable. It was in no sense an alternative strategy.

[2] It is unlikely that this project would have survived an examination of the seasonal and climatic problems involved.

Soviet Russia is forced upon us". It was not until 9 August (when, it will be remembered, bad weather was causing the postponement of "Eagle-day" and there was clearly a strong possibility that invasion might not prove possible in 1940) that OKW were ordered, in a directive which did not mention Russia, to prepare a preliminary outline plan for a campaign in the East; nobody outside OKW saw this plan (although its existence was suspected) at the time.

Hitler was slow to admit that invasion was a strategical necessity and almost equally slow to realise that it was a tactical impossibility. In the intervening weeks he took, as we have seen, little direct interest in the preparations for a novel and important operation; and it is almost certainly true that, in the abstract, a land-campaign against a supposedly weak, Slavonic adversary whom he regarded with pathological detestation made a stronger appeal to his mind and his emotions than an amphibious attack on a fiercely defended island for whose "Aryan" inhabitants he entertained a sneaking esteem.[1] But no respectable evidence, indeed no evidence at all, supports the view that Hitler never really meant to carry out the invasion for which elaborate and costly preparations were made, which for some three months remained the only important item on the operational agenda of his all-conquering forces, about which he boasted to his Italian allies and allowed German propaganda to boast to the world, and to the vital opening phase of which the flower of the German Air Force was, with unhappy results, committed.

[1] The following extract from Hitler's Directive of 13 May 1941, which laid down procedure for dealing with the Russian civilian population during *Operation Barbarossa*, gives a hint of the relish with which he contemplated the conquest of Russia:

"II. Manner of dealing with crimes by members of the armed forces . . . against the civilian population.

(1) There is no compulsion to prosecute actions committed by members of the armed forces against enemy civilians, even when such acts constitute crimes or offences under military law.

(2) In judging such acts it should be kept in mind in each case that the collapse of 1918, the later times of suffering of the German people, and the fight against National Socialism, with the many National Socialists who perished, were mainly the result of Bolshevist influence, and no German must forget that."

The savagery of the German orders dealing with the treatment of British civilians was of a more impersonal and less blatant kind. (See Chapter 18.)

We saw, in Chapters 3 and 4, how the foundations of the German plans were laid in July. The chief burden of the preparations fell upon the Navy, who now began, with more diligence than enthusiasm, to requisition a heterogeneous armada. The economic dislocation which these measures caused throughout Germany and Occupied Europe was one of the stock arguments which Raeder used in his untiring, but cautious, efforts to have *Sea Lion* shelved. His staff estimated the shipping requirements of the invading force, even after it had been sharply reduced in size, as follows:

155 transports
1,722 barges
471 tugs
1,161 motor-boats.

On 26 July he was describing to the Fuehrer "forcefully once again" the damage which would be inflicted on the German economy by the diversion of these resources.[1]

The barges were mostly canal barges, with a loading capacity of 500–800 tons and a draught of six feet, but some river barges, with a capacity of 1,300 tons, were also impressed. Very few were self-propelled, and the indispensable tugs (of which in the end only 386 were got together) were a highly vulnerable part of the whole enterprise. The owners of the barges, of whom more than half were Dutch and Belgian and several hundred French, received compensation at a not ungenerous daily rate based on tonnage and —for powered craft—on horse-power. When *Sea Lion* was finally cancelled, most of the barges were retained by the military authorities for various administrative purposes; but the rate of compensation, which had been worth paying for the sinews of a swift victory, was seen, now that the barges were required not for weeks but for years, to be in need of revision, and in September the rates were much reduced.

The barges were adapted for their role as assault craft by removing the bows and replacing them with collapsible ramps which would act both as sally-ports and as gangways for men and vehicles; they

[1] Raeder was not being merely specious. On 12 October 1940, in one of the directives winding up *Operation Sea Lion*, Hitler decreed that "our war economy must be relieved of some of the present heavy strain placed upon it by our invasion preparations".

were also given concrete floors, so that they could carry tanks, guns and motor vehicles. Neither expedient increased their sea-worthiness or their manoeuvrability, which were in any case—since they were designed only to navigate inland waterways—extremely limited even before conversion. Some of the largest barges, instead of being towed, were to be pushed across the Channel by a pair of small minesweepers lashed on either side of their stern; it is doubtful if these improvised ferries, which had a maximum speed of four knots, could have reached their objectives, or even completed the crossing at all, save in a dead calm, yet they were to carry, in an early wave of the assault, men of two *élite* divisions of the *Waffen SS*.

To a race of landsmen the manning of this remarkable fleet (whose role, it must be remembered, was not to make one reckless descent on England in favourable weather but to cross and recross the Channel continuously for several weeks under conditions which were bound to deteriorate) presented considerable problems. Appeals for men with experience of watermanship resulted in a certain number volunteering or being drafted; but often only very tenuous qualifications (such as a taste for canoeing) fitted these recruits for their new duties, and the placid bargees were sea-dogs by comparison.

But it would be wrong to underrate the drive and resourcefulness with which, in a matter of weeks and starting from scratch, the Germans equipped and assembled the craft they needed; it was a prodigious feat of organisation. In it they were greatly helped by their control of huge labour reserves in the subjugated countries. This is a factor which ought not to be ignored in comparing the respective positions of Germany and Britain in the summer of 1940, for it further weighted the balance of strength in Germany's favour. Everything the British did in preparing their defences they had to do for themselves; they filled their own sandbags, dug their own trenches, drove their own trains, cleared up their own bomb-damage. On the other side of the Channel the Germans could get these and many other things done for them, and French, Dutch and Belgian workmen and officials were perforce harnessed, directly or indirectly, to the task of preparing invasion.

On 19 July, three days after he had received Directive No. 16, Raeder submitted to the Fuehrer a long memorandum setting forth the difficulties inherent in the operation and the dangers to be feared from weather, mines, the British land-defences, the lack of artillery support, and above all from the Royal Navy, which he expected to be committed "fully and decisively", which the Luftwaffe would not be able to deal with, and which, even if the first wave got ashore, might well be able to cut it off from seaward.

On the 21st he had an interview with Hitler, who was still talking in terms of 40 divisions and the "main operation" being "completed" by 15 September. Hitler conceded however that "the invasion of Britain is an especially daring undertaking, because even if the way is short, this is not just a river-crossing, but the crossing of a sea which is dominated by the enemy". He had perhaps begun to suspect that the German Navy's responsibilities were not limited to "doing the work of the engineers" in a river-crossing operation. If Raeder made any comments, he did not record them.

By now OKW had come round to the idea that *Sea Lion*—in which they had not so far taken, and indeed never did take, an executive part of any consequence—was a capital scheme; and OKH were looking forward to "a war of movement on the Island". On 29 June the Navy were given an outline of OKH's requirements: 13 divisions (about 260,000 men) to be landed at dawn between Ramsgate and Lyme Bay and to be followed—in less than the ten days which the Navy considered feasible—by a second wave of unspecified strength. This began a long controversy, the Army adhering to its demands for a wide front, the Navy insisting that a narrow front was operationally essential as far as they were concerned.[1]

On 31 July—with D-day still, on paper, only 15 days away—Raeder was summoned to another conference with Hitler. Besides those military waxworks from OKW, Keitel and Jodl,[2] OKH were represented by von Brauchitsch and Halder. Raeder, whose attitude to *Sea Lion* was not in the current vogue, began by reporting that "all preparations are in full swing" but that 15 September was the

[1] The distance from Ramsgate to Lyme Bay is roughly 200 miles. Four years later the elaborately prepared Allied landings in Normandy took place on a front of roughly forty miles.

[2] Both were hanged at Nuremberg on 16 October 1946.

earliest possible date on which the operation could be launched. He took the opportunity of delivering a short lecture on the influence of tides, weather and darkness on amphibious operations.

The singular composition of the transport fleet [he said] will make it very difficult to carry out the assault in total darkness, i.e. with no moon. Large numbers of slow, unwieldy transport units concentrated in a small space, mixed with motor-boats of the most varied types, and escorted by light units of the Navy and auxiliary vessels, make it necessary to have a certain amount of light for navigational reasons.

Ostensibly Raeder was talking about the dangers of darkness; in fact he was trying, as openly as he dared, to make the soldiers realise that *Sea Lion* was out of the question with the available naval and shipping resources.

He explained to them about tides. "A landing at high tide has the disadvantage that craft are grounded and immobile for about twelve hours . . . and if the next high tide does not reach the level of the previous one, it may not even float them." "Rising water", he went on, warming to his theme, "is unfavourable in any case . . . it causes transport units which are aground to float again and again, thus altering their position and delaying the disembarkation." He recommended the beginning of the ebb, "about two hours after high tide."

The early dawn, he understood, was the best time from the Army's point of view; this meant a night-crossing, whose disadvantages he adumbrated in the words quoted above. He then—and it is difficult to resist the image of a fisherman, who finds he has hooked a salmon on a trout-rod, giving out line lest more obdurate tactics should prove fatal to his purpose—recommended two periods which the moon and the tides would favour. The first (which he said was now out of the question) was 20–26 August; the second, 19–26 September.

More cold water was poured, in politic douches, upon the project. Dawn was a very dangerous time; protected from the Luftwaffe by darkness, the Royal Navy could intervene against the landings from bases as far afield as the Firth of Forth. The alternative was to cross by day. Raeder knew that this was unacceptable to the Army. Lest it should appeal to Hitler's intuition, he drew attention to its main ostensible advantage. "If the crossing is made by day, air reconnaissance can locate the position of enemy naval forces. The operation [which he went on to point out was in any case only possible 'if the sea is calm'] could be stopped if necessary."

Raeder on these occasions prepared notes of what he intended to say. There is no reason to suppose that he did not say it, or that his record of his own part in the proceedings was inaccurate. On 31 July it was the bluff sailor, the expert, speaking. But the bluff sailor spoke, in the interests of his own Service, with considerable astuteness. England was expecting invasion. So were the German Army, the German people and the world at large. Raeder, playing a big fish on light tackle, got as near as he ever did to gaffing it when he suggested that the invasion might have to be called off after the flotillas had set sail. Whether it was pride in his own Service, a sense of duty to his Leader, or a streak of moral cowardice which debarred him from saying plainly that the operation was impossible, we do not know; but he ended, perhaps not uncharacteristically, by recommending that "the best time for the operation, all things considered, would be May 1941."

Raeder's exposition had a considerable and immediate effect on Hitler. "An attempt", the Grand-Admiral recorded him as deciding, "must be made to prepare the operation for 15 September 1940. The decision as to whether the operation is to take place in September or is to be postponed until May 1941 will be delayed until after the Air Force has made concentrated attacks on southern England for one week."[1] These modifications in the plan for *Sea Lion* were crystallised in an OKW order issued on the following day (1 August). Everything was to be ready by 15 September; "8 or 14 days"— second thoughts had made the margin longer but not less arbitrary —"after the launching of the air offensive against Britain, scheduled to begin on approximately 5 August, the Fuehrer will decide whether the invasion will take place this year or not; his decision will depend largely on the outcome of the air offensive".

These orders (which also postponed the move to Ziegenberg and Giessen of the four staffs concerned with their execution[2]) were

---

[1] This estimate of what should constitute a mortal blow well illustrates the nature of German delusions about air power.

[2] See pp. 50–52.

signed by Keitel. They were sensible orders in that they accepted
the inevitable and postponed D-Day from 15 August to (at the
earliest) 15 September. But military orders, though often involun-
tarily unrealistic, should never be demonstrably vague; and to make
everything "largely" dependent on the outcome of an air offensive
with a maximum duration of a fortnight, and a D-day at the mercy
of the weather, was far from practical.

How would the results of that offensive be ascertained in so short
a time? Was it reasonable to hope that Fighter Command, and
Bomber Command as well, would be liquidated in a trice? Granted
his consistent over-estimate of the Luftwaffe's powers, did Hitler
know the capabilities and limitations of their actual plan of attack?

To these imponderable questions the most likely answer is that
Hitler still hoped, obstinately and foolishly, that the British, who
ought to have given in weeks ago, would collapse or disintegrate as
soon as he started to turn the heat on them. At this stage he still in
his heart believed that a display of force would succeed—where an
appeal to reason had failed—in bringing them simultaneously to
their senses and their knees.

It was on the following day that he ordered Goering to prepare, as
a matter of urgency, the air offensive against the island.

While Raeder at the summit discreetly prophesied doom, the
Army addressed themselves without serious misgivings to the task
in hand. It is important to recall that their mood, after the Fall of
France, was one of exaltation; their victories had stupefied the world
and nothing seemed impossible. Their self-confidence, though less
vaunting than the Luftwaffe's, was nevertheless profound. "Without underrating the dangers, we were confident of success",
Manstein wrote afterwards.

On 1 July, anticipating the sense of the OKW "warning order"
issued on the following day, Halder conferred in Berlin with
Admiral Schniewind, who as Raeder's Chief of Staff was his opposite
number. They spoke of the possibility of using railroad ferries to
transport tanks, of the utility of smoke-screens, and of tests which
were being carried out on "Dr Feder-type concrete barges".

These were not in fact barges, but enormous submersible tanks with a minimum length of 90 feet (nearly four times that of a London omnibus); they were built of ferro-concrete and designed to carry no less than 200 men with their arms and equipment. The idea had originated, more than three months earlier, in the brain of Dr Feder, an early Party member who was now a State Secretary in the Ministry of Economics, and had rather surprisingly survived some scrutiny by the technical branches of the Army and the Navy. These interesting engines of war were intended to cross the Channel by creeping upon the sea-bed, and were known as "War Tortoises" or "War Crocodiles".[1]

Though the project came to nothing in the end, it was still being taken seriously at this stage. So was a plan—which did not prove abortive—for using both amphibious and submersible tanks. On 4 July Halder wrote in his diary: "What is maximum distance for *detection of sound* of moving surface craft and underwater movement of tanks?" This early preoccupation with one of the more technical aspects of the final assault bears out other indications that the idea of invasion was not received by the Army with the indulgent scepticism which was later said to have informed their attitude throughout the summer.[2] Halder was a frank though not a voluble diarist, who normally noted the major causes of his discontents and doubts. On 13 July, for instance, he recorded that "the situation is growing intolerable". His outburst was not prompted by dissatisfaction with the invasion plan, but by irritation at the arrangements for a Victory Parade in Paris; in this a leading role had been allotted to a number of Mark III and Mark IV Panzers which should have gone back to Germany to be amphibianised.[3] Throughout

---

[1] R. R. A. Wheatley: *Operation Sea Lion.* (See p. 13.)

[2] A sidelight on the OKH outlook at this time is provided by another item on the Chief of Staff's agenda on 5 July. This was a project for raising and training, in Norway, a "Colonial regiment" of 10,000 men. Halder did not define its role in his diary, but he noted the need for "data on type of automobiles best adapted to use in Colonies". It seems fair to infer that he was counting on the return to Germany, at an early date, of the overseas possessions which she had forfeited after the First World War. On 17 July an American correspondent in Berlin heard that a number of SS men were undergoing tuition in Swahili. (Shirer.)

[3] The Victory Parade was eventually cancelled, partly because of rumours that the RAF intended to mar the celebrations, but chiefly because the war had not been won.

these early days the entries in Halder's diaries referring to invasion strike a brisk, sanguine note; there is no trace of scepticism or misgiving.

Meanwhile training for the operation had started. It was necessarily empirical, and was complicated by the diversity of the invasion fleet, only token elements of which were available for training purposes on the Channel coast. Barges differed in size, type and means of propulsion. Some units were to tranship into them from transports, others were to be towed all the way across. Motor-boats, launches, fishing-smacks, trawlers—craft of all kinds had to be budgeted for; and in advance of their arrival the troops, like Chinese actors mounting imaginary horses, had to learn some form of embarkation and disembarkation drill and be told where they would stow their gear. The experiences of 8 Division illustrate some of the difficulties experienced; this formation reported on 23 August that it had been able to obtain only one steamer to train with, and that this had now been sunk. [1]

Though the morale of the German troops was, and remained, high, it was noticed that men from the Baltic and North German coasts viewed the prospect before them with less enthusiasm than their comrades. An understanding of, or even an acquaintance with, the sea were rare among officers and other ranks. Two Mountain Divisions, raised in the highlands of Austria and Bavaria, were allotted to Army Group A in a cliff-scaling role. The commander of one of them, reaching his training area on the Channel coast, decided that his men must learn to swim, in case of accidents. The order was given that swimming instruction would take place daily at 0900 hours. On the first day, at the appointed time, the battalions jogged smartly down to the sectors of beach allotted to them and swam or floundered according to their lights. Breasting the sand-dunes at 0900 hours on the second day, they were astonished and dismayed to find that the sea had moved; it was much farther away than it had been the day before. A naval liaison officer explained

[1] Wheatley. Among many of the German soldiers one of the strongest impressions made by their invasion-training was the contrast between their own up-to-date, standardised arms and equipment and the old, ramshackle, assorted craft in which they were to cross the sea.

this phenomenon and suggested that—since on this part of the coast at this time of year the ebbing tide receded a long way from the foreshore—the Mountain Division should alter from day to day the time at which it practised swimming. But this officer had a supercilious manner and was not liked; moreover the divisional training programme had been worked out with much thoroughness for a long time ahead, and to adopt his proposal would have involved its complete reorganisation. So the mountaineers continued to seek, punctually at 0900 hours, the embraces of an increasingly coy *Kanal*.[1]

Throughout July, nevertheless, the Army's preparations went forward purposefully; "all ranks [wrote a first-wave corps commander] showed the utmost keenness in training for their unaccustomed task, and we were convinced that, like everything else, it could be mastered in due course". There were many problems to solve, but they were tackled with determination; they were not problems upon whose solution the whole conception of invasion depended for its validity, and the atmosphere at Fontainebleau was bustling and confident. Thence (for instance) on 26 July OKH reported to OKW its view that: "The British operational command, possessing little flexibility, will not be in a position to master the difficult situations arising. The success of the German attacks is thus unquestionable." On the same day Halder was concerning himself with the provision of "75 large pneumatic floats for each main assault group" and with renewed endeavours to cut down the number of horses in the first and second waves; though reduced to 4,200 and 7,000 respectively, the totals were regarded as being still too high. (The British, anxiously awaiting an onslaught in which they expected new and terrible weapons to be employed, would have been very much surprised to learn that the invaders proposed to bring several thousand horses with them, and the disembarkation of these animals under fire would have complicated the tactical

---

[1] It was not only the mountain troops who were disconcerted by the unfamiliar tides. General von Manstein, then commanding 38 Corps, recalls an occasion when he left his car on the foreshore and went swimming with his driver and his ADC. "When we were already far out to sea, the waves suddenly started lapping round our Mercedes on the beach. Only in the very nick of time did we succeed in getting a tractor to tow it out of the incoming tide." (Erich von Manstein: *Verlorene Siege*. Bonn, 1955.)

"Nonsense, my dear Gertrude! They could never swim their horses ashore in a sea like this." *Daily Express*, 22 February 1941

problems of the assault; but in fact horses represented the only available form of motive power with which guns and limbers could be brought from the barges into the beach-head.) [1]

But these halcyon days of planning were almost over, for on 28 July the Navy revealed the full width of the margin which still separated its maximum capabilities from the Army's minimum requirements. Halder stopped counting horses; "We can throw away the whole plan", he reflected. Nobody suggested that this should actually be done, but it was clear that some of the most important assumptions on which the Army had been working were baseless. As escorts or flank-guards the Navy could muster only a flimsy screen of destroyers, torpedo-boats and submarines; the clockwork shuttle-service of barges (which the Army, in the light of some exercises carried out at Emden, expected to cross and recross the Channel with extraordinary celerity) was a land-lubber's dream; it would take ten days to put the first wave across; and nothing could happen before 15 September at the earliest. There followed, on 31 July, the inter-service conference with Hitler at which Raeder, after implying that the operation was impossible, recommended its postponement until 1941.

Now was the time, and here was the excuse, to abandon *Sea Lion*. This course was not discussed. The tenacity with which the Germans

---

[1] At least one infantry division of 6 Army (which was not involved in the assault but which was expected to provide a follow-up force) carried out its training with donkeys requisitioned from the Norman peasants. These animals proved intractable, and were such a nuisance to units on the march that they were always driven to the beaches in lorries.

stuck to a strategy to which fresh drawbacks were discovered almost every day but to which no alternative was seriously pondered is very striking. Legend may assert that they only flirted with the idea of invasion, that they were not really trying; the facts show that they tried very hard indeed.

CHAPTER SEVENTEEN

The Sausage Machine

A frontal attack against a defence line, on too narrow a front, with no good prospects of surprise, and with insufficient forces reinforced only in driblets.

Field Marshal von Brauchitsch, commenting on *Operation Sea Lion* in September 1940

PLANNING for the invasion continued throughout August. It began with controversy, went on to compromise and ended with a great contraction of the front to be attacked.

On 7 August Halder and Schniewind, the two Chiefs of Staff, had a meeting much less harmonious than that at which, five weeks earlier, they had discussed the "War Crocodiles" of Dr Feder. It revealed, according to Halder, "irreconcilable differences" between the Army's and the Navy's points of view. "I utterly reject the Navy's proposals [for landings on a narrow front]," Halder is recorded as exclaiming. "I might just as well put the troops through a sausage machine." A memorandum in which this theme was developed was sent to the Navy.

Schniewind retorted on 14 August with a counter-memorandum, in which he made a vigorous effort to impress on the soldiers the realities of the naval situation and the facts of life in the English Channel. It was sub-acid in tone: "The airborne troops can influence neither the weather nor the sea; they cannot prevent the destruction and incapacitation of the few harbours, nor hold off the enemy fleet or even a small part of it." Two days later Hitler imposed a compromise on the disputants.[1]

[1] This was not the first time that inter-service differences had threatened the success of an invasion of England. In 1588 Medina Sidonia's orders to the Armada included a paragraph specifically designed to limit this threat: "And because it behoveth much, for the preservation and good success of this army, that there be good agreement and friendship between the soldiers and the mariners, and that they behave themselves so lovingly together, that there arise nor happen no

The most westerly of the proposed bridgeheads, in Lyme Bay, was to be discarded, and dispositions were to be made so as "not to exclude the possibility of an attack on a narrow front, should this be ordered at the last minute, and to leave open the possibility of an independent landing in the Brighton area". Within this sketchy and elastic framework the plan for *Sea Lion* slowly assumed its final form. Already in the sky over the objectives the air-battles which were to make its launching possible had begun to rage.

Nobody talked any longer of 40 divisions, but for some time it was hoped that 13 (or roughly a quarter of a million men) could be thrown across the Channel in the first wave, with the second and third waves following hard on their heels; the whole of the first wave would be put ashore in between two and three days.

Study revealed that this was not practicable, and a further reduction in both the scale and the impetus of the assault was reluctantly accepted. In the final version the first wave was to comprise nine infantry divisions, with two airborne divisions in direct support; but it was going to take no less than eleven days to land the whole of these nine divisions, and thereafter they could expect reinforcements at the rate of only two divisions every four days.

One hopeful feature of the plan for the first assault-landings was the amphibious tanks, of which there were some 250, organised in four battalions. They consisted of light tanks, which were truly amphibious and could, as it were, swim ashore from the barges, and medium tanks, which were submersible and with the help of periscopes and breathing-tubes could if necessary travel for a short distance under water.

A weakness in the German arrangements, which they recognised and worried about, was the lack of artillery support to neutralise the

---

differences, tumults, or other occasions of quarrels between them, I command that an ordinance be made, that they wear no dagger, nor that they over-thwart one another, for any occasion, but that they all obey their superiors and officers." (James Bruce: *Report on the Spanish Armada*. State Paper Office, 1798.) Of the 27,128 fighting men embarked in the Armada's 166 ships, 6,128 were sailors. It is Parma's improvised and largely flat-bottomed invasion-fleet mustered canalwise at Dunkirk and Nieuport, rather than the Armada itself, which is the distant prototype of *Sea Lion*. Parma's forces, like Hitler's, never sailed; and Parma, like Hitler, had thought London would be easily reduced "by reason of the citizens' delicacy and discontinuance from the warres".

British beach-defences. The German Navy was not hazarding in these operations anything bigger than destroyers, and it was expected that these vessels, of which there were dangerously few, and the torpedo-boats (which, though comparatively plentiful, carried fewer and lighter guns), would be fully occupied on either flank of the invasion. In mid-August anxious consideration was given to the possibility of employing, in the role of monitors or floating batteries, the two old battleships *Schlesien* and *Schleswig-Holstein*, which had been laid down in 1906; they had been used to bombard forts on the Hel Peninsula in the Polish campaign. It was found however that it would take too long to fit them out with adequate anti-aircraft defences and underwater protection, and the idea was dropped. Various other expedients were canvassed, such as the mounting of 6-inch guns on barges or even on rafts, but none proved wholly satisfactory; and in the event the main fire-power on which the assault would have had to rely was to be provided by a number of 3-inch and 37-mm cannon emplaced on 27 self-propelled coastal craft. On a front which still totalled some 50 miles this was a derisory scale of artillery support; and the complete absence of any heavy guns with the attacking flotillas underlined the importance of ensuring a free hand for the German bombers, fighter-bombers and dive-bombers, which alone could have made any impression on the British pill-boxes and redoubts, let alone on more permanent fortifications.[1]

The nine divisions of the first wave were directed on the following objectives:

(1) Four divisions of 16 Army, embarking at Rotterdam, Antwerp, Ostend, Dunkirk and Calais, were to land in the Folkestone–St Leonards area.

(2) Two divisions of 9 Army, embarking at Boulogne, were to land in the Bexhill–Eastbourne area.

[1] As early as 19 July the Naval Staff, in a memorandum already referred to, had foreseen this weakness in a plan as yet unformulated. "The nature", they wrote, "of anti-invasion defences on the enemy coast, and the detailed preparations which he has been making for a considerable time, cause doubt as to whether the Luftwaffe will succeed in eliminating defensive troops on the coast sufficiently to allow a landing to take place *without any effective artillery support from seaward*".

(3) Three divisions of 9 Army, embarking at Le Havre, were to land between Beachy Head and Brighton.

In addition, on D-Day (or *S-Tag*, as the Germans knew it) 7 *Flieger-Division* was to capture the high ground north and north-west of Folkestone, and having done so was to secure crossings over the Royal Military Canal for the benefit of the seaborne troops in that sector, at the same time establishing a road-block on the Canterbury–Folkestone road. Other airborne troops were provisionally directed on the downs behind Brighton.

The bridgeheads (which the British were not expected to counter-attack in strength until the morning of the fifth day after the landings) were to be expanded in 16 Army's sector to the line Canterbury–Ashford–Tenterden–Etchingham, and in 9 Army's sector to a line running from "the high ground 29 km north and west of Bexhill" through Uckfield to "the high ground west and south-west of Lewes". From these bridgeheads the two armies were in due course to break out and secure their first objective, the line Portsmouth–Petersfield–Guildford–Reigate–Gravesend. In the original plan 6 Army, crossing from the Cherbourg Peninsula to Lyme Bay, was to have carried out a wide encircling movement and placed itself to the north of London. For this useful and attractive manoeuvre no satisfactory substitute was evolved in the final plan; and it is only necessary to glance at the map to understand why the Army always hankered after a wide front, with bridgeheads as far to the west as possible from which a swinging left hook could be delivered at the capital and the Midlands.

When at the end of August this plan was embodied by OKH in an operation order, D-Day was still 21 September. Embarkation would start on the previous day and after a night-crossing the assault would take place at dawn on the 21st. An OKW order of 3 September laid down that final orders for the launching of the invasion would be given on D–10 ("presumably therefore on 11 September" —the small but unsoldierly element of vagueness is typical of OKW, whose leading lights were courtiers first, officers afterwards) and that all preparations would remain liable to cancellation until twenty-four hours before zero hour.

One diversion, ponderous rather than elaborate, was planned to distract the defenders' attention from the main assault and to muddle them while it was being delivered; this subsidiary operation was given the code-name *Herbstreise,* or *Autumn Journey.* On D-2 four cruisers and four liners (the latter included the *Europa* and the *Bremen,* the prewar mainstays of German prestige on the Atlantic routes) were to sail from ports in southern Norway in the general direction of the British north-east coast between Aberdeen and Newcastle. They were to turn back under cover of darkness but would repeat the manoeuvre on the following day if circumstances seemed propitious.

The British, keenly aware that they could neither be strong everywhere nor afford to shift their reserves to meet threats which might prove only to be feints, had pondered deeply the problems of possible diversions by the enemy. They overrated his powers, and thought in terms of diversionary assaults upon their coasts, not of tentative naval demonstrations a long way off-shore. Nevertheless the principle they evolved was a sound one. All diversions, the General Staff reasoned, would have one common characteristic: that their success in diverting or containing British forces would last only as long as the diversion "constituted in the view of the defenders an important threat". This commonsense doctrine might not have been strictly adhered to in a crisis; but it seems unlikely that *Herbstreise* would have caused a prolonged deviation from it. If *Sea Lion* had been carried out, it is debatable which side would have suffered most from the deployment of eight great ships, which had been kept waiting in the wings for weeks, in a perfunctory *tableau vivant.*

A main weakness of the invasion plan was the slow rate of build-up. The assault from seaward at dawn on 21 September was to be carried out, not by nine complete divisions, but by their leading echelons, numbering in each case 6,700 men; this gives the following figures for the three beach-heads, which were much too far apart to be mutually supporting at the outset:

Folkestone–St Leonards	26,800
Bexhill–Eastbourne	13,400
Beachy Head–Brighton	20,100

These totals (which assume, unjustifiably, that no casualties were suffered on passage) show that only the equivalent of three divisions, supported by 250 tanks but by no artillery worth speaking of, would have been involved in the assault, which was to be delivered against an alert, resolute and reasonably strong defence over beaches many of which had been lavishly mined and wired and on all of which accurate and increasingly heavy gunfire could be brought to bear. Even assuming (as the Germans no longer could) that the RAF had been eliminated and that only the British anti-aircraft remained as a deterrent to the Luftwaffe, the initial assault would have been a testing affair for the bravest and most highly trained troops.

The Germans very sensibly took into account a contingency which threatened to bedevil every phase of the operation until one or more ports had been captured. One paragraph in the OKH operation order for *Sea Lion* read: "Commanders and troops must realise that the peculiar conditions of sea transport render the disintegration of formations inevitable." What this meant, briefly, was that divisions and their component units must face the fact that the flotillas, unwieldy and unevenly paced, were bound to lose cohesion during the night, so that some of the troops would be landed on the wrong beaches, and others on the right beaches at the wrong time. The extent to which things would go awry in this manner obviously depended partly on the weather; but the fact that the "disintegration" of formations—before they had made contact with the enemy —was regarded as inevitable augured badly for the success of the enterprise. Moreover, it was not only in the assault that the clumsy barges were liable to make the wrong landfall; all reinforcements and supplies for the bridgeheads would be subject to the same unpredictable margins of error until a port had been captured and the invaders ceased to be wholly dependent on supplies brought in over the beaches.

But the capture of a port would not automatically have solved their problems. Folkestone was the largest of those immediately threatened, and it was threatened by the largest force. In their *Notes on Invasion* M.I.14 considered with some care its utility (together with that of other ports) to the enemy after capture. Their assumptions were generous to the Germans. They allowed them sufficient motor transport, landed over the beaches before the first ships arrived, to clear the quaysides, and they gave them credit for having disembarrassed the harbour entrances of blockships and other obstacles; but they assumed that demolitions would have destroyed all tackle and heavy equipment in the harbour area, that the ships would therefore have to use their own derricks to unload, and that interference by the RAF would reduce handling capacity by 50 per cent.

Under these conditions they calculated that initially 150 tons could be unloaded every 24 hours at Folkestone, but that after seven days, when the place had been put in order, this figure would increase to 600 tons. They worked out the daily requirements of one German infantry division committed to a short campaign at 300 tons, or rather less than the daily requirements of a British division in similar circumstances.

On this basis it will be seen that the *Sea Lion* force (nine infantry and two airborne divisions) would have needed some 3,300 tons of stores, ammunition, rations and other necessities every day. Of this amount less than one-fifth—and for the first week less than one-twentieth—could have reached it through the port it was most likely to capture. Dover, after being put in order, was expected to have the slightly higher capacity of 800 tons; so that if the Germans had taken Dover as well, they would in due course have begun to receive two-fifths of what they needed if they were to resume the conquest of England or indeed remain in being as a force at all.

These figures (in which no allowance was made for the molestation by the Royal Navy and the RAF of the enemy's sea-lanes) were worked out with great care at the time, and any margin of error in them is more likely to favour the attack than the defence. They are a reminder that, even if all had gone well with the assault and if it had proved possible to maintain a regular shuttle-service of supply-ships between the Continent and the bridgeheads, the Germans would still have faced problems of whose nature and importance they seem to have been largely unaware.

In one matter over which the Germans had no control *Sea Lion* had, or would have had, some of the luck that it undoubtedly needed. "Cloudy with rain at times, moderate visibility, light variable winds"—the weather in the Channel on the morning of 21 September 1940 was not unsuitable for the German purpose. On the following day the wind increased to "moderate to fresh" and, blowing onshore from the south-west and therefore making surf, would probably have caused casualties among the barges after beaching. But for the rest of the month it never again rose above "moderate" and was often from a northerly and therefore favourable quarter. So on none of the eleven days required to put the first wave ashore were conditions in the Channel prohibitive, as they intermittently were in October, or even unduly awkward. Nature would not, initially, have been unkind to *Sea Lion*.

All in all, however, the operation's prospects cannot be considered good. It is indeed doubtful whether history offers any parallel example of a victor so nearly offering his vanquished foe an opportunity (the only opportunity that existed in the whole gamut of strategy at the time) of inflicting on him a resounding and well-merited defeat.

CHAPTER EIGHTEEN

"And If Necessary the Island will be Occupied"

We shall have nothing to fear on the part of the inhabitants. They are a dull people, who are absolutely ignorant of the use of arms.... The whole country will rapidly become entirely devoted to us.

Extract from a report on a reconnaissance of south-east England, carried out on the orders of the French Government by Colonel Grant de Blairfinly, Infanterie Légère, in 1767

GERMAN plans for the administration of British territory occupied in the course of military operations on the island were worked out in some detail; but no clear picture survives of how they proposed to govern the United Kingdom after they had subdued it. For this the most probable reason is that they had no means of telling, even very roughly, what the position would be when the British admitted defeat. Up to the last minute there was, or so Hitler believed, the possibility that the British Government would give in, or would be overthrown, before a single German soldier had landed. Failing this happy outcome, how far up the island would the Army have to fight its way before the British asked for terms, and what would be the pattern of territorial occupation imposed upon the vanquished country? Would the United Kingdom be divided, as France had been, into an Occupied and an Unoccupied Zone? What part, if any, would be allotted to the King and to Parliament in the post-war conduct of its affairs?

None of these imponderable problems seems to have been seriously faced. After the war legend put forward two candidates for the viceregal office of *Reichskommissar* of Great Britain. One was Ribbentrop; the other was Ernst Bohle, in 1940—at the age of thirty-five—an Under Secretary in the Ministry of Foreign Affairs and the main architect of the Overseas Organisation of the Nazi

Party, which sought to control German communities in foreign countries. Bohle has denied[1] that he was earmarked for this post or that he knows who was earmarked; he claims only that after the armistice ceremonies at Compiègne, Hitler—who at the time expected a prompt British capitulation—promised him that he should be the next German Ambassador to the Court of St James's "if the British behave sensibly". It seems quite likely that no one was designated to fill an office whose scope and status were inevitably matters for speculation; and it is certain that no establishment (in the bureaucratic sense of the word) was approved by the authorities in Berlin who would have had to sanction the creation of a *Reichskommissar's* staff.

At a lower level policy was more clearly defined. Plunder and sterilisation were its objects. "The able-bodied male population between the ages of seventeen and forty-five will, unless the local situation calls for an exceptional ruling, be interned and dispatched to the Continent with the minimum of delay." The OKH instructions, headed *Orders concerning the Organisation and Function of Military Government in England*, from which this is an extract, were dated 9 September 1940 and signed by von Brauchitsch.

The immediate purpose of these orders was to lay down a procedure for dealing with the civil population behind the German lines while military operations were still in progress; they prescribed, for instance, that "supreme judiciary powers" over the inhabitants would be vested, not in an Army Commander preoccupied with operational problems, but in the general officer responsible for the army's lines of communications. This was eminently practical; it enshrined the experience of invading armies over many generations.

But an army is the servant of the State, and von Brauchitsch's edicts reflect the long-term intentions of the German Government towards a problem which would only temporarily and incidentally concern the forces in the field. They make those intentions clear; Britain was to be cowed and stripped.

"The welfare of the inhabitants and the interests of the country's national economy . . . will be considered in so far as they contribute

[1] Private interview.

directly or indirectly towards the maintenance of law and order and the securing of the country's labour for the requirements of the German troops and German war economy." The Chief Supply Officer (England) was to be responsible for "seizing such stocks of food, petrol, motor transport, horse-drawn vehicles, etc., as have not already been taken over by the Armies". A "Proclamation to the People of England" would have announced that "the following goods are hereby requisitioned: Agricultural Products, Food and Fodder of all kinds, Ores, Crude Metals (including Precious Metals), Cut or Uncut Precious or Semi-precious Stones, Leather, Fur, Hides, and Timber". A rider embodied not, perhaps, so much the Parthian chivalry of a successful highwayman as the hard-won experience of a natural aggressor: "All goods", it said, "are excluded from this regulation which are part of a normal household stock." The British could keep the coal in their scuttles.

It was about all they were to be allowed to keep. The exploitation of the country's economic resources was planned in greater detail than the ultimate form of its political vassalage. On 27 July the nucleus of the *Wehrwirtschaftsstab*[1] ENGLAND was formed as a kind of working party, a month later the working party was replaced by a full-blown bureaucracy, and on 6/7 September its members attended a short but intensive course of indoctrination.

Great Britain was to be divided into six "Military Economic Commands", with their headquarters in London, Birmingham, Newcastle, Liverpool, Glasgow and Dublin.[2] In correspondence dealing with the project all British place-names were given German code-equivalents, London being Hamburg, Edinburgh Danzig, and so on. In the initial stages of the invasion the task of this organisation was largely limited to helping the invading armies to live off the country. In this connection oil and petrol were regarded as particularly important, and a special sub-division of the *Wehrwirtschaftsstab* had the duty of ensuring that all captured stocks were made

---

[1] Military Economic Staff.
[2] The inclusion of Dublin was almost certainly part of a larger deception plan. On the west coast of France five or six divisions not included in the invasion forces carried out amphibious training and were encouraged to believe that they were destined for Eire. Attempts to simulate a threat to the coasts of Scotland and Yorkshire by similar means were also made elsewhere. They were not successful.

available to the fighting troops; any surplus would be allotted to essential industry. After these priorities had been met, the residue (if any) could be used for distributing foodstuffs to the civil population.[1]

The fact that the Military Economic Commands, whose staffs were to be subordinate to the Quartermaster General at OKH, covered the whole of the United Kingdom suggests that the German intention was to occupy the islands in their entirety; but this intention may well have been laid down only as a provisional basis for planning, and is neither more nor less conclusive as evidence than the absence from the invaders' "Baedekers" of topographical details about Scotland. No one in the German camp seems to have looked very far beyond the cross-Channel bridgeheads on whose establishment everything depended.

Von Brauchitsch's *Orders concerning the Organisation and Function of Military Government in England*, though they go into considerable detail, would in fact have created almost as many problems as they solved. How, after all males between the ages of seventeen and forty-five had been deported to the Continent, would British industry have continued to provide the Military Economic Staff with worth-while plunder? "The English authorities may continue to function if they maintain a correct attitude." If they failed to do this, who functioned in their place? At these and other points the German plans appear slapdash.

It is less easy to criticise the practicality of their arrangements for controlling the conquered population. These followed a pattern with which Europe had been familiar since 1870.

"Law and order will be established. Administrative measures will not violate international law unless the enemy has given cause for reprisals. . . . When taking hostages those persons should if possible be selected in whom the *active* enemy elements have an interest. . . . Armed insurgents of either sex will be dealt with with the utmost severity." German criminal law and penal regulations were to be introduced. "When judging acts of juveniles German military

---

[1] At least one German commander admitted after the war that the problem of feeding the British population would have presented grave and perhaps insuperable difficulties. (von Manstein.)

courts may impose the statutory penalty irrespective of the age of the offender, if the latter appears to have reached the stage of development of a person over eighteen years of age." Failure to surrender firearms or wireless transmitters within twenty-four hours was punishable by death, as was the posting of objectionable placards. A drab, impersonal ferocity is the keynote of the regulations on which German Military Government was to be based.

Dieses Haus darf nur mit Genehmigung des Befehlshabers der Sicherheitspolizei für Grossbritannien betreten werden.

———

No entrance without permission of the Chief-in Command of the German Secret Police for Great Britain.

One of the notices prepared in bulk by the Gestapo for use in conquered Britain.

At the time when von Brauchitsch's orders were issued the Germans were already in occupation of a parcel of British territory, which remained in their hands until the end of the war. Although what happened in the Channel Islands provides no reliable guidance to what might have happened in Occupied Britain, this is the place to give some account of the course of events there.

On 19 June, when France was in her death-throes, the War Cabinet decided that the islands, now an untenable and strategically valueless outpost, should be demilitarised. The small garrisons which had been hastily dispatched thither were as hastily withdrawn, and arrangements were made to evacuate as many of the islanders as wished to leave. Roughly a third of the islands' total population of 90,000 decided to do so. Evacuation—to which one of the distressing preliminaries was the slaughter of several thousand dogs and cats—was carried out amid unbecoming scenes of confusion.[1]

Although the British Government had demilitarised the Channel Islands, they omitted to inform the Germans that they had done so, and on the day following demilitarisation the German Navy, on orders from Berlin, set in motion preparations for their capture. On 28 June both Jersey and Guernsey were bombed, a number of civilians being killed. London quickly made good its omission to inform Berlin of the demilitarisation, and on 30 June, after a Luftwaffe officer had landed at the Guernsey airport, the occupation of the islands proceeded in a peaceful and almost amicable manner. The Germans gave pledges, which they later dishonoured,[2] to respect the rights of the inhabitants, and the island authorities, who continued to carry out most of their normal functions, gave corresponding guarantees. These were at times discharged with a punctilio which many thought excessive. A notice, promulgated in July 1940 by the Guernsey authorities and reproduced overleaf, suggests that patriots in the Channel Islands had some right to be critical of the attitude adopted in official circles after the occupation.

There are several reasons why the placid pattern of events in the Channel Islands affords few clues to the probable aftermath of a German occupation of England. The Channel Islands had, on orders from Whitehall, offered no resistance to the Germans. The latter, when they arrived, shared with many of the inhabitants the belief that the war would be over in a few weeks. It was in the interests of both sides to behave in a correct and even considerate way. There had been no fighting, no widespread destruction, to charge the atmosphere with bitterness. The islanders still had everything to lose. Intransigence in any form was directly contrary to the interests of a defenceless community and could do negligible harm to the enemy.

Things could not but have been different in German-occupied

[1] Alan and Mary Wood: *Islands in Danger*. London, 1955. This well-documented account of the German occupation of the Channel Islands has been followed throughout.

[2] All the inhabitants born or normally resident in Great Britain proper were deported to the Continent in 1942. All Jews—they numbered about twenty—were removed in 1940 and were never heard of again.

Britain; the military orders quoted earlier recognised this. There, among the ruins, many desperate men, and probably women too, would have heeded Churchill's suggestion: "You can always take one with you." The Channel Islands were originally a part of the Duchy of Normandy and have always retained a limited autonomy as well as a *patois* of their own; though constitutionally part of the United Kingdom they are not, either by blood or by traditional outlook, as closely identified with England as an English county is. They had in any case been ordered to submit; and although submissiveness was carried, on occasion, to questionable extremes the islands could not in fact have rendered greater service to the British war effort than they did.

 " La Gazette Officielle "

REWARD OF £25

A REWARD OF £25 WILL BE GIVEN TO THE PERSON WHO FIRST GIVES TO THE INSPECTOR OF POLICE INFORMATION LEADING TO THE CONVICTION OF ANYONE (NOT ALREADY DISCOVERED) FOR THE OFFENCE OF MARKING ON ANY GATE, WALL OR OTHER PLACE WHATSOEVER VISIBLE TO THE PUBLIC THE LETTER "V" OR ANY OTHER SIGN OR ANY WORD OR WORDS CALCULATED TO OFFEND THE GERMAN AUTHORITIES OR SOLDIERS.

THIS 8th·DAY OF JULY, 1941

VICTOR G. CAREY,

Bailiff.

For in 1941 Hitler was stricken by what his generals called *Inselwahn*, or island-madness.[1] He became convinced that the British—

[1] Hitler's preoccupation with the defence of the Channel Islands was an early symptom of his "fortress mania". After the Allied invasion of Europe in 1944 the German garrisons in the French ports were ordered to stay behind and fight it

who never attempted anything more than a few abortive commando raids—harboured grand designs upon the islands; they were converted, at great expense, into a fortress and in them was immured a powerful garrison, which was soon badly needed elsewhere but was never redeployed and in the end capitulated without firing a shot.

How long it would have been before the spirit of open resistance among the British population in occupied territory would have been broken and driven underground no one can say. Much, probably, would have depended on the military situation; as long as hostile acts behind the enemy's lines seemed capable of contributing to his defeat, such acts would have been attempted, perhaps widely, perhaps only here and there. But an effective resistance movement is a slow growth which requires to be nourished by material resources; and soon after Dunkirk the British General Staff decided to prefabricate such a movement, so that a small nucleus of well-found guerrillas would already exist in whatever part of the country the enemy succeeded in overrunning.

Before the Second World War the British Army's experience of guerrilla warfare had been largely confined to playing, often on a note of exasperation but generally in the end with success, the Sheriff of Nottingham to a series of exotic Robin Hoods in Asia and Africa. But Lawrence's success against the Turks in Arabia had shown how usefully, and also how economically, irregular operations could further the main aims of strategy. Moreover, in the late Thirties all three Axis Powers had disposed large elements of their forces in situations where they presented—at any rate on paper—suitable targets for guerrilla warfare. Much of the Japanese Army was spreadeagled over half China and the whole of Manchuria; the Italians were holding down Abyssinia with widely dispersed and not over-confident garrisons; and the Germans, who in peacetime had subjugated two European countries against their will, could be

---

out; their command was entrusted to officers who had sworn an oath specially worded to cover this exigency of the service; and the equivalent of ten German divisions, in some respects lavishly equipped, were committed to a role which had small relevance to the most urgent needs of German strategy.

expected to acquire more *Lebensraum*, and with it additional problems of internal security, when the fighting started.

So the British, as in war the weaker side often does, devoted some thought to the possibilities of guerrilla warfare (which at the higher levels of the General Staff was generally referred to as "scallywagging"); and it was because a few minds in the War Office, as well as Churchill's outside it, were already working along these lines that the idea of forming the Independent Companies for employment in Norway found ready acceptance, and that the Commandos, who were directly descended from these units, survived without much difficulty the controversies attending their birth.

Fragmentary though they had been, the reports of the fighting in France had made clear one fact which many people in England found puzzling and disturbing. How was it (the armchair tacticians asked themselves) that the Germans, whenever they had broken through the front, had been permitted to roam without hindrance through the populated districts ahead of them? Were there no desperate men in France? Had everybody simply stood and stared as the *chars* rolled by? Rumours, whether accurate or not, said that this in fact was what they had done; there were reports of gendarmes helping to regulate the flow of their conquerors' traffic and of other discreditable incidents. To the British—who apprehended but dimly the realities of a *Blitzkrieg*—this conception of a vacuum in which you let the enemy have everything his own way appeared all wrong. They were not, perhaps, quite clear as to what they themselves would have done in similar circumstances, but they were quite certain that they would have done something.

These staunch impulses were sublimated for most able-bodied men by the formation of the Home Guard; but the Home Guard was essentially a part of the front. That front might be broken or pierced in England as it had been in France. The screen of regular troops on the coast might be pushed back, the mobile reserve outfought, the Home Guard annihilated or made prisoner, and the enemy left in possession of a deep bridgehead in which to make his preparations for a thrust further inland. Within any sectors thus occupied there would exist the same sort of vacuum from which he had derived important advantages on the Continent.

The first officer to see that it might temporarily be very valuable, and would certainly be better than nothing, if at this stage the enemy in his bridgeheads were harassed by light forces left behind for the purpose, was General Andrew Thorne. Immediately after Dunkirk, Thorne, who had served as Military Attaché in Berlin and commanded a division in France, was given command of XII Corps, which was then responsible for the defence of the whole of Kent and Sussex and part of Surrey. Its strength in early June was made up largely of one Territorial division, one theoretically motorised brigade, 5,000 stevedores armed with rifles, a District Head-quarters and a miscellany of minor units; there was little artillery, hardly any ammunition, and the standard of training was low. The Corps was responsible for a front extending from Greenwich to Hayling Island, and its commander had no illusions about his ability to drive back into the sea, or even to contain, strong German forces if they succeeded in getting ashore.

An advancing army is not normally bothered by guerrillas. They may involve an army of occupation in a costly diversion of effort, and they may be a source of real danger to a retreating army, as they were to the Germans in Russia. But modern warfare is a terrifying business, and an army capable of imposing its will on its adversary and forcing him to retreat moves forward into a region whose occupants are so numbed by alarm and confusion, and so preoccupied with the domestic and administrative cares created by their predicament, that there is little to be feared from them.

This is fortunate for the victors, who as they advance from one battlefield to the next are normally tired, slightly apprehensive and burdened with many cares of reorganisation and replenishment. Thorne expected, if he was pushed back from the coast, to stand and fight, with whatever reserves were available, on the "GHQ Line", a large ditch or fosse then being hastily excavated round the southern outskirts of the capital. It seemed to him that if the enemy's attack on this position could be delayed or interfered with by irregulars operating against the German supply-routes and concentration areas, Home Forces' chances of repelling it would be, however negligibly, improved.

He accordingly made known to the War Office his requirement

for an officer to organise among the natives of Kent and Sussex a network of "stay-behind parties" (or, as it would have later been called, a *maquis* or resistance movement) whose object would be to harass the enemy's preparations for the second phase of his advance on London. The War Office provided an officer for this duty (they chose, oddly enough, the author of this book) and it was not long—for other commanders discovered the same needs as Thorne —before an underground organisation, military in character and secret at any rate in intention, had been brought into being behind the main defences which were beginning to encircle the coasts of the kingdom.

"Auxiliary Units", as they were noncommittally designated, were controlled and administered by a small staff under the aegis of GHQ Home Forces. In the very early days, when they were little more than a bright idea, they were envisaged as being immediately expendable; soon after an area had been overrun, picked members of the Home Guard, led by one or two Army officers with a supposed aptitude for these duties, would emerge from their hiding places and inflict as much damage on the enemy as they could before either being killed or making their way back to the British lines.

The pioneers in the XII Corps area argued that so ephemeral an effort was hardly worth making. Invoking the aid of an imaginary Chinese general of the fifth century BC, to whom they attributed the maxim "*A guerrilla without a base is no better than a desperate straggler*", they submitted a case for the construction of underground hide-outs, to be stocked with rations, blankets, cooking-stoves and so on, as well as with explosives, sabotage equipment and wireless sets. Based on these subterranean retreats, they contended, the guerrillas would have a sporting chance, not merely of inflicting one suicidal pinprick, but of remaining a thorn in the enemy's flesh for weeks or perhaps even in some cases for months.[1]

---

[1] The idea caught the passing attention of the Prime Minister, who on 25 September wrote in a minute to the Secretary of State for War: "I have been following with much interest the growth and development of the new guerrilla formations . . . known as 'Auxiliary Units'. From what I hear these units are being organised with thoroughness and imagination, and should, in the event of invasion, prove a useful addition to the regular forces, Perhaps you will keep me informed of progress."

Higher authority had, for the best of reasons, never heard of the Chinese general but was unlikely, for reasons almost equally good, to admit this. At any rate, the proposals he had been invented to sponsor were adopted as the basis of Auxiliary Units' policy, and all round the coasts of the British Isles a prefabricated underground movement began slowly to take shape.

As a theatre for guerrilla warfare the United Kingdom suffers from the fundamental disadvantage of being much too small. The vast, empty distances of which the Long Range Desert Group made such good use in Libya, the dense jungles under cover of which the Chindits circulated behind the Japanese lines in Burma, are nowhere reproduced in England, Scotland or Wales. Many a would-be Lawrence, surveying a patchwork battlefield laced by ribbon-development and encroached on by suburbia, sighed for the torrid immensities of the Arabian desert. Even in the least promising areas, however, some possibilities existed for operating by stealth against the invaders before they had consolidated their grip on the country; and of these good use was made.

There were in all twenty-odd Auxiliary Units. The basic organisation in the summer of 1940 was one officer, with what was grandiloquently known as a "striking force" of some twelve soldiers commanded by a subaltern; as wireless sets with the necessary range became available, two signallers were added. Some units acquired, and all badly needed, a clerk and a storeman. Loosely affiliated to this military nucleus, and dotted arbitrarily about its sphere of operations (which often covered a whole county) were small "cells" composed of members of the Home Guard, selected for their resourcefulness, their knowledge of the country and their skill in fieldcraft. These men were trained, mostly at the week-ends, in sabotage and the use of high explosive; and as the dumps and hideouts began to be established they assumed responsibility for them.

The technique employed and the problems encountered by these units varied widely in different parts of the country, partly for topographical reasons; it is, for instance, obvious that guerrilla warfare cannot be conducted in the Lincolnshire Fens by the same methods as in the Scottish Highlands. But the invasion, had it been launched, would have fallen on the XII Corps area; and if the

Germans had met with initial success the guerrilla organisation in Kent and East Sussex would have been the first of its kind to go into action.

The underground hide-outs to which both the "striking force" and the far-flung "cells" of the Home Guard would withdraw when the regular forces fell back covered, loosely, the coastal hinterland of the two counties. They were mostly sited in areas of dense woodland or scrub. They varied in design. Some were merely large dug-outs, excavated, roofed and provided with bunks and ventilation by the Royal Engineers. Others made use of existing underground accommodation. One was in the cellars of a house destroyed by fire many years earlier and abandoned; another was made by enlarging the tunnels of a badgers' sett in a derelict chalkpit where generations of these animals had made their home; a third consisted, basically, of a huge oval pit, dug in the corner of a deer park to house a small and presumably secret airship during the First World War. The domestic economy of these lairs bore a general resemblance to that of the Lost Boys' subterranean home in the second act of *Peter Pan*. They were well stocked with the necessities of life and with ammunition, high explosive and various booby-trap devices.

The amateur guerrillas in Kent and Sussex took pains to familiarise themselves with the demesnes of the larger country houses in their area.[1] They reasoned that these were likely to be used by the Germans as unit and formation headquarters, and as they reconnoitred the shrubberies and the ha-has they had tuppence-coloured visions of German generals being mysteriously shot down as they took their ease on the terrace after dinner.

It seems unlikely that in practice the Auxiliary Units would have been able to achieve very much. Their main operational handicap would have been lack of communications; between the tiny "striking-force" and the widely scattered "cells" the only method of transmitting orders or intelligence would have been by messengers, moving cautiously across country at night, so that very

[1] According to local legend, one of these—Eastwell Park near Ashford—had been selected by the Kaiser as his field headquarters during the invasion of England which the Germans were mistakenly believed to have planned in the First World War.

little co-ordinated action would have been possible. As long as the leaf was on the trees—for six or seven weeks, that is, after the first landings on 21 September—their hide-outs might well have remained undiscovered, and any serious attempt to search for them would have involved the invaders in a major diversion of effort. But with the onset of winter low-flying reconnaissance aircraft, aided by improved intelligence, would sooner or later have located the well-defined tracks which by that time would have converged on every woodland lair, and—in Kent and Sussex, at any rate—it would only have been a matter of time before the guerrillas were hunted down.

Even more damaging—and more swiftly damaging—to their prospects would have been the policy of reprisals from which, as we have seen, the Germans had no thought of shrinking. The offensive spirit of an isolated group of half a dozen Home Guards, living in a hole in the ground, could not indefinitely have been proof against the terrible retribution which would have followed such forays as they made, and of which their neighbours and often their own families would have been the victims. Nevertheless, even assuming that the British resistance movement would have melted away in the white heat of German ruthlessness, it might have struck some useful blows before doing so; and within a bridge-head under heavy counter-attack its diversionary activities would have had a value wholly disproportionate to the number of guerrillas involved. It is difficult to find fault with Churchill's estimate of Auxiliary Units as "a useful addition to the regular forces".

CHAPTER NINETEEN

The Eleventh Hour

Never in the field of human conflict was so much owed by so many to so few.
Winston Churchill in the House of Commons, 20 August 1940

As the bad weather at the beginning of August gave way to an almost unbroken succession of golden summer days, a feeling of suppressed and curiously pleasurable excitement communicated itself to the British people. The atmosphere was quite different from that of the period immediately after Dunkirk. There had then been an element of desperation in the nation's defiance, a frantic air about its ill-coordinated activities, and behind its stout-hearted demeanour a fear of perils which loomed monstrous, new and unassessed.

But many things had changed in two and a half months. In early June the main cause of inward misgiving had been the fact that nobody knew what to do; now everybody had his or her duty, and those who would have to fight held arms of a sort in their hands. Their arch-enemy, moreover, had dwindled in stature as week after week went by and he failed to resume his juggernaut advance or to implement the vague threats with which—sometimes in terms found risible—he bombarded his prospective victims. Their view both of Hitler and of his amphibious aspirations is well reflected in a poem by A. P. Herbert which a Sunday newspaper printed in those crucial mid-September days:

> Napoleon tried. The Dutch were on the way,
> A Norman did it—and a Dane or two.
> Some sailor-King may follow one fine day;
> But not, I think, a low land-rat like you.

More important, the people had by now an implicit faith in their leader; Churchill had tempered the national spirit into a true and well-balanced blade, and in the main the British awaited the outcome of events with something of the relish which they noted in their Prime Minister, and something of the unassuming fortitude which they admired in their King and Queen.

The German air offensive began on 13 August. On the 18th headlines in the German press, quoted by London newspapers on the following day, proclaimed: "Conclusive Phase of the War Begun" and "Closing Act of this Conflict Opens". On 22 August Dover was shelled for the first time by the heavy batteries on and around Cap Gris Nez.[1] On the 24th the Luftwaffe opened its attack on the Sector Stations covering London; these successful and potentially decisive operations have been described in Chapter 15.

The British, who had grown accustomed to living in a perpetual state of emergency, were interested rather than perturbed by these developments. By now not even the most inexperienced unit or formation would have referred in its war diary to "tension", let alone to "flap". As for the civilians, the following extract from a letter, not intended for publication but quoted in the *New Statesman and Nation* of 31 August 1940, gives a glimpse of their attitude to the impending storm:

We have two or three air-raids [the writer meant "air-raid warnings"] most days and we had seven German bombers swoop a few feet over our roofs machine-gunning only six days before our fête in aid of the Red Cross—so we know something about the *Blitzkrieg*. But we held our fête on Saturday with stalls, side-shows, dancing on the lawn, and the acting of scenes from *Twelfth Night* under the old mulberry tree, which is a stone's-throw from the path still called Princess Gap because Princess Elizabeth used to walk there when she stayed in our village in the days before she became Shakespeare's Queen Elizabeth. So it was all very much in the English order, and we felt quite secure with one foot in the sixteenth and the other in the twentieth century as we listened to the Rector's wife and Tom and Dick and Joyce and Annie transformed under the mulberry tree into Olivia, Malvolio, Sir Toby, Maria. The sun shone from a clear sky and there were some 250 of us sitting on the lawn. There were mothers with babies and there were about 20 or 30 children playing about and sometimes getting mixed up with the actors. And then just when the Clown was singing "Come

[1] A few rounds were fired, for ranging purposes, into the Dover area during the preceding ten days; but 22 August was the date of the first bombardment.

away, come away, death", the sirens began to wail. Not a soul moved; the play went on. I thought to myself that at least a mother or two would take her children off to shelter. But not a bit of it; they sat there and watched the children sprawling on the lawn as if Goering and his Luftwaffe were as unreal and innocuous as Malvolio.

Goering was, both then and in retrospect, a good deal more unreal than Malvolio; but it was never his aim to be innocuous. By the beginning of the last week in August a kind of bargain or compromise had perforce been arrived at between the hyperbole of his original claims (in July these had envisaged the liquidation of Fighter Command in four days and the total breaking of British resistance in four weeks) and the more realistic appreciation formed in battle by his crews and the staffs controlling them. This compromise guided German air strategy on to worthwhile objectives; and by 6 September the Luftwaffe was well, though tardily, on its way to making invasion possible by crippling Fighter Command.

But at the very moment when German strategy was ceasing to pivot on the vanity of a single braggart, and was finding a surer basis in the hard-won lessons of a hard-fought slogging-match, its future was blighted by an accident whose causes are never likely to be revealed. The onslaught on the Sector Stations began during daylight on 24 August. On that night the best part of two hundred German bombers were sent to attack targets in many widely separated parts of England and Wales. None of the pilots had London on his bombing orders; but about a dozen of them were directed on aircraft factories and oil installations on the extreme perimeter of the capital.

These bombers missed their mark by a wide margin. A sharp attack was carried out on the City of London and on residential districts in the northern and eastern parts of the capital; there were, for those days, heavy casualties, and many Londoners were made homeless. Whether these substantial errors of navigation were due to inexperience, to irresponsibility or to some aberration either in *Knickebein* or in the counter-measures to it (some of that night's raids on the Midlands also went askew) we shall never know. What was immediately clear was that this apparently deliberate attack on the capital called for a riposte.

It was delivered with Churchillian alacrity on the following night, and the British were greatly heartened by a communiqué describing, in over-optimistic terms, the RAF's first attack on Berlin, a city over which its leaflet-dropping activities in the early days of the Phoney War had aroused negligible enthusiasm. Eighty-one aircraft were despatched; despite dense cloud about half found the target; very little material damage was in fact done. But honour was satisfied.

For the Germans, who had not intentionally invited this tit-for-tat, the consequences of the first RAF raids on Berlin (they were continued on every night when the weather was at all favourable) were far more serious than the trifling damage inflicted on the target. For in Hitler's mind they diluted strategy with domestic politics; upon his dream of conquering Britain was suddenly superimposed the nightmare of losing the always dutiful and often idolatrous respect of his compatriots. To them he had often implied, and Goering had proclaimed, that no bombs would ever fall upon Berlin; and now several had. Hitler had lost face.

The vigour of his reactions to the small British raids on Berlin may be gauged by the scale on which the capital's anti-aircraft defences were hurriedly reinforced. These defences had originally been perfunctory. They were now increased to the following totals:

	Heavy Batteries	Light Batteries	Searchlight Batteries
By 11 September to	29	14	11
By 26 September to	32	22	14
By mid-October to	45	24	18

The British bombers (whose capabilities were known to the Germans) had to fly five times as far to reach Berlin as the German bombers had to fly to reach London; they carried, in consequence, smaller bomb-loads and accepted greater risks from the weather and from intermediate defences. The heaviest attack on Berlin at this time was carried out on 23/24 September by 119 aircraft (Whitleys, Wellingtons and Hampdens), of which 84 reached the target area. Richards gives this account of the results achieved: "The only significant success was at Charlottenberg, where incendiaries set fire to a gasometer. Many of the bombs failed to explode, including one which dropped in the garden of Hitler's Chancery. . . . Twenty-two Germans were killed—ten more than our own losses in aircrew." In terms of strategy, however, these forlorn forays by Bomber Command were sounder and more rewarding than the mass attacks delivered by their opponents at less risk on an easier target.

The operational consequences of the RAF attacks on Berlin were almost inevitable. On 4 September, in a speech already quoted, Hitler promised devastating reprisals to a delirious audience; and on the late afternoon of 7 September the aircraft of *Luftflotten* 2 and 3, abandoning their attacks on the Sector Stations, converged in massive formations on the British capital.

There can be little doubt that this switch in German strategy saved Fighter Command from acute peril, or that its immediate cause was the RAF raids on Berlin, which in their turn were directly attributable to the accidental German attacks on London on the night of the 24th. No one can say for certain that the switch might not have been made in any case, without the benefit of provocation; for terror was a weapon equally dear to Hitler and to Goering. But all the evidence suggests that without provocation it would not have been made so soon. The bombing of London had always been an integral part of the *Sea Lion* programme, but it had been regarded as something of a *pièce de résistance* and as such allotted a place of importance at the climax of the proceedings; an OKW directive of 16 August, which put finishing touches to the main plan for the invasion, had laid down: "On D-1 day the Luftwaffe is to make a strong attack on London, which should cause the population to flee from the city and block the roads." This makes it clear that the opening of the air offensive on London was planned as an operation whose object was to provide direct support for the Army's assault on the island.

The inference seems inescapable that Hitler's decision to start bombing London D-15 instead of on D-1 was not a military but a political decision, taken in defence of his personal position and prestige. It was an extremely unwise decision.

Before we examine its repercussions it will be convenient to review various developments on land and at sea which even the sceptic Churchill found "impossible to watch . . . without a sense of awe" and which, in the great multitude who were only fractionally aware of what was going on, induced a quizzical expectancy.

Earlier in the summer a rumour had been widely current that Hitler had given assurances to the Germans that the war would be over by 15 August (the original D-day of *Operation Sea Lion*)[1]: and the mystic significance attached to this date may have reinforced the anxieties aroused by circumstantial intelligence, received from Stockholm on 13 August, that the Germans had begun embarking "along the whole of the Norwegian coast" on the previous night. At any rate an important Army training exercise on the 14th was cancelled, although no other special precautions seem to have been taken.

By the first week of September the main German plan was beginning to reveal itself, as small but numerous flotillas of transports, barges, tugs, launches, drifters and other craft steamed down the European coast or glided through the waterways towards the ports and estuaries of Holland, Belgium and northern France, where their presence was revealed to the British by photographic reconnaissance. From 5 September Bomber Command, whose daylight activities during the past few weeks had been dissipated over too wide a range of targets, began to concentrate its attention on the inert phalanxes of shipping and the supply-dumps on the quays. Air Ministry communiqués mentioned these targets and the public knew what was toward; on clear nights people living on the south coast could see the flash and flicker of explosions as the nearest French ports were assailed.

On 3 September the four spies whose arrest was described in Chapter 12 were picked up near Rye in Kent; it will be remembered that their mission was to provide intelligence which would help the leading troops in an invasion of south-east England. On the 6th yet another spy, equipped with a wireless set, a Swedish passport and a British identity card, was captured soon after he had landed by parachute near Denton in Northamptonshire. It was scarcely necessary for the New British Broadcasting Station to assure its listeners,

[1] In a GHQ Home Forces Operational Instruction of 27 June this rumour was given the status of a fact.

the same evening, that "Hitler may at any hour give the order for invasion to begin". There was thunder in the air.

When the storm broke on London the Chiefs of Staff and their principal advisers were assembling for a meeting in Whitehall. It was 5.30 p.m. on the afternoon of Saturday, 7 September, and the leading elements of a force of more than 300 German bombers escorted by twice as many fighters were droning through an almost cloudless sky towards the docks and other Thames-side objectives. In the circumstances the Chiefs of Staff may be forgiven for neglecting their agenda and gazing out of the windows. They had come to the meeting primed with evidence that the invasion might be launched at any moment. The spectacle they now witnessed—or, more probably, the noises they now heard—seemed to reinforce this evidence. Nothing appeared likelier than that Hitler would make a heavy air-raid on London the immediate prelude to his main attack; indeed, as we have seen, this was exactly what he had, only a fortnight earlier, planned to do. The Chiefs of Staff completed their somewhat *distraits* deliberations and went on to a further meeting at No. 10 Downing Street, over which Churchill presided as Minister of Defence. At an early stage of this meeting it was decided to bring the country's defences to the alert. The consequences of this decision were greatly to enrich the folklore of the period; for this was the night on which the codeword *Cromwell* was issued.

The Royal Navy and the Royal Air Force were already virtually at a state of maximum readiness. On the previous night, after the sighting of a concentration of 60 vessels off Calais, the Admiralty had ordered all cruisers, destroyers and small craft to be kept at immediate notice during darkness and all boiler-cleaning to be stopped until further notice; and the issue to the RAF of Alert No. 1 ("Invasion imminent, and probable within 12 hours") made little difference to the arrangements already in force. The Army was less tensely poised. All units in Home Forces automatically "stood to" at dawn and dusk and were at eight hours' notice (i.e. ready to move and if necessary to fight within eight hours). But on the evening of 7 September 1940 eight hours seemed an unconscionably long time, and it was rightly felt that the situation demanded a higher state of alertness. The only method of achieving this was by the issue of *Cromwell*.

It was sent out by the Deputy Chief of Staff at GHQ Home Forces shortly after eight o'clock that night. It was addressed to Eastern and Southern Commands: IV and VII Corps (in GHQ Reserve): and HQ London District. It was repeated, for information only, to all other Commands. It seems to have taken the best part of four hours to reach troops on the coast. It created much excitement and confusion.

A great deal of this was due to the fact that hardly anybody knew what *Cromwell* really meant.[1] The 7th, it will be remembered, was a Saturday, and by the late hour at which the dread codeword reached them most headquarters were sparsely manned. To some of the night-duty-officers who received it *Cromwell* meant nothing at all; but by the majority it was believed to signify that an invasion was actually in progress. Many of the junior staff officers serving with field formations (and somehow it is generally a junior officer who does night-duty at the week-end) were inexperienced, and not all the forces in Western, Northern and Scottish Commands realised that the message had been sent to them for information and not for action.

The Home Guard, though not among the message's official addressees, were quickly aware of what was, or was supposed to be, afoot; they rose to the occasion with gusto. Church-bells were rung; in many parts of the country road-blocks were closed with concrete bollards, *chevaux de frises* and other obstacles held ready for this purpose; telephone operators refused to accept non-official calls;

[1] *Cromwell* dated from Ironside's tenure of command at GHQ Home Forces, where on 5 June it superseded *Caesar*, a codeword with similar implications. It was defined as a warning on receipt of which:

    (*a*) the troops were to take up their battle stations;
    (*b*) certain civilian telephone and telegraph lines were to be taken over by the military;
    (*c*) liaison officers were to take up their duties (presumably with branches of the civil administration).

Many units and formations not under command of Home Forces on 5 June had since come into being, and the general lack of clerical and filing facilities in those days probably contributed to the oblivion in which the letter, and in some cases the spirit, of the original order had here and there been engulfed.

in one sector of Eastern Command several bridges were demolished
by the Royal Engineers; in a Guards brigade serving in Lincolnshire
three officers were blown up and killed by mines laid in the roads
along which they were driving. On the other side of the Channel,
while all this was going on, the Chief of Staff of the German Army
High Command spent an "evening filled with most unpleasant
conversations with the Foreign Office about a diplomatic contretemps in Rumania".

On the morning after *Cromwell* the country was alive with
rumours, of which the most prevalent was that the Germans had
launched an invasion but that their forces had been cut to pieces on
passage by the Navy and the RAF. These rumours persisted until
after the war, when they were scotched (but not, as research in
this field has made clear, killed) by a long statement on the whole
incident given by Attlee to the House of Commons on 18 November
1946. *Cromwell* remained in force until 19 September, by which date
it was producing unacceptable effects on the Army's training programme and unpopular repercussions on the leave-roster. A modified
form of alert, known as *Stand To*, had meanwhile been devised.
This was brought into force on 22 September and cancelled on the
following day. It seems to have been about this time that a short
communiqué was prepared for issue immediately after the first
German landings; a gap was left in the wording of this document
(which has unfortunately not survived) so that the areas undergoing
invasion could be inserted at the last moment.

Ever since Dunkirk what Richards has called "the brute fact that
the world's largest air force was now within an hour's flight of the
world's largest target" had seldom been far from the thoughts of
the British; and they found it impossible to contemplate without
dismay the effects of the first deliberate attack on London. For
eleven hours, of which only the first three were hours of daylight, more than 600 bombers showered high explosive and
incendiaries on the capital almost without a pause; and although
Fighter Command shot down 40 aircraft (mostly fighters) before
darkness fell, the destruction of only one machine was claimed by
the night-defences. These were in fact all but non-existent. Night-
fighters—at this stage Blenheim bombers were employed in this

role—were few, and were still entirely dependent on luck and the searchlights for their chance of a kill; the anti-aircraft guns had been much thinned out to protect aircraft factories and other targets and were in any case forbidden to fire barrages while the night-fighters were aloft. The huge fires caused by the early attacks ruled out the possibility of navigational errors by the Luftwaffe.

The next day—Sunday the 8th—had already been designated as a day of national prayer. "Damage", said a communiqué on the London raids, "was severe but judged against the background of the war is not serious." In Britain any attempt at euphemism in official statements always defeats its own purpose; no surer way could have been found of informing the provinces that the capital had been hit very hard indeed. An official historian[1] thus summarises the main results of the German operations against London on 7 and 8 September:

Between five and six o'clock on the evening of Saturday, 7 September[2], some 320 German bombers supported by over 600 fighters flew up the Thames and proceeded to bomb Woolwich Arsenal, Beckton Gas Works, a large number of docks, West Ham power station, and then the City, Westminster and Kensington. They succeeded in causing a serious fire situation in the docks. An area of about $1\frac{1}{2}$ square miles between North Woolwich Road and the Thames was almost destroyed, and the population of Silvertown was surrounded by fire and had to be evacuated by water. At 8.10 p.m. some 250 bombers resumed the attack, which was maintained until 4.30 on Sunday morning. They caused 9 conflagrations, 59 large fires and nearly 1,000 lesser fires. Three main-line railway termini were put out of action, and 430 persons killed and some 1,600 seriously injured. After the fire brigades had spent all day in an effort to deprive the enemy of illumination, some 200 bombers returned at 7.30 in the evening to carry on the assault. During this second night a further 412 persons were killed and 747 seriously injured, and damage included the temporary stoppage of every railway line to the south.

The summer of 1940 is full of legends, and some of them have been shown at earlier stages of this narrative to be insecurely rooted in fact. But London's courage under bombardment is a legend which

[1] O'Brien.
[2] On the morning of this day *The Times*—in moments of crisis perhaps the greatest character-actor on the stage of public life in Britain—had reported the discovery in a public air-raid shelter in Euston of a Great Crested Grebe.

runs no risks from reappraisal. The Londoners were very brave, and they went on being brave for a long time. "The largest target in the world" was recommended to its assailants not merely by its size (which is roughly 800 square miles) but by its irreplaceability as a centre of communications, of administration and of seaborne supply. Bisected by a river spanned by too few bridges, dotted with railway termini and criss-crossed by thousands of acres of permanent way, its subsoil laced with tunnels, drains and cables, its heart sheltering the seat of government, its port indispensable to the island's survival and its residential areas to the continued presence at their posts of the men and women who made the metropolis work, London offered not so much one huge unmissable target as a congeries of interrelated bull's eyes. Damage to any of these bull's eyes seemed likely to result in indirect damage to the others.

And if targets abounded in London, so did totems. The targets were made of stone, brick, concrete, timber, slate, glass, and other substances vulnerable, in greater or less degree, to high explosive and incendiary bombs. The totems, unlike the targets, could not be destroyed; but they could perhaps be toppled or shifted and in the process would lose some of their magic and their power to hold the tribe together. To drive the King and his Parliament out of London, to close the banks, to shift *The Times* from Printing House Square to Kettering and the other national newspapers to their respective emergency stations in the provinces, to compel a withdrawal from Broadcasting House, to put the London railway termini out of action —all or any of these achievements by the Luftwaffe would have struck at the roots of national confidence and would have furthered the prospects, cherished by Hitler, of voluntary collapse or involuntary disintegration.

None of these things was brought about. Parliament, which had reassembled on 7 September, continued to sit, although its deliberations were often interrupted; "I am informed", the Speaker would say on these occasions, "that an air-raid is now considered to be imminent and I will accordingly suspend the sitting." The newspapers continued to appear, the BBC to transmit programmes from Broadcasting House, the Royal Standard to fly over Buckingham Palace. Somehow the great wounded city went on discharging not only its manifold duties to its six or seven million inhabitants but its wider, symbolic function as the capital of a Kingdom and the hub of a Commonwealth.

Like several other aspects of British resistance, London's staunchness has come in retrospect to be taken for granted, as though it were (so to speak) part of the furniture of the period. But it seems worth pointing out that there were alternatives to staunchness. When the attacks started there was no telling how long they would continue, nor to what extent their fury might increase (the Germans were insisting that so far only a small part of their available air force had been committed).[1] There was on paper a strong case for moving the seat of government from the capital and for declaring London, on humanitarian and cultural grounds, an open city, as the French had done with Paris. This course (which does not seem to have been considered) might not have deflected the Luftwaffe's attacks from London; but if it had, it would almost certainly have deflected them back on to the Sector Stations, with serious consequences for Fighter Command. Moreover, the people would not have liked it if the Government had given ground in this way; and an official announcement, issued on 13 September and probably provoked by German propaganda,[2] that the Government had no intention of leaving London was received everywhere with approbation.

During the week which began on 8 September the weather was never again so favourable to the Germans as it had been on the 7th, and their attacks on London were made in less strength and with less effect than on that day. But their hopes were high. Not only was Fighter Command believed to be very near the end of its resources in pilots and aircraft, but the material and moral damage inflicted on London was exaggerated. Hitler opined that "our attacks up to now have had an enormous effect, though perhaps chiefly upon nerves",

[1] The *New York Times* reported from Berlin on 9 September that "authoritative German quarters assert that 'as yet, in spite of the tremendous numbers involved in the present battles, only part of the forces of the Reich's air army has been sent into action. The attack will be carried further, systematically, and the possibilities of increasing its force are obvious'."

[2] Two days earlier, for instance, the New British Broadcasting Station had implored its listeners to "leave London now. The central districts are marked down for destruction as surely as was the riverside".

and he contemplated with glee the possibility that "the English may yet be seized with mass hysteria". At OKW the reports of the German Military Attaché in Washington gave particular satisfaction; they spoke of heavy civilian casualties, widespread destruction, sinking morale, and severe damage to—among other objectives—the important railway stations of "Sherrycross and Waterloo".[1] Suitable conditions for another large-scale effort were eagerly awaited.

They were present on 15 September, a Sunday. Dispensing—ill-advisedly—with the feints and diversions over the Channel on which they usually relied to blur the radar picture and confuse the defending squadrons, more than 200 heavily escorted bombers crossed the English coast about midday, headed for London. Two hours later they were followed by an even larger force. Elements of both formations, fiercely harried, reached the target area, but bombing was scattered and indiscriminate. The results achieved did not compare with the havoc wrought eight days earlier, and the Luftwaffe's loss of 56 aircraft—believed by the British to have been 185—illuminated with a bleak glare the fools' paradise in which its High Command had been living. The RAF lost only 26 machines; and the nation's jubilant conviction that a famous victory had been won was perhaps due as much to some sort of tribal intuition as to the exaggerated claims of German casualties. Whatever its origins, it was not misplaced.

Old countries, like old men, tend to have a bad memory for dates. In the British calendar (upon which an unsuccessful attempt to blow up the Houses of Parliament is, thus far, the only event to have left a completely indelible mark) victories are given shallow niches. Though both are still celebrated, the date of Trafalgar Day, which for several decades seemed unforgettable, is now no easier to remember than the date of Shakespeare's birthday, which for several centuries was forgotten altogether. It remains to be seen whether Battle of Britain Day, which since 1941 has been celebrated throughout the British Commonwealth and Empire on 15 September, will eventually sink into oblivion. It will be in good company if it does.

[1] Wheatley and Greiner.

While these decisive but for the time being imponderable events were taking place four miles up in the sky above south-eastern England, the German plans for landing a large army in that area had been going purposefully forward. Von Brauchitsch's final orders had been issued from Fontainebleau on 30 August. A week later Goering arrived at Beauvais to take personal command of the last phase of the Luftwaffe's operations. On 4 September, in Berlin, Hitler delivered the "he-is-coming" speech in which he publicly pledged himself to invasion. The German Navy, though unhappy about the air situation over the Channel, were prepared on 10 September to "guarantee provisionally" the completion of their final preparations in time for D-Day.

This, it will be recalled, had been postponed at the Navy's request from 15 to 21 September, when the first landings were to be made at dawn, the troops having embarked on the 20th. But there was also a kind of satellite D-day: 11 September. Mainly because the Navy needed ten days in which to complete its mine-sweeping and mine-laying programme (a hazardous series of operations which were indispensable if *Sea Lion* was to be carried out but superfluous if it was to be cancelled) Hitler had undertaken to ratify the date of D-day ten days in advance. When the 11th came, therefore, he should have issued an order or directive either confirming D-Day as the 21st or postponing it. He did not do so; and in the German camp there was a brief period of uncertainty during which nobody quite knew how matters stood.

Hitler's failure to take a decision on 11 September was the first instance of his wavering in the execution of Directive No. 16. He had misgivings about the invasion, to which the men close to him were privy; and he took small interest in its planning. But as Supreme Commander of the German Armed Forces he was ultimately responsible for mounting the complex operation which was now all but ready to be launched. Innumerable difficulties had been discovered; there had been much bickering, many changes of plan. All this had not deflected his purpose, announced eight weeks earlier, to "prepare for and, if necessary, to carry out an invasion of England". Now everything was ready, and he had only to give the word.

Despite its shifts of emphasis, its quirks, its compromises and its setbacks, Hitler's strategy against England had remained true to the pattern it had reluctantly assumed in July. But it now showed signs of bankruptcy. On the 11th (one of the rare days on which the Luftwaffe's losses were lower than the RAF's) Hitler postponed his final decision until the 14th. It seems unlikely that he any longer seriously hoped for that victory in the air which was nearly a month overdue. Even if in the next three days the last Spitfire were shot out of the sky, there remained Bomber Command and the Royal Navy to deal with; both were already attacking the invasion flotillas while they lay at anchor, and neither had been weakened by the German air offensive.

Hitler was still gambling on a collapse. The mind which had expected a single attack on the British capital to "cause the population to flee from the city and block the roads" found it impossible to jettison the seductive conception of a sudden universal panic. He had adapted his original thinking on this point. "Not one attack is decisive," he told Raeder on 14 September, "but the *total* effect produced." Raeder agreed that the bombing of London "may have a decisive outcome". On the same day Hitler once more postponed his final decision for three days, and D-Day automatically slid back to 27 September.

The short OKW order which dealt with this postponement is a revealing document. The first of its two paragraphs is headed *Operation Sea Lion*, but in it the only reference to arrangements which might further the operation reads: "The Air Force is to carry out the attack on British long-range batteries firing on the French Coast as soon as preparations to that effect are concluded." This attack was never delivered. Even if it had been its success or failure would not materially have altered the odds against the landings. The order reads like a sop thrown to inter-service disputants in an issue which no longer mattered.

The second paragraph ("Air attacks on London") ordered that these attacks should be intensified, "continuing primarily against important military objectives and those vital to the city (including railway stations) *as long as there are worthwhile targets*. Terror attacks against purely residential areas are to be kept as a last resort, and are not to be used for the time being".

The words italicised suggest how seriously Hitler and his military advisers overrated the scope and the nature of the damage which one week's bombing had inflicted on London. They imply a belief that everything worth destroying in London was already within measurable distance of being destroyed. Had Hitler used these words in a private or even a public boast they might have been dismissed as vapourings; but their inclusion in an operation order issued at a juncture which was critical for German strategy should not pass without remark.

The 27th of September was a very late date, just outside the period (19–26 September) laid down by the Naval Staff as being suitable from the point of view of tides. The weather forecasts for the end of the month were bad. Eleven days were required to land the whole of the first wave of nine infantry divisions. Air supremacy over the Channel had not been established. Nightly attacks by the RAF and intermittent bombardments by the Royal Navy were creating in the invasion ports a situation which could be met only by the dispersal of the shipping and supply-dumps. It must, in a word, have been clear to Hitler by 14 September that to begin the invasion of England on the 27th was for practical purposes out of the question. Why did he not call off the operation? Why, on the 14th, did he tell a conference of his commanders-in-chief that "a successful landing followed by an occupation would end the war in a short time" and therefore "the operation will not be renounced yet"?

During the war Hitler's inner thoughts were never revealed to his closest associates; their posthumous analysis can only be conjectural. But all the evidence points one way. It suggests that between 8 and 14 September Hitler dismissed from his mind the idea of an opposed landing on the English coast. (He may conceivably have dismissed it earlier; the deliberate compromising of his objectives in clandestine broadcasts at the end of August suggests this, though in so faint and indirect a manner that it can hardly be called a clue.)

Firmer indications of his attitude to *Sea Lion* in the final stages emerge on 13 and 14 September. On the 13th, after being assured at a midday conference by the commanders of 9 and 16 Armies that their preparations were beset by "no especial difficulties", Hitler gave a dinner to a number of officers recently promoted to the rank of Colonel-General; in an address afterwards he "took [according to Greiner] a very optimistic view and said that in the present favourable situation he would not think of taking such a great risk as to land in England. The Fuehrer [Greiner added] has promised 30,000 tons of shipping space to Colonel-General von Falkenhorst." This officer, commanding in Norway, suffered chronically from a shortage of shipping to supply his isolated garrisons; and four days later, on 19 September (by now D-8), OKW released eight large merchantmen forming the dummy fleet which, by carrying out a diversion (*Herbstreise*) against the Scottish coast, was to fulfil the requirements of strategic deception when the invasion was launched. The cancellation of this feint, which had always been an integral part of the *Sea Lion* plan, suggests that the operations from which it was designed to draw off attention were already in the discard.

Why, then, were preparations for them actively continued, to the inconvenience of all concerned, if Hitler had decided in his own mind that *Sea Lion* could not be carried out during 1940? The RAF's attacks on the ports obliged the Germans to thin out the denser concentrations of shipping; this process began on 19 September, reinforcement of the anti-aircraft defences along the invasion coast being ordered on the same day. But the orders for *Sea Lion* remained in force for the best part of a month longer; although it was known at OKW on 17 September that Hitler had finally abandoned the project as far as 1940 was concerned, it was not until 12 October that he decreed that the elaborate apparatus of invasion should be dismantled as unobtrusively as possible.

The most probable explanation of these outwardly unpractical arrangements is a comparatively simple one. Hitler still hoped against hope that British morale would crack. He reasoned—and indeed told Raeder on 14 September—that if invasion were cancelled the fact would be immediately known to the British Intelligence; "a counter-order", he said, "cannot be kept secret". The cancellation of *Sea Lion* would therefore "make the German air attacks easier to bear" and was thus unthinkable before the weather ruled out the possibility of a cross-Channel operation.

To sum up: until about 13 September Hitler fully intended to invade England if she failed to collapse or give in before the last week of that month; after the 13th he realised that invasion could not be carried out in 1940, but still believed that the pressure on British morale (to which he supposed, wrongly, that the threat of invasion was making an important contribution) would yet prove unbearable and that British resistance would break or buckle under its manifold stresses. Invasion, throughout the summer a dagger pointed at his enemy's heart, became for a month thereafter merely another of the magician's wands—like peace, and terror, and sub-version—which Hitler waved successively or simultaneously over his enemy's head. But his spells failed to work upon the British, and he beat the air in vain.

Meanwhile on the British side of the Channel, as the sequent D-days for *Sea Lion* approached, the spectre of invasion was becoming less rather than more intimidating. "One could not help being in-wardly excited alike by the atmosphere and the evidence of Hitler's intention which streamed in upon us," wrote Churchill afterwards; but he added darkly "there were indeed some who on purely technical grounds, and for the sake of the effect the total defeat and destruction of his expedition would have on the general war, were quite content to see him try."

This sentiment was perhaps not widely shared; but there was by mid-September a very general mood of confidence combined with scepticism. Perhaps *Punch* hit it off best with a drawing, published on 11 September, of an elderly lady confiding to her friend: "These raids give me the feeling that Hitler appears to be a great deal more worried than he seems." The country glowed with pride in the exploits of the outnumbered RAF, and Londoners in particular derived a keen satisfaction from news of the raids on Berlin. London was the centre of interest in those days. From it an inexhaustible anthology of anecdotes diffused itself over the islands. Some were tales of courage, some of hideous disaster, some of strange coinci-dence; but most were funny though often macabre stories of experiences undergone, if not by the *raconteur* personally, then by the *raconteur's* niece's charwoman or by his dentist's mother. For a time the whole country talked about little save bombs, and the provinces were thus able to identify themselves, in however indirect a way, with the ordeal of the capital.

In these circumstances it was natural that, except on the south and east coasts, the idea of invasion should have receded from the forefront of men's minds. The great scare of 7 September had left a legacy of rumours; their gist was that the Germans had tried and had catastrophically failed. In a broadcast on 11 September —that in which his grasp of the German preparations earned the respect of OKW—Churchill ranked "the next week or so" with "the days when the Spanish Armada was approaching the Channel, and Drake was finishing his game of bowls; or when Nelson stood between us and Napoleon's Grand Army at Boulogne. We have read all about this in the history books; but what is happening now is on a far greater scale and of far more consequence to the life and future of the world and its civilisation than those brave old days". The people heeded him, as ever; but they could not help remembering what happened to the Spaniards and the French, and almost all felt in their bones that the conquest of England was no longer on the cards.

At this stage each side had in reserve a weapon not hitherto employed. The Germans used theirs; the British did not, since the contingency which was held to justify its use never arose.

The German weapon was delayed-action bombs. These were known to the Civil Defence Services and the police as UXBs, or unexploded bombs; but there was often no ready means of telling whether a projectile which had buried itself in the ground was a UXB or merely an ordinary bomb which had failed to explode. A few had been used here and there in sporadic raids as early as July, but the Germans first began to drop them in important quantities on 7 September and they created many new and unattractive problems. An official historian's verdict is that "the UXBs dropped in such unexpected numbers formed at this stage, it is probably not too much to say, one of the largest threats to normal civil activities and war production".[1] On 17 September a report from the German Military Attaché in Washington, giving them credit for yet another

[1] O'Brien.

decline in British morale, was studied with satisfaction at OKW.

But counter-measures were devised and put into effect, mainly by officers and men of the Royal Engineers of whom was required a high and rare form of courage; for to grapple, in cold blood and in silence, with an infernal machine which may at any moment blow you to smithereens calls for great steadiness and resolution. The most dramatic episode to which at this time the UXBs gave rise was that of the bomb, eight feet in length and weighing a ton, which buried itself in the outer foundations of St Paul's Cathedral, near the south-west tower, on 12 September. A Bomb Disposal Squad of the Royal Engineers, under a subaltern, dug to a depth of 27½ feet, with a six-inch gas-main burning inextinguishably in the heart of their excavations, before they were able, after three days, to extract the huge incalculable missile and transport it through cleared streets to Hackney Marshes, where it was detonated. If they had not performed this duty, the bomb would have brought down the west portico of St Paul's besides doing other serious damage; and thereafter Army vehicles bearing the letters BDS and having their mud-guards and bumpers painted red aroused feelings in which the thrill evoked by a fire-engine mingled with the respect due to a hearse. [1]

Ruminating afterwards on what would have happened if the Germans had got ashore in strength, Churchill wrote: "They would have used terror, and we were prepared to go to all lengths." This would seem to be a veiled reference to the British decision, surrounded by secrecy at the time and ever since, to attack the German beach-heads with mustard gas if the need arose; the gas was to be sprayed from low-flying aircraft, and was regarded as a last resort, to be used only if more conventional methods of defence looked like being overcome.

In the small circle to whom it was known this expedient aroused controversy. One of the main arguments used by its critics was that it was certain to lead to retaliation in kind and that as a target for

[1] Though they attracted less attention, the exploits of the Royal Navy's Mine Disposal Units equalled in heroism those of the Royal Engineers. These units had the task of rendering harmless huge mines which were dropped by parachute. The mines were equipped with a wide variety of acoustic, magnetic and other fuses, and each was in effect a booby-trap, so designed that (in theory) anyone who discovered the secrets of its mechanism was automatically blown to bits.

chemical warfare Britain was many times more vulnerable than Germany, and must remain so as long as the powerful German bomber force threatened the islands at point-blank range. But these objections were outweighed by the paramount importance of denying the invaders a lodgement; and although in the event it is likely that this would have been achieved by the normal weapons of the three fighting services, the British would not, in a crisis, have forgone the use of gas. The German, like the British, soldiers were provided with gasmasks, but in the assault-wave they were carried as unit stores in large zinc-lined boxes equipped with wheels and straps for hauling up the beach; these chests also contained rations, wireless sets and other gear which it was essential to keep dry. It is thus probable that in the initial stages of a landing comparatively few of the invaders would have had their gasmasks ready to hand.

"The enemy's ports are our first line of defence," Nelson had once said, and on the tense night of 7 September British heavy bombers made their first attacks on the invasion bases; the light bombers had been at work on these targets since the 5th, and thereafter raids on what the RAF knew as "Blackpool Front" were continuous. "It was," one of the pilots wrote, "an amazing sight. Calais docks were on fire. So was the waterfront of Boulogne. . . . The whole French coast seemed to be a barrier of flame broken only by intense white flashes of exploding bombs and vari-coloured incendiary tracers soaring and circling skywards."

The layman in Britain, who visualised the European littoral in terms of *plages* off which the massed invasion fleet rode conspicuously at anchor like the vessels in a print of the Napoleonic era, had small idea of the difficulty of attacking barges and other craft in the recesses of a modern harbour heavily defended by anti-aircraft guns and searchlights. The RAF disturbed rather than disrupted the German preparations. The following shipping was sunk or put out of action after being concentrated in the invasion ports:

Transports	21 out of	170
Barges	214 out of	1,918
Tugs	5 out of	386
Motor-boats	3 out of	1,020

In addition a good deal of damage was done ashore, an ammunition train being (for instance) blown up on 17 September and the water supply at Le Havre put out of commission a week later.

But if the total volume of destruction wrought was not prohibitively great over the whole of the invasion-front, its effects were often locally most serious. The number of men and the tonnage of stores to be embarked at each port remained constant, but the amount of shipping in the port declined; in the worst-hit ports it declined to a point at which the original loading-tables, movement-orders and so forth became so much waste paper, and there was every reason to expect that it would go on declining. Nor was it easy to visualise the orderly embarkation of troops, horses and equipment under the conditions nightly prevailing along the "Blackpool Front". It was with the detailed German plans, rather than with their *matériel*, that the attacks of Bomber Command may be said without exaggeration to have played havoc; and the claim made by Marshal of the RAF Sir Arthur Harris that "it was definitely Bomber Command's wholesale destruction of the invasion barges in the Channel ports that convinced the Germans of the futility of attempting to cross the Channel"[1] is not strictly in accordance with the facts.

The effect of these attacks was on occasion increased by salvoes from the guns of His Majesty's destroyers, but the Navy's role off the invasion coast was, though important, unrewarding. Regular sweeps were carried out by destroyers, motor torpedo-boats and the little ships of the Auxiliary Patrol, which for one night (8/9 September) were joined by the 2nd Cruiser Squadron; but encounters with enemy shipping were rare and engagements inconclusive. The Germans however knew that the Royal Navy was out and they largely discontinued, much to their inconvenience, the coastwise movement of shipping by night. The deterrent effect of aggressive patrolling which the enemy was in no position to challenge made, as in history it so often had before, a traditional contribution to the thwarting of invasion.

Thus September drew on towards October, and a short, strange chapter of British history came to its unperceived end. The bombs

[1] *Bomber Offensive.* London, 1946.

still rained on London, though now almost all by night. Other cities were attacked in force, and the roll of civilian dead grew steadily longer.[1] Along the coasts the islanders continued to strengthen their defences, and the great guns still fought an intermittent duel across the Channel, without ever doing any damage to each other or very much damage to any other worthwhile target. On the Continent the RAF dropped leaflets in German, French and Dutch; they took the form of a phrase-book or conversational guide entitled *Wir Fahren Gegen Engelland*. "Was that a bomb—a torpedo —a shell—a mine? . . . We are seasick. Where is the basin? . . . How much do you charge for swimming lessons? . . . See how briskly our captain burns! . . . Why is the Fuehrer not coming with us?"

The Fuehrer by now was busy with other plans. *Sea Lion* was postponed not for days but for an indeterminate number of months. Other islands ephemerally succeeded Great Britain on the German agenda—Gibraltar, the Azores, Madeira, the Cape Verdes. Nothing came of these projects. They were dwarfed by the grand design—a conquest of Russia; and *Sea Lion* was still kept outwardly in being as a gigantic bluff—"the greatest deception in history"—to distract attention from Hitler's purposes and preparations in the East.

At the end of that year he began suddenly to toy with the idea of seizing Ireland. "The occupation of Ireland", he told Raeder on 3 December, "might lead to the end of the war." The Naval Staff demonstrated, easily and unanswerably, the unsoundness of this whimsical scheme, but Hitler showed a marked reluctance to abandon it. On 23 January 1941, in an interview at which Goering was the only other person present, he discussed with the airborne commander Student the possibility of invading Ireland by air; he hoped

[1] Casualties to the civilian population in Britain during the whole of the 1939–45 war were 146,777 killed, missing believed killed, or seriously injured. This total includes 15,358 children under sixteen and 537 human beings who were never identified. It does not include civilian casualties in British overseas possessions or Japanese internment camps, nor any lives lost at sea. (O'Brien.)

Official German figures put their civilian losses at just under 3,000,000. Of these 500,000 were killed in air-raids and ground fighting; the remainder are said to have perished in the great fluxes and deportations which followed the Russian advance into Germany. It is not clear whether the total of 3,000,000 includes the large number of German civilians who were put to death during the war by the German Government.

that the Irish could be induced to invite him to do this. If he held Ireland, he could quickly strangle Britain by cutting her Atlantic life-lines and destroying their termini on the west coast.[1]

Hitler was already deeply preoccupied with the attack on Russia, for which the directive was issued on 18 December; and if British sea and air power could prevent the capture of Kent, a German expedition to Ireland faced prospects which (as Raeder pointed out) were bleak indeed. Yet Hitler's interest in this far-fetched project does not redound wholly to his discredit as a strategist. It shows that he was aware how cardinal had been his failure on the Channel coast, and how vitally important it still was to end the war in the West before beginning the war in the East; he reminds one of a small child tiptoeing downstairs in the darkness to tidy up a cupboard which it knows it should never have left in disarray. As Hinsley has put it: "The striking thing about the three months which followed the postponement of *Sea Lion* was not the ease but the reluctance with which the idea was abandoned."

It was not in fact until 13 February 1942 that the German forces earmarked for invasion were officially released from their role; and in Britain precautions continued to be taken until, and in some cases even after, the tables had been turned by the Allied landings in Normandy in June 1944. (It was not, for instance, until five months later that the Invasion Committees were dissolved, road-blocks dismantled, and authority given for the exhibition on railway-stations of their names.) But in fact the invasion of England was never again contemplated by Hitler after the end of September 1940. He had had his chance, but he had not made the most of it; he had failed. Time was to show how serious were the consequences of this failure; but time's verdict had, not for the first or last time, been anticipated by Churchill. On 18 June he had told a House of Commons half-stunned by the Fall of France: "Hitler knows that he will have to break us in this island or lose the war." As winter closed in on Europe Hitler turned his back on the unbroken island. Before him stretched a summer of thunderclap victories; but on him lay—irremovable, not to be exorcised—the curse of ultimate defeat.

---

[1] It was about this time that the spy Goertz was instructed to report urgently on Irish defences and told that this order came from "the highest authority". See p. 183.

CHAPTER TWENTY

The Reckoning

His first great failure, of far greater ultimate consequence than all his victories.
    Chester Wilmot: *The Struggle for Europe*. London, 1952

THE foregoing chapters have made clear the view that *Operation Sea Lion*, as planned and mounted, was doomed to failure and, had it been launched, could only have ended in disaster. Two questions remain to be answered:

Were there any circumstances in which, during the summer of 1940, Hitler could have successfully attempted the invasion of England?

What would have been the probable results of a successful invasion upon the subsequent course of the war, and what were the consequences of Hitler's failure to carry it out?

Although the answers to these questions must necessarily be speculative, both require to be examined.

(1) *Were there any circumstances in which, during the summer of 1940, Hitler could have successfully attempted the invasion of England?*

There can be no doubt as to *when* a German invasion would have had the best prospects of success. Had the Germans been able to put quite a small force—say three or four divisions—across the Channel early in June (that "very dark hour," as Churchill called it two months later) they might have done the trick. The reinforcement, and indeed the maintenance, of this force would have presented serious difficulties, but some of these could have been overcome by the capture of airfields in south-east England, which in those days would not have been a hard task.

At this time—immediately after Dunkirk, whence the last troops were taken off on the morning of 4 June—there simply did not exist in the islands the physical means of repelling, or even containing, a determined attack. The BEF, dead tired, disorganised, without artillery or transport, had temporarily ceased to cohere as a force; units, much depleted, could have gone into action, but formations existed as such only on paper. A few half-trained and much less than half-equipped divisions, which had not been fit to send to France, could have been moved—by rail—to meet the incursion, whose progress would not have been seriously hindered by the Local Defence Volunteers, most of whom were still in the brassard-and-shotgun stage. Reserves of fighter aircraft were dangerously low, and the Civil Defence services had not been given the mild, prolonged baptism of fire which saw them through their teething troubles.

Almost more important, the nation, though outwardly defiant, had not really got its second wind. It was on its feet and still full of fight; but, like a man who has just been knocked sprawling in the gutter twice in rapid succession, it was dazed and off balance, and without a breathing-space might have gone down again to a blow which a little later it could have parried.

In order to carry out an invasion at a time from which he would have derived psychological and operational advantages of the first importance, Hitler would have had to take two decisions which he did not take. The second (which, as events turned out, he had the opportunity of taking but which would have been useless since he had not previously taken the first) was, after Dunkirk, to contain the French armies along the Somme instead of attacking across it on 5 June. This would have left the main strength of the Luftwaffe available to support the invasion.

But no invasion, on however limited or improvised a scale, could have taken place unless it had been planned, well in advance, as a sequel to *Operation Yellow*; flimsy though the British defences were at the time, no cross-Channel assault could have been launched on the spur of the moment. A failure in foresight was the basic reason for the abortion of *Sea Lion*. It was an error in psychology rather than in pure strategy. As a result of *Operation Yellow* Hitler expected, as Directive No. 6 shows, to "acquire as great an area of Holland, Belgium and Northern France as possible, to use as a base offering good prospects for waging aerial and sea warfare against England and to provide ample coverage for the vital district of the Ruhr". He meant to get what was in fact a jumping-off point, but he failed to see the point of jumping. It did not cross his mind that he would have to do so in order to eliminate Great Britain from the war; and the real, the ultimate reason why Hitler failed to invade England was because he failed to understand her.

(2) *What would have been the probable results of a successful invasion upon the subsequent course of the war, and what were the consequences of Hitler's failure to carry it out?*

Certain consequences could scarcely have failed to follow a German conquest of the British Isles in the autumn of 1940. The main sufferer from them would have been Russia.

Apart from the Royal Navy—or whatever was left of it—which would have withdrawn across the Atlantic to Canadian bases, the only British forces still left in contact with the enemy would have been Wavell's Army of the Nile. In the circumstance even that bold and resourceful commander would hardly have felt justified in launching, in December 1940, the desert offensive which destroyed the vastly superior Italian armies confronting him; for although he would still have had useful sources of reinforcement in India and Australia, his troops, and in particular his small air forces, were almost wholly dependent on British industry for their equipment.

The necessity for Hitler to send Rommel and the *Afrika Korps* to Mussolini's rescue would thus not have arisen. Much more important, there would have been no British intervention in Greece in March 1941, and no need for Hitler to divert forces already earmarked for the invasion of Russia to forestall it. The orders which set in motion his essentially preventive operations in the Balkans (*Operation Marita*) were issued as early as 13 December 1940, five days before the Directive (No. 21) for the invasion of Russia. At that time only a small RAF contingent was helping the Greeks to bring about what the directive called "the dangerous situation in Albania", and Wavell had barely begun the dazzling operations which were to obliterate a huge Italian army in Libya and Cyrenaica.

Nevertheless, the first paragraph of the orders for *Operation Marita* shows that it was the British gadfly which drove Hitler into this digression; his main purpose was defined as being "to keep the British from establishing an air base under the protection of a Balkan Front, which would be a threat especially to Italy, as well as to the Rumanian oilfields".

Four months later a *coup d'état* in Belgrade against the pro-Nazi Government of Yugoslavia gave Hitler the excuse for altering—in Directive No. 25 on 27 March 1941—the route to be followed by an expedition which was originally to have advanced through a complaisant Bulgaria to attack Greece. But it is, to say the least, doubtful whether the Belgrade *coup d'état* (in which British agents played some part) would have taken place if the Yugoslavs had not been as well aware as were the Germans[1] that British troops had been disembarking at the Piraeus for several weeks.

The German campaign in the Balkans was swift and successful. Nevertheless it imposed an important delay on the launching of *Operation Barbarossa*. D-Day, originally set provisionally for 15 May 1941, was put off until 22 June.

To say, as General Blumentritt does, that "the Balkan incident postponed the opening of the [Russian] campaign by five and a half weeks"[2] is probably an exaggeration; for the thaw was late in 1941, some East European rivers were in flood until early in June and the Germans could not in practice have adhered to their original timing. But the margin by which their armies failed to capture Moscow— outside which they were halted in their tracks by the onset of the Russian winter, against whose rigours they were unprovided—was a matter of a very few days. If Hitler had not felt himself compelled to thwart British designs in Greece, he could have launched his attack on Russia earlier; and if he had launched it earlier, even by as little as ten days or a fortnight, it is at least highly probable that he would have taken Moscow before the weather baulked him.

[1] "It is hard to picture a more ridiculous situation in war than that of the German Military Attaché [in Athens] standing on the quay and counting the British troops." (Major-General Playfair and others: *The Mediterranean and the Middle East, Vol. II*. London, 1956.)

[2] Guenther von Blumentritt and others: *The Fatal Decisions*. London, 1956. In the same work General Westphal estimates the delay at "a good six weeks".

The capture of Moscow would not in itself have meant the collapse of Russian resistance nor even an eventual German victory over Russia; but it would have gravely weakened the Russian cause. With Britain prostrate, moreover, German strategy would not have been hobbled, as it increasingly was, by the need to turn the long littoral of western and north-western Europe into a fortress,[1] and there would have been no German theatre of war in North Africa. Resistance movements would doubtless have come into being in occupied territory; but they would not have been nourished from the United Kingdom with arms, with leaders and with hope, and their diversionary effect (which in the event eroded if it did not deflect German strategy) would have been much smaller than in the event it was.

His failure to conquer Britain before he attacked Russia involved Hitler in a war not on two fronts, but on half a dozen. It was as a direct consequence of this failure that—during 1941, while Britain still stood alone—he felt himself obliged to impose upon the German Navy, Army and Air Force the following tasks and duties:

(1) The bombardment and blockade of the United Kingdom. (Navy and Air Force.)

(2) The maintenance of an invasion-threat. (Army.)

(3) The defensive garrisoning of Norway, the Channel Islands and—later—the whole coast of Occupied Europe. (All three services.)

(4) The dispatch of a German expeditionary force to Libya. (This was ultimately to lead to—among other serious losses—the surrender of 150,000 German and Italian troops in Tunisia in December 1942. All three services were involved.)

(5) The provision of armies of occupation for Greece, Yugo-slavia and Crete, where they were soon engaged in costly and

[1] Less than four months after the cancellation of *Sea Lion* an OKW order of 15 February 1941 laid down the measures to be taken, as a matter of urgency, "in order to prevent British successes, even prestige successes" in operations against the coast of Occupied Europe, and particularly against Norway. The first paragraph of these orders ended with the words: "Daring British action can be expected."

inconclusive operations against guerrillas nourished mainly from the United Kingdom. (Army and Air Force.)

(6) The attempt to prevent British convoys from carrying arms to north Russian ports. (Navy and Air Force.)

All these commitments became part of German strategy before Germany declared war on America when the Japanese attacked Pearl Harbour on 10 December 1941, some fourteen months after the cancellation of *Sea Lion*. All stemmed directly from Hitler's failure to eliminate Britain from the war, and of the six only the third—the defence of the Western European littoral—could conceivably have been undertaken in 1941 (in a modified form) if Britain had ceased to be a belligerent in 1940. The necessity for the other diversions of effort from the Russian front would not have arisen; and although the need to provide occupation forces for Great Britain and some of her colonies would have represented a small drain on the total German war effort, it would have been more than offset by the material advantages reaped from the territories occupied.

These are not abstract or theoretical contingencies. We do not know with certainty what would have happened if Germany had successfully invaded the United Kingdom; but we can point to a number of things which could not possibly have happened if she had. They are listed above. They did happen. They were a direct result of Hitler's failure to knock out his only remaining adversary. They were all immediately harmful to Germany and helpful to Russia.[1] None of them could have been brought about at the time by any other agency, or any other combination of circumstances, than that to which all owed their common origin: the fighting spirit of a small kingdom, unconquered and uncowed.

It is now necessary to turn to the other side of the world. Supposing Britain had been occupied by the Germans in 1940, what would Japan have done? We hardly need to invoke the image of the jackal, or the squalid precedent of Italy's declaration of war on France. The British possessions in the Far East would have lost

[1] The destruction of the Italian Empire in Africa was a by-product of Hitler's failure to conquer Britain.

their status as the targets of a laborious strategy, and would—along with the French and Dutch colonies—have become so much loot; and the only rule in looting is to grab before anyone else can. Hong Kong, Malaya, Borneo, and Burma, the Dutch East Indies and French Indo-China—it is difficult to believe that these would not have been swiftly taken over by the Japanese; and it is probable that the authorities in the British territories would have been ordered—by the Exiled Government in Canada, on humanitarian grounds—to offer no resistance.

Australia and India would thus have become the immediate objectives of Japanese strategy. However expeditiously plundered, her vast new domain (which, when she took it by force, she called the "Greater East Asia Co-Prosperity Sphere") would have absorbed much of Japan's energies. In the circumstances it seems unlikely that anything corresponding to the surprise attack by carrier-borne aircraft on Pearl Harbour in December 1941 would have been carried out: partly because America, alarmed by the *dégringolade* on both her flanks, would have looked to her defences, partly because Japan would have had her hands full.

This is not to say that she would have abandoned her aggressive designs upon America, but she would have had cogent reasons for not embarking on them prematurely. Had Britain been occupied in 1940, the position of the three Axis powers a year later would have been one of overwhelming strength. With the Germans in Moscow, Italy mistress of the Mediterranean, and Japan consolidating blood-less conquests all over East Asia, the world would have been presented with a *fait accompli* of the most daunting kind.

America's defence programme would by then have got into its stride, and by December 1941 she would have disposed of very large armed forces. At that date the bulk of these would have been only partially trained and devoid (through no fault of their own) of combat experience. Their primary task would have been to defend American territory. In this duty the whole nation would have been no less resolute than the British had been. But until the threat of a simultaneous invasion of America's Atlantic and Pacific coasts could be discounted it is difficult to imagine circumstances in which any American Government would have felt justified in sending a large expeditionary force to wage offensive warfare overseas; nor is it easy to suggest where it could usefully have been sent.[1]

But enough has been said to show how very great would have been the benefits to Germany and her associates of a successful invasion of England. No one can say for certain that Hitler would have won the war if he had carried out the invasion, or that his failure to carry it out made his defeat inevitable; but this failure left in the hands of his enemies the tools with which they laid the foundations of his ruin, and without those tools, though it is possible to proclaim a blind faith in Hitler's eventual downfall, it is not possible to reconstruct the circumstances in which it could have been brought about.

A war is not like a game of chess. We cannot, when it is over, replace the pieces on the squares they occupied in some critical situation and show that, had one of the players made a different move, the result of the game must infallibly have been reversed. We can sometimes go so far as to show how it *might* have been reversed; but when half the pieces on the board have to be redeployed in order to ensure victory for the loser, the business becomes tedious. This would be the fate of any attempt to demonstrate in the light of after-knowledge how Hitler could have conquered England in 1940.

But it cannot be too strongly emphasised that Hitler did not want, nor did he need, to conquer England. He wanted to eliminate her as an opponent; that was all his strategy demanded, though his ego would have liked to see her humbled in the process. Invasion was the crude, dangerous and (as it turned out) impracticable method to which he reluctantly turned. It is at least arguable—though it has not, oddly, been argued before—that he could have chosen another expedient which would have offered better hopes of success.

After the Fall of France Hitler did three things, each of which failed to produce the results he hoped for and each of which, failing, contributed to the failure of the other two. He threatened invasion: he prepared invasion: and he launched the aerial bombardment

[1] Cf. von Manstein: "The conquest of Britain by Germany would have deprived the other side of the very base that was indispensable—in those days at any rate—for a seaborne assault on the continent of Europe. To launch an invasion from over the Atlantic without being able to use the island as a springboard was beyond the bounds of possibility in those days."

which was to make invasion possible. Nothing obliged him to do any of these three things, and it is scarcely disputable that he would have been better off if he had done none of them.

Idiotic is not too hard a word to apply to the minatory tone adopted by German propaganda towards the islanders after the Fall of France. Some allowance must be made for the fact that the Germans were suffering from what Lenin once called "dizziness from success". It was, nevertheless, sheer folly to try to browbeat the British with the threat that their country was about to be occupied by force. If Hitler wanted the British to throw up the sponge this was the way to deter them from doing so; and if he wanted to invade England, this was the way to arrange the hottest possible reception for his troops.

So profound was the distrust which he inspired in them that Hitler had in reality small chance of lulling the British into a sense of false security. But none of his purposes was served by doing the opposite. Even before he actually decided on invasion his propaganda machine was working for the British Government, instilling in even the sceptic, the slacker and the dullard a sense of the immediacy of the danger, providing a background of drama against which it was both easy and becoming to make sacrifices and submit to restrictions, to fill sandbags and to stand in queues.

The British first began to worry about invasion in mid-May; by the end of July Hitler had realised that *Sea Lion* could not be launched before mid-September. Four months is a long time for a whole nation—and particularly one whose character has a streak of feckless-ness in it—to remain on the alert; as Churchill suggested to the House of Commons on 17 September, "the process of waiting, keyed up to concert pitch day after day, is apt after a time to lose its charm of novelty". Throughout this period German propaganda had upon the British much the same effect which a matador's scarlet cape has upon a wearying bull. Not for a moment were they allowed to suppose that the elaborate, costly and inconvenient pre-cautions which they were taking might be superfluous. "Do not be deceived", the New British Broadcasting Station implored its listeners on 6 August, "by the present period of relative calm. The attack is not abandoned, it is only postponed." A week earlier the same station had been pointing out that every delay in launching the attack meant only that it would be more terrible when it came. If there had ever been any prospect that this fee-fi-fo-fum bluster would cow the islanders into submission, it had long since vanished; its continuance, on a note of fluctuating stridency, throughout the summer was directly contrary to German interests.

It required no profound knowledge of the British character to realise that threats would strengthen rather than weaken their will to resist; but it did require more imagination than Hitler possessed to see what immense advantages might have been gained if in June 1940 he had turned his back on England instead of shaking his fist at her. Had he, in his hour of victory, left the British severely alone, it is difficult to resist the conclusion that he would have improved his chances of securing their withdrawal from the war.

The menace of invasion was at once a tonic and a drug. It braced the islanders to exertions whose necessity seemed beyond question, and it expunged from their minds the memories of the disasters they had suffered. The wider, more imponderable issues of the war receded into the background of their thoughts. It would be time to speculate about ultimate victory over two power-ful enemies, at whom for the time being they were all but impotent to strike, after their homeland had been preserved. The extreme and disheartening bleakness of their long-term prospects was obscured by the melodramatic nature of the predicament in which—as their leaders prudently, and their enemies imprudently, lost no oppor-tunity of reminding them—the fortunes of war had placed them.

What if they had lacked this tonic, these stimuli? We have seen how, in May and June, they first visualised invasion in terms of air-borne attacks: how for some three months their intelligence re-ceived no reliable indications that a seaborne landing was being prepared: and how in the meantime it was as much as anything else the enemy's own assertions and hints which fixed in their minds the conviction that invasion was probable if not certain. Supposing that Hitler, instead of bringing their patriotic instincts to the boil, had left them to stew in their own juice?

It would have meant a return to the Phoney War. Save at sea, where the full resources of the German Navy could have been profitably employed on the blockade instead of being largely diverted to the makeshift preparations for *Sea Lion*, there would not only have been no fighting but no prospect of fighting. Bomber Command could have inflicted on German industrial targets pin-pricks of a slowly increasing severity, though the RAF would have had to contend with the powerful German fighter force behind its own radar screen and under conditions far more favourable than its pilots enjoyed in the Battle of Britain. The Army's training would have benefited from its relative freedom from urgent defensive commitments; but what would it have been training for?

It would have been a lacklustre situation. America, so generous with her moral and material aid to an island closely beleaguered and quite possibly doomed,[1] would have offered less comfort to a nation which, after being decisively defeated, was wordily pretending that nothing of the sort had happened. The loyalty of the Dominions would have been qualified with a certain caution, the embittered reproaches of France would not have been tempered with admira-tion. Churchill's tenacity of purpose would have kept defiance alive —but for how long, when there was nothing tangible to defy? It is worth remembering, too, that some 40,000 British prisoners of war had fallen into German hands. If Hitler had made a contemp-tuous offer to send them home, could any British Government have refused it? And for how much longer, after it had been accepted, would the nation have continued to face the prospects—which on a short view were all this Phoney War would have had to offer—of boredom, bankruptcy and blockade?

[1] In May 1940 America had a small regular army of 75,000 men, a one-ocean navy and an air force with a total strength of less than 25,000 men. When the spec-tacular German successes in Europe brought home to her the urgent need for expansion, her industry was not producing armaments in any important quantity; and the long-term arrangements which harnessed so much of its nascent strength to the British war effort may all be said to have stemmed directly from the threat of invasion in 1940. "The immediate sale [of ships, aircraft and arms] is of the utmost importance," urged the British Ambassador, Lothian, on 2 July, "*if the impending attack on Britain is to be beaten off before the winter sets in.*" (H. Duncan Hall: *North American Supply*. London, 1955.) This was a much-used and cogent argument in Washington, where British observers—and many American ob-servers too—reported a pessimistic atmosphere and where the need to hold the United Kingdom as an outpost of American defence came to be an axiom of policy.

A truly cunning man who wished, as Hitler fervently did, to eliminate Britain from the war would have grasped these possibilities, would have left the islanders after Dunkirk to lick their wounds, to formulate and reformulate their war aims, to awaken slowly to the realisation of their impotence. It might not have worked; but it involved no unacceptable risks. (There was the risk that Russia might have realised more clearly and more quickly than she did what was in store for her; but this ought not, in all the circumstances, to have been unacceptable to the Germans.)

If Hitler had shaped his political strategy in the West on these aloof and noncommittal lines, it seems unlikely that by the end of the summer either his air force, or his prestige, or the German economy would have sustained the damage which they suffered for the sake of *Sea Lion*: while Britain, though she might still have been a belligerent, would not have been tempted to remember as her finest hour a summer in which swift disaster had been followed by protracted anticlimax.

FINIS

APPENDIX

THE CHAIN OF COMMAND IN THE GERMAN ARMED FORCES: SUMMER, 1940.

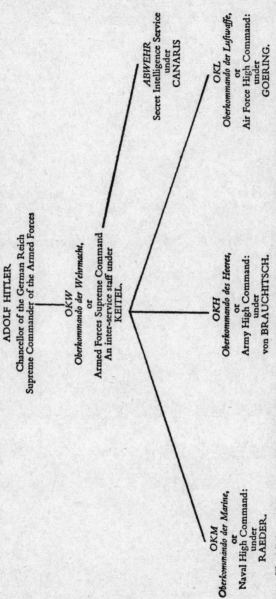

ADOLF HITLER
Chancellor of the German Reich
Supreme Commander of the Armed Forces

OKW
Oberkommando der Wehrmacht,
or
Armed Forces Supreme Command
An inter-service staff under
KEITEL.

ABWEHR
Secret Intelligence Service
under
CANARIS

OKM
Oberkommando der Marine,
or
Naval High Command:
under
RAEDER.

OKH
Oberkommando des Heeres,
or
Army High Command:
under
von BRAUCHITSCH.

OKL
Oberkommando der Luftwaffe,
or
Air Force High Command:
under
GOERING.

NOTE.—The Ministry of Foreign Affairs (under Ribbentrop), the Propaganda Ministry (under Goebbels) and other key government departments had permanent representatives at OKW. Arrangements for liaison between OKW and its three subordinate headquarters, or between any two of them, were irregular and perfunctory.

Bibliography

Titles preceded by ** are volumes of the *History of the Second World War*, edited by Professor J. R. M. Butler and published by Her Majesty's Stationery Office. Those preceded by * are histories produced under British official auspices but not forming part of the above series.

The place of publication is London except where otherwise stated.

ALLINGHAM, MARGERY: *The Oaken Heart* (1941).

ANON.: *The London Irish at War* (privately printed, 1949).

BANKS, SIR DONALD: *Flame Over Britain* (1948).

BANSÉ, DR EWALD: *Germany, Prepare for War!* (1934).

BIRDWOOD, LIEUTENANT-COLONEL THE LORD: *The Worcestershire Regiment, 1922–1950* (Aldershot, 1952).

BLAKE, J. W.: ** *Northern Ireland in the Second World War* (1956).

BRIGHT, JOAN: *The Ninth Queen's Royal Lancers, 1936–1945* (Aldershot, 1951).

BRUCE, James: *Report on the Spanish Armada* (State Paper Office, 1798).

BUCKLEY, Christopher: *Norway: the Commandos: Dieppe* (1951).

BULLOCK, ALAN: *Hitler: A Study in Tyranny* (1952).

BURT, KENDAL, AND LEASOR, JAMES: *The One That Got Away* (1956).

CHURCHILL, SIR WINSTON S.: *The Second World War*. Vol. II. "Their Finest Hour" (1949).

——: *Into Battle* (1949).

——: *My Early Life* (1930).

CIANO, GALEAZZO: *Ciano's Diary, 1939–43* (1947). Edited by Malcolm Muggeridge.

COLVIN, IAN: *Chief of Intelligence* (1951).

COWIE, CAPTAIN J. S., RN: *Mines, Minelayers and Minelaying* (1949).

COWLES, VIRGINIA: *Winston Churchill: the Era and the Man* (1953).

CREASY, E. S.: *The Invasions and Projected Invasions of England, from the Saxon Times: with Remarks on the Present Emergencies* (1852).

DE JONG, DR LOUIS: *The German Fifth Column in the Second World War* (1956).

DERRY, T. K.: **Campaign in Norway (1952).

DESBRIÈRE, EDOUARD: Projets et Tentatives de Débarquement aux Iles Britanniques (Paris, 1902).

DE WOHL, LOUIS: The Stars in War and Peace (1952).

DU MAURIER, MAJOR GUY: An Englishman's Home (1909).

ELLIS, MAJOR L. F.: **The War in France and Flanders (1953).

GALLAND, ADOLF: The First and the Last (1955).

GIBBS, AIR MARSHAL SIR GERALD: Survivor's Story (1956).

GIBSON, WING COMMANDER GUY: Enemy Coast Ahead (1946).

GILBERT, FELIX: Hitler Directs his War (New York, 1950).

GOEBBELS, JOSEPH: The Goebbels Diaries (1949). Edited by Louis P. Lochner.

GRAHAM, HARRY: Ruthless Rhymes for Heartless Homes.

GRAVES, CHARLES: *The Home Guard of Britain (1943).

GREINER, HELMUTH: Die Oberste Wehrmacht Fuehrung 1939–43 (Wiesbaden, 1951).

GUDERIAN, HEINZ: Panzer Leader (1952).

HALDER, GENERAL FRANZ: Hitler as Warlord (1950).

——: Diaries (unpublished).

HALL, H. DUNCAN: **North American Supply (1955).

HANCOCK, SIR W. K. and M. M. GOWING: **British War Economy (1949).

HARRIS, MARSHAL OF THE RAF SIR ARTHUR: Bomber Offensive (1947).

HART, CAPTAIN B. H. LIDDELL: The Defence of Britain (1939).

——: The Other Side of the Hill (1951).

HILL, B. J. W.: Eton Medley (1948).

HINSLEY, F. H.: Hitler's Strategy (Cambridge, 1951).

HOFFMANN, H.: Hitler Was My Friend (1955).

ICKES, HAROLD L.: The Secret Diary of Harold L. Ickes. Vol. III (New York, 1955). Edited by Joseph Barnes.

JOWITT, THE EARL: Some Were Spies (1954).

"JUDEX": Anderson's Prisoners (1940).

KESSELRING, GRUNDFELDMARSCHAL ALBERT: Memoirs (1953).

LE QUEUX, WILLIAM: The Great Invasion of 1910, With a Full Account of the Siege of London (1906).

MACDONAGH, MICHAEL: In London During the Great War (1935).

MUNRO, H. H. ("Saki"): When William Came (1913).

O'BRIEN, T. H.: **Civil Defence (1955).

PLAYFAIR, MAJOR-GENERAL I. S. O. and others: **The Mediterranean and Middle East. Vols. I (1954) and II (1956).

RAUSCHNING, HERMAN: *Hitler Speaks* (1939).

RICHARDS, DENIS: *★The Royal Air Force 1939–1945*. Vol. I. "The Fight at Odds" (1953).

RICHMOND, ADMIRAL SIR HERBERT W.: *The Invasion of Britain* (1941).

ROSKILL, CAPTAIN S. W., RN: *★★The War at Sea*. Vol. I (1954).

SCHELLENBERG, WALTER: *The Schellenberg Memoirs* (1956).

SHERWOOD, ROBERT, E.: *The White House Papers of Harry L. Hopkins* (New York, 1948).

SHIRER, W. L.: *A Berlin Diary* (1941).

SPAIGHT, J. M.: *★The Battle of Britain* (1941).

STACEY, COLONEL C. P.: *★The Official History of the Canadian Army in the Second World War*. Vol. I (Ottawa, 1955).

STIRLING, MAJOR J. D. P.: *The First and the Last: A History of the 4/7 Royal Dragoon Guards* (1950).

TITMUSS, R. M.: *★★Problems of Social Policy* (1950).

VON BLUMENTRITT, GENERAL GUENTHER, and others: *The Fatal Decisions* (1956).

VON MANSTEIN, ERICH: *Verlorene Siege* (Bonn, 1955).

WAUGH, EVELYN: *Put Out More Flags* (1942).

WESTPHAL, GENERAL SIEGFRIED: *The German Army in the West* (1951).

WHEATLEY, R. R. A.: *Operation Sea Lion* (as yet unpublished).

WHEELER-BENNETT, J. W.: *The Nemesis of Power* (1954).

WILMOT, CHESTER: *The Struggle for Europe* (1952).

WOOD, ALAN AND MARY: *Islands in Danger* (1955).

YOUNG, DESMOND: *Rommel* (1950).

Documents on German Foreign Policy 1918–1945. Series D. Vol. IX (1956).

The Fuehrer Conferences on Naval Affairs. Reprinted in *Brassey's Naval Annual* (1948).

Index